Into the Labyrinth
Essays on the
Art of Lawrence Durrell

Challenging the Literary Canon

Into the Labyrinth
Essays on the
Art of Lawrence Durrell

Edited by
Frank L. Kersnowski

U·M·I Research Press
Ann Arbor / London

Copyright © 1989
Frank L. Kersnowski
All rights reserved

Produced and distributed by
UMI Research Press
an imprint of
University Microfilms Inc.
Ann Arbor, Michigan 48106

Library of Congress Cataloging in Publication Data

Into the labyrinth : essays on the art of Lawrence Durrell / edited
by Frank L. Kersnowski.
  p. cm.—(Challenging the literary canon)
  ISBN 0-8357-2024-1 (alk. paper)
  1. Durrell, Lawrence—Criticism and interpretation.
I. Kersnowski, Frank L., 1934- . II. Series.
PR6007.U76Z69 1989
828'.91209—dc20   89-20164
                                                      CIP

British Library CIP data is available.

The paper used in this publication meets the minimum requirements of
American National Standard for Information Sciences—Permanence of Paper for Printed
Library Materials, ANSI Z39.48-1984. ∞ ™

Nadia Blokh, *In the Mirror of the Cecil Hotel,* 1987
Ink drawing.

Contents

Acknowledgments

To thank Lawrence Durrell for the works of his lifetime, for the intense involvement of his existence in ours is a large task for any one person. To thank him as well, as I must, for his willingness to encourage without expecting assent increases the difficulty of the task. But I, as well as all the contributors to this volume, are indebted to the genius and generosity of Lawrence Durrell. I am clearly indebted as well to all the contributors for their readiness to commit time and intellectual energy. My colleagues at Trinity University, especially Norman Sherry and Peter Balbert, have facilitated this venture with encouragement and advice more than they can guess. I am grateful to Ronnie Swanner and Pat Ullmann of the Trinity University Library. The scrutiny of Skip Eno was very important. I am also grateful for permissions to reprint: Jean Fanchette's essay previously appeared as the introduction to *Lawrence Durrell. Letters to Jean Fanchette. 1958–1963* (Paris: Editions Two Cities Etc., 1988), and is here reprinted with the permission of Jean Fanchette. Steven G. Kellman's essay was previously printed in a slightly different form with the title "The Reader in/of *The Alexandria Quartet*" in *Studies in the Novel* (Spring 1988) and appears here with the permission of the editor.

And I owe much gratitude to Nell Robertson Kersnowski, my mother, to whom this book is dedicated.

Introduction

With the approach of Lawrence Durrell's seventy-fifth birthday, I began to plan a present for him: a small gathering of essays by people whose lives had been affected by Durrell and his writings. From such a familiar beginning grew this volume, a complex and quite comprehensive collection. The original plan was to combine studies of the genres in which Durrell has worked with critical reminiscences by such close friends of his as Alfred Perlès, Jean Fanchette, Nadia and Alexandre Blokh, and F. J. Temple.

The initial pieces were so provocative that I decided to expand the volume and invite other acquaintances of Durrell and scholars significantly concerned with Durrell's writings to contribute. After two years of gathering, winnowing, and revising, the volume is complete—or as complete as a study of Durrell and his writings is likely to be.

Even though Durrell has said that his oeuvre was completed with *Quinx, or the Ripper's Tale*, he has already begun work on another book which suits the genre best called literature of residence rather than travel literature. And when I visited with him in 1986, he said he might well paint more paintings and write more poetry, though he planned to write no more fiction—a questionable resolve. As important as the books he continues to write is the way Durrell wrote the earlier ones. Durrell's "Author's Note" to *Clea*, the last volume of *The Alexandria Quartet*, explains his inclusion of a section entitled "Workpoints" after the completion of the narrative itself:

> Among the workpoints at the end of this volume I have sketched a number of possible ways of continuing to deploy these characters and situations in further instalments—but this is only to suggest that even if the series were extended indefinitely the result would never become a roman fleuve (an expansion of the matter in serial form) but would remain strictly part of the present word-continuum. If the axis has been well and truly laid down in the quartet it should be possible to radiate in any direction without losing the strictness and congruity of the continuum. (7)

Though *The Alexandria Quartet* is complete, Durrell makes possible its imaginative continuation by the curious reader—though I have never heard of this actually happening. Instead, the books of Durrell involve readers in inquiries into the nature of fiction and even life itself. In the shifting overlays of fictional events and characters in Durrell's varied writings are as many questions as answers.

Though the spirit of inquiry so essential to Durrell's writings must be shared by involved readers, the contributors to this volume have written to establish the achievement of Durrell. The essays consider the complexity of Durrell's career as a writer from the poems and fiction praised by T. S. Eliot and Henry Miller, such as *The Black Book,* to the short stories about life in the diplomatic service which Miller censured, stories which continue to please Durrell. Clearly, though, *The Alexandria Quartet* introduced most Durrell readers to him and made him a household name, not only a point of reference for critics concerned with the literature which developed after the twenties.

The union of the exotic, even the bizarre, with the spiritual quest that is central to *The Alexandria Quartet* informs as well the most intriguing, and disturbing, of Durrell's creations. In such settings as Alexandria and Provence, Greece and even England (which Durrell calls Pudding Island), the merely mundane is given a place of significance with matters that have global import. To eat, to drink wine, to love, to give birth, these have the power to continue life beside which the efforts of the military-industrial complex seem mere gestures—unless they release evil, as happened with the rise of totalitarian powers in our century.

Durrell, the author, might have disappeared in the complexity of the fictional technique he used to present the paradox and ambiguity of a reality shifting from place to place, from point of view to point of view. Yet he is undoubtedly present as a moral voice reminding readers that the tender, the obscene, the expected, and the unthinkable are part of reality; that a toe stubbed by a stone, a fragmented conversation, a book can interfere with reality so strongly as to shatter any philosophic assurance.

Chronology

1912	Lawrence George Durrell is born in India to Anglo-Indian parents on 27 February.
1924–25	Attends St. Olave's and St. Xavier's in England.
1925–26	Attends St. Edmund's in Canterbury.
1931	Publishes his first book in London, *Quaint Fragment,* a collection of poems, with the Cecil Press.
1935	Publishes his first novel, *Pied Piper of Lovers*, with Cassell and Company.
1935	Marries Nancy Myers.
1935–39	Durrell, his wife, his mother, his sister, and two brothers move to Corfu from England. They remain there until 1939, when the advancing German army causes their departure.
1937	Publishes *Panic Spring* under the pseudonym of Charles Norden with Faber and Faber.
1937	First meets Henry Miller and Alfred Perlès in Paris.
1937–39	*The Booster. The Monthly Magazine of the American Country Club* (Paris) edited by Durrell, Henry Miller, and Alfred Perlès.
1938	Publishes *The Black Book* with Obelisk Press in Paris.

1939–41	Lives in Athens with Nancy and teaches at the Institute of English Studies.
1940	Birth of a daughter, Penelope Berengaria Durrell.
1941–45	Foreign Press Service officer in Cairo.
1944–45	Press Attaché in Alexandria.
1945–47	Moves to Rhodes, where he is Director of Public Relations, Dodecanese Islands.
1945	*Prospero's Cell: A Guide to the Landscape and Manners of the Island of Corcyra* published by Faber and Faber.
1946	*Cefalû. A Novel* published by Editions Poetry London. Rev. ed. published in London by Ace Books in 1958 under the title *The Dark Labyrinth*.
1947	Marries Eve Cohen.
1947–48	Director of the British Council Institute in Cordoba, Argentina. The lectures he gave there were published under the title *A Key to Modern British Poetry* in 1952 by Peter Nevill in London and by the University of Oklahoma Press in the United States.
1949–52	Press Attaché in Belgrade, Yugoslavia.
1950	*Sappho: A Play in Verse* published by Faber and Faber.
1951	Birth of a second daughter, Sappho-Jane.
1953–56	Lives on Cyprus, where he teaches and is Director of Public Relations for the government of Cyprus.
1953	*Reflections of a Marine Venus* published by Faber and Faber.
1954	*Pope Joan* by Emmanuel Royidis, translated by Durrell, published by Derek Verschoyle. Originally translated by Durrell for publication by Rodney Phillips and Green in 1948 but did not appear because the press ceased publication.

1956	*Selected Poems* published by Faber and Faber in London and New Directions in the United States.
1957–Present	Lives in Provence.
1957	*Justine, White Eagles over Serbia, Bitter Lemons,* and *Esprit de Corps* published by Faber and Faber and Dutton.
1957	Awarded the Duff Cooper Prize for *Bitter Lemons*.
1958	*Balthazar* published by Faber and Faber and Dutton.
1958	*Stiff Upper Lip* published by Faber and Faber.
1959	*Mountolive* published by Faber and Faber and Viking.
1959	Prix du Meilleur Livre Etranger for *Justine*.
1959	Edits *The Henry Miller Reader*, published by New Directions.
1960	*Clea, Acte,* and *Collected Poems* published by Faber and Faber.
1961	Marries Claude-Marie Vincendon.
1963	*An Irish Faustus: A Morality in Nine Scenes* published by Faber and Faber.
1967	Claude-Marie, Durrell's third wife, dies.
1968	*Tunc* published by Faber and Faber and Dutton.
1969	*Spirit of Place: Letters and Essays on Travel,* edited by Alan G. Thomas, published by Faber and Faber.
1970	*Nunquam* published by Faber and Faber.
1974	Marries Ghislaine de Boysson.
1974	*Monsieur, or the Prince of Darkness* published by Faber and Faber and Viking.

1977   *Sicilian Carousel* published by Faber and Faber and Viking.

1978   *The Greek Islands* published by Faber and Faber and Viking.

1978   *Livia, or Buried Alive* published by Faber and Faber and Viking (1979).

1979   *Constance, or Solitary Practices* published by Faber and Faber and Viking (1982).

1980   *Collected Poems. 1931–1974* edited by James A. Brigham and published by Faber and Faber.

1980   *A Smile in the Mind's Eye* published by Wildwood House (London).

1983   *Sebastian, or Ruling Passions* published by Faber and Faber and Viking.

1985   *Quinx, or the Ripper's Tale* published by Faber and Faber and Viking (1986).

1985   *Antrobus Complete* published by Faber and Faber.

1988   *The Durrell-Miller Letters, 1935–80* edited by Ian S. MacNiven and published by Faber and Faber and New Directions.

1

Happy Birthday, Larry

Alfred Perlès

And many happy returns.

Many happy returns indeed! Why, he has a happy return every morning he wakes up, with or without a hangover. He was strong as an ox when I first met him. Food and wine were his greatest joys in life, and he denied himself nothing. He was no health-food faddist. He was too healthy to worry about health. And he didn't mind taking a little risk when, as happened occasionally, he ate and drank a little more than was strictly good for the health.

I have a clear recollection of the day I first set eyes on him. That was in the already legendary Villa Seurat. He had left his Ionian paradise for the express purpose of meeting Henry Miller, whose residence was No. 18 of the now famous cul-de-sac. I just happened to be there when he showed up, and our friendship dates from the first glass of wine we drank together.

Of course, Henry and I had known each other for nearly ten years before Larry arrived in our midst. Often, when we were short of funds, we walked together to Montparnasse. We hoped some of our friends would treat us to a meal, and our hopes were seldom in vain. I was known as Henry's "sidekick" among our mostly American friends.

It is hardly necessary to make a special point of the tremendous impact Larry made on Henry and me. Henry was already brushing the forties and I was only a few years younger, but Larry still looked like a bright, handsome school-boy. He is seventy-seven now. But he was no schoolboy. He had already a novel and a number of poems to his literary credit. He had published the novel under a pseudonym, for he didn't think it was good enough to be signed with his real name.

He was exalted and exultant. And how he could talk! In that beautiful English accent which I only much later came to appreciate. He was scintillating all the time; there was a punch to every sentence he uttered. Nothing could abate his exuberance and enthusiasm. We had always been gay and exuberant; it seemed impossible our gaiety could reach a higher point. And yet, Larry, with his inexhaustible reserve of *joie de vivre,* pushed our gaiety to a new height; it was a gaiety that could only be matched by the combined efforts of a Rabelais, a Restif de la Bretonne and an Apulieus—with a push from Robbie Burns.

The feasts of eating, drinking, talking, and laughing in Villa Seurat went on uninterruptedly, often until late at night. Every day was a holiday; we didn't have to wait for Christmas or New Year's or birthdays. And yet we managed to carry on with our writing at our usual rhythm and with undiminished speed. It's amazing how much can be packed in a day. Time seemed to have lost its tyranny over us.

Even our writing seemed to improve. Henry wrote in American, Larry in English, I in French, and it was all the same language, the language of the heart. Is Larry to be given credit for that? Somehow he seemed to have access to a novel source of inspiration, the overflow of which he pumped into us, as if we hadn't enough of our own already.

It was the luckiest period of our lives. All our undertakings proved success-ful, our love life flourished, there was no shortage of women in Villa Seurat, food and wine were in abundance, and we had a little literary magazine of our own, *The Booster,* in which we put juicy excerpts from our works in progress—titles to follow.

I was perhaps a more avid and grateful recipient of Larry's influence than Henry, because I needed it more than Henry. Everything that happened to me turned out lucky. Of course, I can't give Larry credit for the successful love affairs I had at the time, nor for the publication of my second novel, but the fact is that nothing bad happened while he was with us in Paris. While he was with us, everything was fine and delightful in the world, though there were already war clouds discernible in the distance.

I was no longer Henry's sidekick; I'd become one of the triplicity, I might almost say triumvirate, of a single unit in spirit and mind. Soon people began to call us "The Three Musketeers," a rather unsuitable name, were it not for the literary association, for a trio of writers, none of whom could handle a musket, not even I, though I had already one world war behind me.

Maybe I should mention at this point an odd idiosyncrasy Henry and Larry had in common. Neither of them had much love for his homeland. Henry especially spoke vituperatively against America, and his *Air-Conditioned Night-mare* was a veritable indictment of the American way of life. Nevertheless, the American Academy of Arts and Letters finally made him a member of that august institution.

Larry was born in Nepal, which is much nearer the stronghold of the Dalai Lama than to the center of the British Empire, to which he belonged by parent-age, education, and language. And yet he found life in England unsupportable and always settled down in foreign parts—Greece, Cyprus, and France. The reason for this, as I soon found out, was that English life was too familiar to him, and boring, totally devoid of the exoticism his nature couldn't do without.

I remember spending a few days with him in Bournemouth, where his mother lived. He couldn't understand my taking so much interest in this little seaside town, in the ways and habits of the people there, in the manner in which the kids played hopscotch on the sidewalks, in the pubs, and even the traffic signs. Larry found this extraordinary, and I had to remind him that having never before been to an English provincial town, I found Bournemouth as exotic as certain places in foreign lands were to him.

The last time I saw Larry was a couple of years ago in Paris when we were both signing copies of our books at the old bookshop Shakespeare & Co., originally founded by Sylvia Beach in the rue de l'Odéon. It was there that I met James Joyce on the day his *Ulysses* came out, published by Shakespeare & Co. The shop has since moved to the quai de la Seine, exactly opposite Nôtre-Dame.

On the occasion of our booksigning, Larry and I were supposed to reminisce about Henry Miller, our old friend, who had departed a few years previously from this earth, without leaving a forwarding address. I wonder if he listened to our chatter from high above, smoking a Gauloise Bleue in one of God's many mansions.

That event was widely reported in the Paris press. And surprise—there was a cartoon in one of the papers depicting us as The Three Musketeers welded together like Siamese triplets, with Henry, the musketeer-in-chief, in the center, and Larry's and my profile to the right and left of the master. A briar pipe was hanging out of the mouth of one of the profiles—mine.

I haven't seen Larry since that booksigning in Paris, but Ian MacNiven, a mutual friend of ours, sent me a recent snapshot of him holding on to a signpost as to dear life. The sign read "Sodom School," a boys' school somewhere in Pennsylvania. The schoolhouse is still standing, but is no longer in use since 1915. Larry probably wondered if there hadn't also been a Gomorrah School for girls. The image of the Angel of the Lord raining fire and destruction on the two corrupt, iniquitous cities might have flitted through his mind, but he must have realized that we no longer needed an Angel of the Lord for this purpose; we can do it now ourselves, if not better at least as thoroughly.

And on this rather sour note I conclude my birthday greeting. So once more, happy birthday to you, dear Larry, and, just for the hell of it, many happy returns.

Somerset, England

2

A Critical Friendship: Lawrence Durrell and Henry Miller

Ian S. MacNiven

Henry Miller once defined his literary relationship with Lawrence Durrell in terms of the ancient Greek complementary opposites: "There are two types always—one working with & in Chaos, the other with law, form, etc. No use comparing them or putting one above another—systole & diastole: Apollonian & Dionysian, what!" (15 October 1948/MacNiven 225).[1] Theirs was not always a tranquil relationship, intellectually, nor did the roles remain fixed. In May 1937 we find Miller arguing for more authorial control in *The Black Book*: "There are passages of minor importance where you elaborate for no good reason—perhaps because the machine was geared up and you couldn't apply the brakes. Throw a cold searchlight on it! You will lose nothing by cutting" (3 May 1937/MacNiven 74). "Now that I know there is verbiage about I have something to clean up—it does me good to be sat on. Thanks a lot," replied Durrell (May 1937/Wickes 94). More often Durrell assumed the Apollonian role, taking Miller to task for his supposed carelessness, for the lack of "form" in his longer works, for unnecessary and irrelevant passages.

Behind, alongside, and beyond the literary wrangles was a friendship of such steadfastness, such uninterrupted mutual support and love, that, until Miller's death in 1980, it furnished a fixed axis to the turbulent lives of both men. To start reading the correspondence between Durrell and Miller at any randomly chosen point is to gain the impression that the frequent letters and obviously close affinities must have been fueled by frequent meetings. Yet such was not the case: this was a friendship that not only survived long separations but seemed to thrive on distance, an intellectual communion between a some-times reluctant letter writer—Durrell—and an almost pathologically driven cor-respondent whose overall output is estimated to have been somewhere between one hundred thousand and two hundred thousand letters.

Appropriately, it all began with a letter, the 1935 fan letter Durrell on Corfu wrote to Miller in Paris. Durrell had just discovered *Tropic of Cancer*, and he composed an astute tribute. Miller responded, "You're the first Britisher who's written me an intelligent letter about the book" (1 September 1935/MacNiven 3), and the flow started. By the time they met in August 1937, Durrell had taken up the cause of Miller's reputation, and was promoting the publication of a collection of letters from the famous, who were to be dunned to support Miller; the American had undertaken to see Durrell's *Black Book,* unpublishable in America or England, through the Obelisk Press in Paris. It is not surprising that within minutes of their meeting, as reported by Alfred Perlès—the "Joey" or "little Joe" of the correspondence—they were fast friends, and the formal last names or initials of the epistolary greetings and closings gave way to "Larry" and "Henry."

Perlès's eyewitness description of the two principals at 18 Villa Seurat, Paris XIV, was never to lose its currency: two brother monks from a Lhasa of the mind, or a master/disciple pair, interchangeable in roles.

> Larry was squatting on the floor, Confucius-fashion, or perhaps rolled up in a ball on the carpet. I forget which. A ball with the face of an angel, looking younger than his age: oval face, eyes of stainless steel, long golden hair jewed down by the sun to nine carats. I recognized him at once from the ceiling frescoes in the Italian museums, picked him up from the floor and gave him the accolade, not bothering about sizing him up. There never was a better buy of a cat in the bag: our friendship incepted that far-off summer Sunday has lasted ever since.
>
> Henry, wrapped in his mocha dressing gown that always gave him the air of an inquisitive friar straight from Tibet, hadn't recovered yet from the surprise caused by the materialisation of his guest from Greece whom he had so far only known through his letters. Larry seemed a source of constant fascination for him, he kept staring at him open-mouthed, listening to the boy's scintillating chatter that brought tears of affection and admiration to his eyes. Even at that early stage, when Larry was as yet unfulfilled promise, Henry treated him with the sort of reverence one might have for a beloved child, a wonder child. (Perlès 11)

Another image is needed to fill out the Paris picture of Durrell and Miller beside those of their sitting at ease in the Villa Seurat rooms or in the flat Nancy and Larry rented near the Parc Montsouris, and that is their long walks across Paris "at the old break-neck speed," as Durrell was to recall after a meeting with Miller some twenty years later. North at the end of Villa Seurat, up the rue de Tombe Issoire, left onto boulevard Raspail, left again at Montparnasse—Miller of average height but looking taller because of his slenderness and the worn felt hat settled off-true over his bald spot, Durrell's muscular shortness emphasized by his bulky sweater, Miller's pleasantly rough Brooklyn accent pitched above the traffic, Durrell answering in his tenor of mocking subtlety. Explorations of Paris under the experienced guidance of long-term expatriate Miller, the Villa Seurat Series publishing venture, wine, good food, and talk, talk, talk. Durrell, Miller, Perlès, and Anaïs Nin took over *The Booster,* official organ of the

American Country Club, and in three issues turned it from a stodgy carrier of social gossip into a lively avant-garde literary magazine—and lost their sponsor amid threats of a lawsuit.

After a few months alternating between London and Paris, Larry and Nancy returned to Corfu where they remained until their return to France late next summer. They took Miller with them to London for Christmas and meetings with Dylan Thomas and T. S. Eliot. This series of encounters lasted until early 1939, and in July of that year Miller overcame his inertia and his fear of the onrushing war sufficiently to meet the Durrells in Greece, where he stayed through 26 December, sometimes alone on Corfu, sometimes with Larry and Nancy in Athens or touring the Peloponnesus. (Miller described his visit to Greece in *The Colossus of Maroussi,* his best non-fiction and according to some his finest book.) Durrell and Miller were not to meet again until the summer of 1959, when Henry, his children Val and Tony, and his third wife, Eve, stayed for a couple of months in a flat on the market square in medieval Sommières, about twelve miles from the Durrells' Mazet Michel near Nîmes. There were short meetings in France during 1960, 1961, 1962, and 1967, and in the United States in 1968, 1970, 1972, and 1973, but Durrell and Miller were not to live near one another again until 1974, when Durrell accepted a teaching post for January through March at the California Institute of Technology in Pasadena. These facts and dates, like X-ray plates, show only the bare bones of the friendship.

The literary development of Miller and Durrell can also be reduced to a revealing outline. Miller's artistic direction remained fairly constant throughout their relationship: his method had been autobiographical from the time of "Crazy Cock," his unpublished early novel; he wrote with one voice, a narrator-observer-actor persona that varied only slightly. "My own kind of flap-doodle," he once termed his style. Durrell, on the other hand, went from the clearly autobiographical *Pied Piper of Lovers* (1935) to *The Avignon Quintet* (1974–85), in which history and sheer invention far outweigh such details as may have been derived from events in the author's experience. It is ironic that the novel which shows most overtly Miller's influence (via *Tropic of Cancer*), *The Black Book,* the manuscript which Miller and Nin retyped and helped edit for publication, is in fact the most significant transitional book in the Durrell canon. *The Black Book* demonstrates Durrell's shift from confessional writing—Durrell had lived through most of the experiences attributed to his character and sometime narrator, Lawrence Lucifer—to the *heraldic* mode, as he termed his invented universe. In fact, *The Black Book* contains most of what were to become the hallmarks of Durrell's subsequent fiction: multiple narrators, internal diarists, inserted letters, the retrospective stance, indulgence of his fascination with the pathology of disease, patches of highly colored writing to set mood and tone, concern with structure (in the original typescript, the three main sections are headed "ego and id," "EGO," and "EGO AND ID" respectively), and so on. Thus, exactly at the time of the most intense association with Miller, both in number of letters per year and in hours spent together, Durrell was in the process of pulling away in his own direction.[2]

Durrell's brief flirtation with surrealism also coincided with his early association with Miller. He wrote "Asylum in the Snow" under the spell of Miller's *Hamlet* correspondence with Michael Fraenkel, and "Zero" after reading Nin's *House of Incest*. By 1937 David Gascoyne, the English poet and acknowledged surrealist, had become a friend of both Miller and Durrell. While Miller and Nin gave extravagant praise to "Zero" and "Asylum," Durrell resisted any suggestion of a surrealist label: "So far I've never managed to honestly become anything more than an ardent Durrealist," he wrote (Fall 1936/Wickes 24).

If I may risk a geographical generalization, Miller in Paris provided an epicenter for seismic shocks to Durrell's artistic system, even when Durrell buttressed and reinforced himself against giving in to Miller. During the Corfu-Paris-London period the praise flowed both ways; the literary criticism, gentle at that, came only from Miller. When the war drove Miller back to the United States, the independence Durrell had demonstrated with *The Black Book* became even more pronounced; and, while the reciprocal appreciation continued, Durrell criticized certain aspects of Miller's writing as he saw him embracing what Durrell perceived to be the American vices of formlessness and dispersion.

What I would like to examine closely, then, are the ways in which Durrell and Miller viewed one another as writers and tried to influence each other's work. Although Durrell was to have published two novels by the time he met Miller, *Pied Piper of Lovers* and *Panic Spring* (under the pseudonym Charles Norden), he regarded them as bastard offshoots of his true bent and refused to submit them to Miller's critical eye. When he tried to justify to Miller "my double Amicus Nordensis" on the ground that "Norden would keep me in touch with the commonplace world which will never understand my personal struggle" (21 July 1937/MacNiven 81), Miller devoted most of a three-page, single-spaced typed letter to setting his junior straight: "Alors, 'I want to begin here and now to talk about your future work!' . . . (Ahem) Don't, my good Durrell, take the schizophrenic route! . . . You can't write good and bad books. Not for long. . . . The toll is 'disintegration.' You must stand or fall either as Charles Norden or as Lawrence Durrell." Among other advice, Miller told his friend to have the courage of silence: not to write when he had nothing to say. However, it was permissible to make mistakes, as long as they occurred while he was attempting to follow his major vein: "Homer nodding" was okay, but not "Homer pseudonyming" (29 July 1937/MacNiven 84–85).

There is some irony in the fact that Miller, who penned many flippant and admittedly minor works on the order of the pamphlet *What Are You Going to Do about Alf?*, should warn Durrell against schizophrenia, against frittering away his talent. After Durrell had broken his teaching contract with the British Council to return to England from Argentina in 1948, ill and exhausted, Miller told him what to do—and, emphatically, what *not* to do:

> Wrote you a tremendous letter (in my head) two days ago at the sulphur baths here. Felt something was wrong. . . . Take a good rest. Don't worry about literature. I often think the Consular Service must be the ideal solution for a writer. But evidently it doesn't pay enough to keep two wives and a kid. Writing books & articles *to make money* is what essentially destroys one, I believe. Do anything else, if you can, rather than that. (18 February 1949/ MacNiven 228)

Miller, at least through 1945, could seldom be accused of writing for money— he usually made, so he claimed, less than five hundred dollars a year from his books. However, personal advice is generally easier for a writer to swallow than attempts to alter his art, and Durrell had already embarked on his effort to analyze and, if necessary, to reform Miller's writing. Durrell must have been amused to receive a warning from Miller against prostituting himself, since only a few years before he had similarly cautioned the American:

> I must say Henry that as a dissipater of talent and profit you are hard to beat; I have had letters from every poet and writer under sixteen in England asking for poetry or prose: and all ending up, "Mr Henry Miller has allowed us to issue his book so and so. It will be off the press soon!" There go your first copyrights! I think sympathy with cranks and young writers an admirable trait but I don't think you can do it. Unless you start a correspondence agency. And think of the waste! It's worse than being a psychoanalyst. (ca. February 1947/MacNiven 204)

Durrell was in fact much better than Miller at giving his art a rest, at permitting periods of inactivity between books. Indeed, this practice seems to be the secret of his own very rapid composition—*Balthazar* in six weeks, *Mountolive* in twelve. Once the idea for the book has matured, he often does the actual writing very quickly. In 1951 Durrell told Miller how to get himself into the mood for the masterwork he was sure could succeed the flawed *Rosy Crucifixion:* come to Europe! "Ah! if you could only lie fallow for a year, not writing, not thinking, by the Mediterranean, it would come, this book full of the innocence, amorality and ripeness of old age" (early September 1951/MacNiven 256).

Before he left Alexandria for Rhodes in early 1945, Durrell wrote his first formal criticism of Miller, the title essay for *The Happy Rock,* Bern Porter's collection of essays about Miller. While he ranks his friend with Melville and Whitman, and says he "completely overtops the glazed reflections cast by those waxworks of contemporary American fiction—Hemingway, Dos Passos, Faulkner" (1), he recognizes Miller's lack of structure. Durrell writes of *Tropic of Cancer,* "Formally the book was a chaos. . . . It was chaotic in the way that *Leaves of Grass* is chaotic; it dramatized and ranted: it was cold-blooded and terrifying and upsetting. It defied every rule of taste and construction. It completely came off" (1). In this essay, of course, Durrell makes a triumphant virtue of Miller's supposed main failing.

Durrell's negative criticism of Miller's writing began some years after the imposition of the Atlantic between them, and seemed to become more intense as his friend's popular success grew. Like some Tiresias warning against hubris, Durrell launched an attack on what he saw as Miller's deteriorating grasp of form: "I see your reputation is riding higher and higher these days; glory in your well-deserved security, your studio, infant and secretary; hope the new books follow through. You have a tendency to splay rather these days, which is perhaps the influence of the US" (ca. mid-February 1946/MacNiven 194). In Durrell's view, the warning turned out to be all too direly needed, though it went unheeded: *Sexus* was to strike him as "disgracefully bad" (10 September 1949/MacNiven 233).

Durrell planned an expansion of "The Happy Rock," and cleverly found in Miller's own practice exemplar of what he was to campaign for:

> I have just started and read you all the way through again. I think it's time someone did a serious critical essay on your prose: it has some very curious elements—quite new to prose I think. For example the amount of double talk and non sequitur you indulge in is really incredible; it's the perfect packing for the image. . . . What a disastrous effect Whitman has had on his imitators! The egoismus cult is very bad for young men! You should know, you've had a wicked effect yourself on the young of England. They think if they splash about in the bath it's interesting because it's THEM. Little do they realise what practice and technique and elision goes into making your free-and-easy effect. May I say that the first draft of TROPIC was some 600 pages long and that had it been published as it stood it would have been a very near miss as compared to the bullseye you put out? (ca. November 1946/Wickes 233)[3]

Durrell asked for some of Miller's most recent writing in manuscript, and got a reply that was at once a defense and an evasion: the guerrilla fighter of American letters hiding on Big Sur ridge. "But about my style, etc. . . . I don't want to ship you the ms. of *Rosy Crucifixion* for the reason that as it stands it is in the first writing, with not a correction and I may delete whole pages or sections when I get down to it. You are wrong, I think, to judge from excerpts you saw: there is every sort of style and treatment in the 750 pages I have written, and a good bit is diffuse, opaque, rambling, hugger-mugger" (12 July 1947/MacNiven 213). In "Studies in Genius VIII—Henry Miller," which expands upon and does not simply repeat "The Happy Rock," Durrell showed that he recognized the type of writer Miller was, and also that he realized it was not rational to expect change: "There seem to be two distinct types of creative man. The first controls his material and is shaped by it. The second delivers himself over, bound hand

and foot to his gifts. . . . With this second type of artist it is useless to agitate for measure, form, circumspection" (45). Being as stubborn in his beliefs as Miller was resistant to change, Durrell continued to agitate for measure and form, and even for circumspection: he found entire passages of *Sexus* embarrassingly "vulgar."

With equal stubbornness, Miller stuck to his self-chosen scatter-gun: "When it comes to the autobiographical narrative I really don't change much. Also wrong of you, I think, to consider Rimbaud, *Hamlet,* etc. as 'peripheral.' It's all one. If one lived long enough the whole man would come through in the work—ideas, sensations, experience, philosophy, aesthetic, and everything. . . . Certainly you may quote from books and letters—but I do want to see the passages and approve, of course" (12 July 1947/MacNiven 213). This points to a main cause of Durrell's critical difference with Miller. Durrell consistently refused to see Miller "whole," knowing that he himself could be two or three or more writers: Lawrence Durrell, poet and serious novelist; Charles Norden, popular writer in a light romantic vein; a Wodehousian humorist gamboling in the halls of the Foreign Office; and so on. Durrell apparently believed at this time that he could keep the roles separate. Miller, on the other hand, always saw his work as unified, even when most diverse: he saw no real contradiction between his lucid, clear writing and his rambling, "bad" writing. Is this because Miller *became* his work in a way Durrell never has, nor ever intended to?

When Durrell reached South America he thought he had found a clue to Miller's lack of control over form: it was not simply Miller's individual nature as an artist, it was that of the entire hemisphere!

> So much is explained here about the American struggle, the struggle not to get de-personalised. Because this is a communal continent; the individual soul has no dimensions. In architecture, in art, religion, it is all community—skyscrapers, jitterbugging, hyperboles—it is all of a piece. I understand now why the American artist has no sense of form—because his soul is continually being siphoned off into the communal soda water fountain, and his struggle is to concretise it enough to suffer. . . . All this is quite understandable the moment you hit Rio. (ca. late November 1947/MacNiven 218–19)

Durrell has made no secret of his faith in Georg Groddeck, the German contemporary of Freud who believed that people produce their illnesses according to inner needs. Bored and unhappy in Cordova, Argentina, Durrell became overweight and ill, and fled the "formless" Americas for form-conscious Europe. Eventually he was to settle in France, appreciating the form-adherence of French intellect, courts, government, and literature.

Durrell's criticism was by no means confined to form: toward the end of 1947 he wrote to Miller complaining that some of his work was becoming facile, that he was repetitive, that he sometimes appeared to strain after images:

The *Remember to Remember* episodes are some of the most moving things you have ever done: also you capture little Joe perfectly. I think you still write better about France than about anything else: and it seems to me that you are doing too much intimate portraiture of the "Rattner" style. It comes easily to you, but it is also getting a little bit repetitive . . . you will see that you have said almost the same things and in almost the same way of Anaïs, of Benno, of Reichel etc. . . . . The tone of voice is familiar, and I feel that this type of portraiture corresponds in you to what would be, in a lesser sized man, journalism. It comes easy, too easy, and though it's delightful and breath-taking to read if you are new to it, if you are an old Miller fan of the 38 vintage as I am, you long for more of the new Miller (*Remember to Remember* and the "Washboard Veteran") where the integration is flawless and smooth, and where you don't have to reach for an out of the way image, it lies inherent in the matter. (December? 1947/MacNiven 220)

Miller's response to this letter has been lost; in any case, life at Big Sur was not going well: the brilliant, perfumed, and feckless French astrologer Conrad Moricand was living with the Millers, a disaster brought about, as described by Henry in *Devil in Paradise,* by Miller's compassion; Lepska Miller was pregnant for the second time; Henry, expecting another war, was planting vegetables and fruit trees. That his writing at this time should strike Durrell as "too easy" must have seemed to Miller a crazy irony.

Durrell's teaching at the Asociación Argentina de Cultura Británica in Cordova was very important for his understanding of Miller: he taught Miller's books and set out to explain him to students and local intellectuals. His strictures now went beyond form and facility to the lack of "tightness":

Sure, and we wouldn't be after asking you to impose a Form of the outer, the reasoned, the Willed—sorry if I gave such a silly impression. No, I meant that we had a right to expect work of a certain horse-power from you now, and that here and there you allow some lesser jobs to creep in. For example the essay on American bread in the last book, and the story about astrology. The *writing* ain't tight enough . . . . Of course I know 100 years from now we'll be treasuring the smallest fragments—but that don't excuse you not making them as powerful as only you know how to. And sometimes you do run on and worry an unrefreshing theme to death—*Murder the M.* contains much that [you] might excise, thinketh the heretic who has just completed a course on you. (ca. November 1948/MacNiven 225–26)

This complaint about the writing itself was to become the crux of Durrell's fault-finding with *Sexus*.

The first volume of *The Rosy Crucifixion* was heralded by Miller's joyous approbation—and a hint of defensiveness. Although his tendency had been to ignore Durrell's admonitions, finally the repeated accusations that his writings lacked form—and therefore presumably were flawed—provoked him into an earnest if good-natured setting forth of his views, a patient explanation more than a defense: "Just preparing Vol. I. (*Sexus*) of *The Rosy Crucifixion* for Girodias to publish, in English, then French. A great work!!! Have read it thru several times & am still making revisions. No order—yes and no! I see now what is my order—at least in this work. It is the picture of 'germination' in all its phases. That other, *imposed,* order—by the brain or will—will never be mine" (15 October 1948/MacNiven 225).

When an advance copy of *Sexus* reached Durrell, his reaction was to write his disappointment before he had finished reading, and then, in his agitation, to overtake the letter with a more blunt telegram: "SEXUS DISGRACEFULLY BAD WILL COMPLETELY RUIN REPUTATION UNLESS WITHDRAWN REVISED LARRY" (10 September 1949/MacNiven 233). This time it was not so much formlessness as a failure of judgment, a failure to prune, that distressed Durrell:

> I must confess I'm bitterly disappointed in it, despite the fact that it contains some of your very best writing to date. But my dear Henry, the moral vulgarity of so much of it is *artistically* painful. These silly, meaningless scenes which have no raison d'être, no humour, just childish explosions of obscenity—what a pity, what a terrible pity for a major artist not to have critical sense enough to husband his forces, to keep his talent aimed at the target. What on earth possessed you to leave such twaddle in? I understand that with your great sweeping flights you occasionally have to plough though an unrewarding tract of prose. But the strange thing is that the book gives very little feeling of real passion. (5 September 1949/MacNiven 232)

Miller must have been deeply disappointed at the disapproval of his closest literary ally, yet he replied calmly enough, "I laugh and shake my head bewilderedly, that's all." And he did not back down but asserted, "I am writing exactly what I want to write and the way I want to do it. Perhaps it's twaddle, perhaps not" (28 September 1949/MacNiven 233–34). Meanwhile, Durrell was in a lather of remorse; Perlès had scolded him for being hard on "the Master," and he had sent another telegram: "DEEPEST APOLOGIES UNJUST CRITICISM WRITING NOTHING SAID QUALIFIES ADMIRATION YOUR GENIUS HOPING FRIENDSHIP UNAFFECTED" (29 September 1949/MacNiven 237). Durrell need not have worried. Henry scolded Fred for imagining him "going gaga soon," and told Larry, "In these matters friendship can only be asserted and maintained by the strictest probity" (3 October 1949/MacNiven 238). All was well.

Some years later Durrell realized the counter-clockwise pattern of *The Rosy Crucifixion*—that the trilogy was moving backward into the spiritual and artistic development of the author—and admitted to Miller that the presentation of the callow, unformed, undiscriminating mind of the proto-artist did indeed have a certain justification. Thus far, outside criticism seems to be running in agreement with Durrell's first impression, but, if the Melville parallel Durrell claimed for Miller holds, there will be upward reevaluations of the huge sequence.

The year after the *Sexus* flap, Miller read Durrell's first published play, *Sappho,* and wrote approvingly:

Sappho in a new guise, most enchanting and very much you. (With a tincture of Eliot's gray foreboding wisdom.) But somehow Shakespeare comes out in this—the flavor of him, his essence, his magic of language. Yet it's Greek—and of no time, or all time. "We" are not deceived by tyrant-and-mob business. What wots here is the poet—his fate. It's secure. There are passages on the role and effect (of poet) which are revelatory & personal. It's very alive, your play—and the drama itself thrilling. (4 November 1950/MacNiven 252)

Then Miller turned the tables on Durrell, who had so often criticized him of failure to trim and cut. "Don't *cut* as suggested in back of book—cut down on some of the sometimes too florid, vague, too beautiful (precious) speeches. But it's your *poetic* utterance I like—and the poetic feeling. Do more plays, yes! Hallelujah!" (252). The appreciation of poetry Miller apparently learned from Durrell: a frequent refrain in the correspondence is Miller's inability to understand verse, but, out of sheer loyalty, one imagines, he kept reading Durrell's poems until he could say, "I take your poems to the woods now, when I go for my constitutional. They read well there" (2 July 1945/MacNiven 182).

Although Durrell's friendly offensive against Miller's lack of form was for many years the main critical note in their correspondence, Miller's minatory voice reappeared too, periodically, and his most earnest later denunciation of a book by Durrell came over *Esprit de Corps,* the volume of "Diplomatic Sketches" featuring Antrobus, Durrell's playfully caricatured British Foreign Service officer. Durrell had not expected Miller to like these stories, and wrote in early 1958, "I didn't send you *Esprit de Corps;* thought you mightn't find it funny. I had to pay for the baby's shoes somehow" (before 20 January 1958/ MacNiven 306). Emboldened by the British success of the book, Durrell added that he was "sending it along for you to see." Miller replied categorically: "Don't write any more *Esprit de Corps* stuff. That's really terrible. Not even for money!" (6 March 1958/previously unpublished). And don't give me the baby excuse, he implied in a later letter: "Don't buy any more shoes for the baby! Believe me, they are better off without" (3 April 1958/MacNiven 317).

Miller's complaints about the Antrobus stories, however, coincided with his panegyrics about each successive volume of *The Alexandria Quartet.* Indeed, from 1960 on, neither writer was to say much in literary admonition to the other. Was Durrell really won over to accept *The Rosy Crucifixion,* and did Miller come to tolerate *Stiff Upper Lip* and *Sauve Qui Peut*? More likely, there were affectionate Gallic shrugs in Provence—"Ah, that Henry! What can one do?"— and bemused head waggings along the California coast as each author received a work from his friend in the style or genre he disliked.

Tolerance in friendship is fine, but most pleasing of all, perhaps, is the gratitude which flowed both ways, from early years until late. Debts were invariably acknowledged, and in the most unequivocal manner for men chronically plagued by overwork and shortage of time: they wrote letters, edited books, and actively campaigned for one another. Their meetings were mutually cherished, as any reader of the correspondence knows. In 1957, when Durrell was on the edge of achieving financial independence through his writing—with *Bitter Lemons* a Duff Cooper Memorial Prize winner and a Book Society choice, *Justine* winning plaudits and sales, and lucrative contracts for future books— Larry paid Henry the handsome tribute of crediting him with responsibility for his success. Rowohlt, in part through Miller's urging, had just contracted to publish *The Alexandria Quartet* in German, and Durrell wrote: "THIS REALLY DOES OFFER ME THE CHANCE TO FREE MYSELF FROM DIRTY JOBS AND SEE AT LEAST A YEAR AHEAD. A VERY BIG TURNING POINT IN MY LIFE—THOUGH OF COURSE THIS ADVANCE WILL SOUND CHICKEN-FEED FROM THE U.S. POINT OF VIEW [about 1400 dollars]. NOW THE REST IS UP TO ME AND UP TO BOOKS. MARVELLOUS. AND OF COURSE I REALLY OWE IT ALL TO YOUR HARD HITTING CHAMPI- ONSHIP OF ME. WAS EVER A WRITER LUCKIER IN A TRUE FRIEND I WONDER?" (August 1957/previously unpublished).

Notes

1. Quotations from published letters of Durrell and Miller *not* found in the 1988 *Durrell-Miller Letters* have been taken from the originals and follow the authors' usages; in some cases they differ from versions printed in the Wickes *Correspondence* of 1963, listed here only for those letters not included in the 1988 edition. All the Durrell letters quoted herein are to be found in The Henry Miller Collection, University Research Library, University of California, Los Ange- les; the Miller letters are in The Lawrence Durrell Collection, Morris Library, Southern Illinois University at Carbondale.

2. The typescript of *The Black Book,* identified by Durrell as "the one and only," is in the Durrell collection at Morris Library.

3. Approximately one-half of this text appears in Wickes.

Works Cited

Durrell, Lawrence. "The Happy Rock." *The Happy Rock*. Ed. Bern Porter. Berkeley, California: Packard, 1945.
_____ . "Studies in Genius VIII—Henry Miller." *Horizon* 20:115 (July 1949), 45–61.
Durrell, Lawrence, and Henry Miller. *The Durrell-Miller Letters, 1935–1980*. Ed. Ian S. MacNiven. New York: New Directions, 1988.
_____ . *Lawrence Durrell–Henry Miller: A Private Correspondence*. Ed. George Wickes. New York: Dutton, 1963.
Perlès, Alfred. *My Friend Lawrence Durrell*. Northwood, Middlesex: Scorpion, 1961.

3

The Uncommon Ground

James A. Brigham

To decode even the narrow and finite Stuff of life is to tumble upon answers.

In an early interview with Kenneth Young (1959), Lawrence Durrell made it clear that it was for the English that he wrote and to the English that he addressed his work (6). The English, unfortunately, have not always returned Durrell's interest. The volumes of his verse, for example, have always been *succès d'estimes,* but otherwise the poet has suffered such perennial neglect that Peter Levi was prompted to.ask, "Why are we not told more often that Durrell, except perhaps for Empson, is the most faultlessly musical of modern poets, and yet not trivial, not facile, not unreal?" (102). Why, indeed?

Throughout the late thirties, the forties, and the early fifties, and despite his prolonged absence from England, Durrell's poems appeared regularly in the pages of *The New English Weekly, Poetry (London),* and *The New Statesman and Nation.* Here were clear signs of a good poet getting better, yet the neglect continued. Durrell the poet was suffering from his decision to identify with a tradition which the writers and critics who were his contemporaries had rejected: although he wrote *for* the English, he refused to write *about* the English and the England which were then in vogue. "Dealing with [a] set of realities other than those bankrupt ones still obsessing the British left," says Derek Stanford, "his poetry could claim to be in every way as authentic as that of the school of Lehmann. In fact, one could argue that it dealt with universals in a way that the latter writers in their topical concerns with contemporary history did not do" (103).

Tradition and individual talent, according to T. S. Eliot, must coexist in a balance so delicate that each irrevocably changes the other:

[Tradition] cannot be inherited, and if you want it you must obtain it by great labour. It involves, in the first place, the historical sense, which we may call nearly indispensable to anyone who would continue to be a poet beyond his twenty-fifth year; and the historical sense involves a perception, not only of the pastness of the past, but of its presence; the historical sense compels a man to write not merely with his own generation in his bones, but with a feeling that the whole of the literature of Europe from Homer and within it the whole of the literature of his own country has a simultaneous order. This historical sense, which is a sense of the timeless as well as of the temporal together, is what makes a writer traditional. And it is at the same time what makes a writer most acutely conscious of his place in time, of his contemporaneity. (49)

I suspect we will not find a better statement than this of the sense of tradition which has infused Durrell's poetry and prose for the past fifty years. Following the guidelines which Eliot laid down in *The Sacred Wood* and then illustrated in *The Waste Land,* Durrell has used the traditional figures of European literature and myth for educative rather than ornamental purposes. He has also roamed the corridors of ancient and modern thought, finding resonances between seemingly disparate ideas. In those resonances, he has discovered the "philosophy of metaphysic" which Stanford finds hidden in the depths of the poetry.

Profoundly transcendental, Durrell's metaphysic is founded in what Leibniz called the *philosophia perennis,* to which the best introduction in English is Aldous Huxley's *The Perennial Philosophy* (1944). "We are moving towards a new metaphysics—at any rate new for us," Durrell tells us in *A Key to Modern British Poetry* (1952):

In a recent anthology Aldous Huxley tries to show that non-attachment is the philosophic basis of all religions, and that all mystics agree about it. If you look at the book honestly and carefully, without sectarian prejudice, I think you will be forced to agree. "The Perennial Philosophy" stretches like a bridge between Lao Tzu and St. John of the Cross, between Eliot and Rilke, between Auden and John Donne. (85)

Durrell discovered that the same philosophy nourished visions as diverse as those of the Gautama Buddha and Eugene Marais, and much of his concern has been to point out that realization to those who could profit from understanding the premise which underlies the world's cosmologies. As he says elsewhere in *A Key to Modern British Poetry:* "When you look at the art of an epoch in any of its modes you see that, taken in the round, it constitutes a cosmology, an overall interpretation of the universe we inhabit" (2).

In the connections between the cosmologies of different ages, Durrell has found the resonances that inform his work and upon which his metaphysic is based. According to Huxley, the perennial philosophy is "the metaphysic that recognizes a divine Reality substantial to the world of things and lives and minds; the psychology that finds in the soul something similar to, or even identical with, divine Reality; the ethic that places man's final end in the knowledge of the immanent and transcendent Ground of Being" (vii). Metaphysics, psychology, ethics: these have been Durrell's subjects and concerns from the beginning. They have prompted his many allusions to Plato and Emerson, to Orpheus and the Buddha, to Groddeck and Jung, to Marais and even Einstein. Each of these he has found deeply rooted in the idea of a common "Ground of Being" which is immanent in all things.

In Durrell's system, very different concepts are broadly similar: the individual talent and tradition, the *phenomenal* and *noumenal* worlds, the individual psyche and the It, the individual and the collective unconscious—these relationships are variations of the relationship of the many and the One described by Lao Tzu in the *Tao Te Ching*. Similar associations occur in nature—in the *siphnophora,* a composite animal to which Durrell refers in *A Key to Modern British Poetry,* and in the African termitary which Eugene Marais describes in *The Soul of the White Ant.* The control of the queen over individual termites is one model Durrell used for the relationship of the Alexandrians to their city in *The Alexandria Quartet,* and was also, perhaps, a basis for the interconnection of the individual and the spirit of place in "Landscape with Literary Figures" (1960).[1] Another, more clearly cosmological model which Durrell adapted to the *Quartet* is Einsteinian relativity. Durrell's relativity is one without the indeterminacy of Planck and Heisenberg: his Einstein is the Einstein who believed in a unified field, a universal "common ground" to which all things are ultimately relative. The most fundamental statement of this correlation is the "As below, darling, so above" of "The Reckoning" from 1971 (*Collected Poems* 303). Although in 1934 he could entertain the thought that we may be only "sick hack-satires on meaning by Infinity, / With not one working sense / That does not illustrate our own / And all humanity's impertinence" (*Collected Poems* 37), by the time of "The Reckoning" he had concluded that "the feeble human finite must belong / Within the starred circumference of wonder." Like his good friend Theodore Stephanides, Durrell has come to understand mankind as a function of the universe, and this realization underlies and informs his work.

Even *White Eagles over Serbia* (1957), considered a minor work by most, contains clear references to the perennial philosophy. Methuen, the hero, carries a copy of Thoreau's *Walden* when on missions for "the Awkward shop," and is haunted by passages such as "Time is but the stream I go a-fishing in. I drink at it; but while I drink I see the sandy bottom and detect how shallow it is. Its thin current slides away, but eternity remains" (103). The first edition of *The Dark Labyrinth* (1947) contains an epigram from Plato's *Phaedo* which questions the nature of reality by questioning the true nature of life and death. Hogarth the psychologist is clearly modeled on Groddeck, and his theories are founded in part on Groddeck's claim that we should say not "I live," but "I am lived by the It" (11). And the plateau to which the Trumans ascend is clearly the plateau of Cupid and Psyche from Ovid's *Metamorphoses,* a place where Elsie Truman learns more about her own relationship to what is permanent in existence and where her husband comes to feel that he is "O. C. Universe" (255–56).

The transcendent river of time in *Walden* and the labyrinth of life and death suggested by the *Phaedo* are models of Plato's false, imperfect phenomenal world behind which stands a perfect noumenal one; or as Durrell wrote in *White Eagles over Serbia:* "Shams and delusions are esteemed for soundest truths, while reality is fabulous!" (103). Durrell had found a similar message in Groddeck's theory of the *Es,* the It of whose wishes our own desires are mere reflections, and of whose presence we can have clear proof only if the veil that separates us is lifted as "the mist that dulls the vision of mortals" was lifted for Aeneas so he could briefly see the gods, those "huge and mighty forms, that do not live like living forms" (Vergil 46) and so see his own condition in cosmological terms. Twentieth-century man has been brought to a similar realization through the efforts of Groddeck and of Jung, among others.

As the universe has become increasingly subjective in this century, the mythic systems through which the ancients understood the cosmos have been internalized. The essential duality of the Goddess and her Consort has become the *anima-animus* relationship of Jung's system: the fruitful union of Isis and Osiris has become the equally desirable union of the female and male elements of the self. "This inner duality," Jung says, "is often symbolized by a hermaphroditic figure, like the crowned hermaphrodite . . . from a 17th-century alchemical manuscript" (30n). In *The Alexandria Quartet,* Durrell's own mythopoesis produced a blending of the archetypal duality with modern science and psychology. "I can imagine a form," Pursewarden tells Darley, "which, if satisfied, might raise in human terms the problems of causality or indeterminacy. . . . And nothing *recherché,* either. Just an ordinary Girl Meets Boy story" (*Clea* 136). *The Alexandria Quartet* is a love story, certainly—perhaps a collection of love stories—or variations upon one love story, the story of the Goddess and her Consort as Rhea and Kronos or Cupid and Psyche, which modern physics calls the space-time continuum. *The Alexandria Quartet* is an investigation of modern love.

The Revolt of Aphrodite (1974) is a "culture reading" of the male-dominated Western society in which both the real and the symbolic roles of the female have become distorted ("Postface"). The dual nature of mankind is exemplified both in the dual structure of the novels and by various traditional dichotomies (light and dark, blonde and brunette, East and West, and so on). More importantly, however, the sickness of Western society is personified by the illnesses of Benedicta and Iolanthe, illnesses which mirror one another in the most instructive way. For "she who confers blessing" is psychologically ill, and the "screen goddess" has tuberculosis, emblematic of sickness of the spirit.

Using a system of equivalents found in both Groddeck and Jung, Durrell uses mythic and near-mythic figures as avatars of the collective unconscious. Indeed, the gods and goddesses inhabit Durrell's works as they were once supposed to walk the ancient world: they are personifications of the forces at play in the universe, and their presence in Durrell is instructive as it is in the ancient myths.

The poetry is a more personal statement of the philosophy propounded in the prose. Durrell's verse illustrates his long-held belief that art is just as much "an overall interpretation of the universe we inhabit" as is science (*A Key to Modern British Poetry* 2). He combines successfully the observed detail and the reflective response and subtly appropriates mathematical and scientific terms ("the calculus of prayer" and "the permutations of a rose") to his own use just as he has incorporated the ancient deities and their meanings into the modern context. The earlier poems are derivative and awkward in style. Although there are hints of the later style in lines such as "There is a great heart-break in an evening sea" (*Collected Poems* 25) and the "lithe God" (25) of "Dark Grecian" (1934), they lack the power of, say, Lais (260) in "Poemandres" (1964), and there is no suggestion of the preoccupations of the later poems.

Beginning in 1938, however, the perennial philosophy appears increasingly, so that the bulk of Durrell's verse constitutes a document of nonattachment. "The new metaphysics—at any rate new for us" toward which in the later thirties Durrell already sensed that Western man was moving was a system beyond European arts and science. "Faut-il enfin dépasser le point de tangence qui sépare l'art et la science," asks a character in "Solange" (1969), "tout en les traitant comme les religions primitives en faillite? Oui mais comment?" (269). Durrell's bankrupt European culture is one dominated by Cartesian dualism in "Cities, Plains and People" (1946), and he proposes Taoism as a solution: "Duality, the great European art subject, which is resolved by the Taoist formulas" (107n). Throughout "Cities, Plains and People," his most autobiographical long poem, he identifies increasingly with Shakespeare's Prospero and with "the mythical Yellow Emperor, first exponent of the Tao" (169n). As in Taoism, "All bearings are true" according to the Admiralty Pilot (163n), and Durrell adopts a stance of simple acceptance, understanding that "no saint or seer unlocks / The wells of truth unless he first / Conquer for the truth his thirst" (162). In "On the Suchness of the Old Boy" (1972), the Sage advocates that we "live the life of a stowaway in this world" (327). "If so things are, why let them be," he says: "Look not for reason anywhere; but keep / Revelation for those who least care" (325). Here the nonattachment and simplicity which are the central tenets of the perennial philosophy are presented through the gentle humor of the old man, who has come to see all deities as manifestations of the Divine and all selves as manifestations of the self.[2] "Suchness" is a synonym for Buddhahood in Huxley's *The Perennial Philosophy*.[3] And in Durrell's poem, "The Sermon," the sage has reached that level of understanding which "is to become wholly aware, to become holy, / To stand between the causal and the casual" (80). What was once understood intellectually has become an intuited knowledge: the tragic dualities of a European culture based on the will can be resolved through the simple acceptance of being as a part of the universal process.

In the One, all opposites are reconciled, all manifestations joined: this is the message of the perennial philosophy, and of Durrell's poetry and prose for nearly fifty years. Moving against the tide of his contemporaries, he has chosen to write in an older tradition than the one founded by Auden, rejecting the myopia of those who were caught up in contemporary events. "Procounsuls should be taught to leave art alone," the Roman speaker of "In Patmos" (1948) tells us:

> Before we came the men of the east
> Knew it contained a capital metaphysic,
> As chess once founded in astronomy
> Degenerated into the game we know.

(Collected Poems 207)

In keeping with his sense of his own place in tradition, Durrell has built upon the figures of ancient myth, returning them to the streets of his "personal world" and reaffirming their place and importance in the twentieth century. With Lao Tzu, Thoreau, and the others whose work has been such a rich source for his own, Durrell understands that "the Many and the None" are "base reflections of the One," and his art shows the sheer delight taken in the commonplace (169). But throughout a long and illustrious career, he has also tried to lift a corner of the curtain which separates the finite from the infinite, teaching his readers that "the fullness of being is not in refinement, / By the delimitation of the object, but / In roundness, the enbosoming of the Real" (204).

Notes

1. Lawrence Durrell, "Note in the Text," *Balthazar.* In the context of Durrell's use of the composite animal as a model in *The Alexandria Quartet,* we should also recall that Melissa is the name of the Bee-Goddess.

2. Huxley, pp. 102 and 112, for example.

3. Huxley, p. 53, for example.

Works Cited

Durrell, Lawrence. *Balthazar.* London: Faber; New York: Dutton, 1958.
———. *Clea.* New York: Dutton, 1960.

———. *Collected Poems, 1931–1974.* Ed. James A. Brigham. London: Faber, 1980.

———. *The Dark Labyrinth.* Harmondsworth: Penguin, 1978.

———. *A Key to Modern British Poetry.* Norman: University of Oklahoma, 1952.

———. *The Revolt of Aphrodite.* London: Faber, 1974.

———. *White Eagles over Serbia.* Harmondsworth: Penguin, 1980.

Eliot, Thomas Stearns. "Tradition and the Individual Talent." *The Sacred Wood: Essays on Poetry and Criticism.* London: Methuen, 1960.

Huxley, Aldous. *The Perennial Philosophy.* New York: Harper and Brothers, 1945.

Groddeck, Georg. *The Book of the It.* Trans. V. M. E. Collins. Intro. Lawrence Durrell. New York: Vintage, 1961.

Jung, Carl Gustav. "Approaching the Unconscious." *Man and His Symbols.* Ed. Carl Gustav Jung. London: Aldus, 1964.

Levi, Peter. "Lawrence Durrell's Greek Poems." *Labrys* 5 (1979), 101–3.

Stanford, Derek. "Lawrence Durrell as Poet: Some Retrospections & Presumptions." *Labrys* 5 (1979), 104–9.

Vergil. *The Aeneid.* Trans. Patrick Dickinson. New York: New American Library, 1961.

Young, Kenneth. "A Dialogue with Durrell." *Encounter* 13:6 (December 1959), 61–68.

4

The Poetry of Lawrence Durrell

Michael H. Begnal

Despite international acclaim as one of the greatest novelists of the twentieth century, Lawrence Durrell has said many times that he had always expected to be known as a poet. He has written poetry continuously throughout his life and still continues to do so. G. S. Fraser has described him as "a minor poet, though of a very distinguished sort" (45). Perhaps this is something of a fair assessment, since Durrell's body of verse has not attained the stature of that of T. S. Eliot or W. H. Auden, whom he considers to be the giants of modern English poetry. Still there is a depth and solidity to his work which makes it more than worthy of consideration. If Lawrence Durrell is a distinguished poet, as indeed he is, then just what kind of poet is he? By drawing on a representative poem or two, and by considering some of the statements Durrell himself has made about poetry, perhaps we can come to a balanced evaluation.

Just as *The Alexandria Quartet* was heavily influenced by the thought of Albert Einstein, as well as by that of Sigmund Freud, so too has the poetry been likewise affected. In a series of lectures delivered in Argentina for the British Council, later collected as *A Key to Modern British Poetry,* Durrell comments extensively on his apprehension of the space-time continuum. At one point he says, "Time has become a thick opaque medium, welded to space . . . but an always-present yet always recurring thing. . . . To think according to the terms of relativity one has to train the mind to do something rather extraordinary: to accept two contradictory ideas as simultaneously true." He goes on: "If there is any movement at all it is circular, cyclic, and significant only because it is repeated" (31).

Keeping in mind D. H. Lawrence's dictum that we should trust the tale, and not the teller, let us consider "Rain, Rain, Go to Spain," first published in 1971:

That noise will be the rain again,
Hush-falling absolver of together—
Companionable enough, though, here abroad:
The log fire, some conclusive music, loneliness.
I can visualize somebody at the door
But make no name or shape for such an image,
Just a locus for small thefts
As might love us both awake tomorrow,
An echo off the lead and ownerless.
But this hissing rain won't improve anything.
The roads will be washed out. Thinking falters.

My book-lined walls so scholarly
So rosy, glassed in by the rain.
I finger the sex of many an uncut book.
Now spring is coming you will get home
Later and later in another climate.
You vanished so abruptly it took me by surprise.
I heard to relearn everything again
As if blinded by a life of tiny braille.

Then a whole year with just one card,
From Madrid. "It is raining here and
Greco is so sombre. I have decided
At last to love nobody but myself."
I repeat it in an amused way
Sometimes very late at night.
In an amazed way as anyone might
Looking up from a classic into all the
Marvelous rain-propelled darkness.

As if suddenly you had gone
Beyond the twelfth desire:
You and memory both become
Contemporary to all this inner music.
Time to sift out our silences, then:
Time to relay the failing fire.

(Collected Poems 305)

The poem is divided into four sections, and at first it seems firmly rooted in both time and space—the speaker is alone, late in the evening, listening to the rain drumming on the roof. The poem is a meditation recounting the thoughtful progress of the mind, and, though the initial calm and peacefulness of the moment are disrupted by the intrusion of the memory of a past love, the voice struggles to forget. With a conscious effort to control his thought processes, he wrenches his attention away to the practical now: "this hissing rain won't improve anything. / The roads will be washed out." Though "Thinking falters," he begins again in something of a Prufrockian fashion, resetting the manageable scene with "My book-lined walls so scholarly," until the subject of the woman surges to the fore, and the speaker is undone by his own language: "I finger the sex of many an uncut book." With a jolt, the voice which has been musing to itself in the present now suddenly addresses the female "you" in lines which fuse both the future and the past in the immediate present: "Now spring is coming you will get home / Later and later in another climate. / You vanished so abruptly it took me by surprise." Though he is aware of time and the passing seasons, it seems that at this point spring will bring with it no promise of rebirth.

G. S. Fraser, describing Lawrence Durrell the poet, calls him "the solitary dancer in a self-walled enclosure" (60), an apt portrait of the speaker of this poem. The essential subject here is not the lover who has disappeared, not a celebration or a rueing of past pleasures, but rather a consideration of what the poet is to do with the present and the future. He has begun the process of regeneration, and it seems to be working well: "I heard to relearn everything again / As if blinded by a life of tiny braille." The initially curious choice of "heard" when we expect "had" serves to portray a reeducation of the senses, a revitalization of sight and sound which goes beyond the books in the library or "some conclusive music." This is picked up in the poem's final section by "this inner music," which incorporates the speaker, the lover, time, and memory. Learning is depicted as a process of inner listening. The fracturing of the relationship is ultimately of little consequence, underscored by the pompous and silly postcard: "It is raining here and / Greco is so sombre. I have decided / At last to love nobody but myself."

While on a basic level the final section seems quite apprehensible, it is also fraught with doubleness and puzzles. Commenting on the structure of Durrell's poetry, Derek Stanford points to "the element of order in his work; an order not of traditional forms, of some external arbitrary law, but one inherent in the mind that creates—an indigenous, elegant harmony" (40). Describing the movement of a poem, Durrell has said, "Thought-clusters, constellations of ideas linked by private associations, characterize poetic thinking as against the ratiocinative, poetical operations of philosophers" (*Red Limbo Lingo* 12). Here, the speaker is released from his reverie by realizing that the lover "had gone / Beyond the twelfth desire," a phrase which makes sense while yet remaining elusive. Perhaps the twelfth desire has to do with time, implying either the midnight hours when one attempts to recall and give meaning to the events of the previous day, or the twelve months of a year and the beginning of a new one. Cyclic recapitulation lies at the heart of the poem. An answer might also be found in the Burmese Theravada school of Buddhism, with which Durrell is familiar, and which lists twenty-four conditions "which the monk had to apply systematically to all the data of his experiences. It must be noted that they are chiefly concerned with elemental processes and their conditions because of the overriding importance of mental attitudes" (Conze 150). The twelfth condition in this scheme is "recapitulation": "When such repetition takes place, a thought-moment assists the one which follows immediately upon it by making it more familiar and strong. . . . Each wholesome volition facilitates the emergence of another wholesome volition immediately following upon it" (Conze 153). Yet another possibility is that Durrell is referring to the twelve terms of the "Chain of Dependent Origination" of the Pali scriptures, the twelfth of which is the more-than-fitting "rebirth."

Without insisting upon the incontestable rightness of any of these interpretations, it is still clear that, in going over and over the same experience, the poet has ultimately accomplished a resolution through the fusion of time itself: "You and memory both become / Contemporary to all this inner music." Past, present, and future have all become one, and the poet incorporates their disparities. As Durrell has noted, "It is one of the paradoxes of the new space-time that, if time is really spread out in this way, *we can just as easily situate death in the present as in the future*. It is this multiple state birth-life-death in one which the poet is trying to capture" (*A Key to Modern British Poetry* 36).

The oneness of birth and death is underlined directly in the last two lines of the poem, coming together in the doubleness of the word *relay*. The poet is left with the healing qualities of time, a measure of time in an archetypal sense which brings a resolution to this past situation. In one way, the poem is relaying, or sending on, the message that the relationship is dying a natural death, that it is in essence a "failing fire." This is the thought that the poem sends outward to the woman in Madrid, almost an afterthought. Yet the lines are directed inwardly to the speaker himself as well, with the realization that it is now time to relay, or reconstruct, or start rebuilding his essential self anew. His own "failing fire" will not be allowed to go out. Any extinguishing of his passion in the past must be complemented by a spiritual and a physical rebirth, a relocating of himself in the present. Ian MacNiven places a great deal of emphasis on the role that biography plays in the poetry, and he says that "there are at least three main points to consider: the importance of chronology and biography; the depth of introspection revealed; and the quality of the later poetry, especially with respect to 'the highly praised early verse'" (82).

In several ways, the ending of this poem explains the beginning, its title. Certainly we can hear an echo of the song from "My Fair Lady" which Professor Higgins used to reeducate Liza Doolittle, "The Rain in Spain Falls Mainly on the Plain," and one aspect of the poem is indeed the speaker's attempt to pass something on to the woman, to explain the two of them to each other. The children's nursery rhyme "Rain, Rain, Go Away, / Come Again Some Other Day" would seem, in its lightheartedness, to demonstrate the poet's rising above his initially lugubrious situation, while the command to the rain to "Go to Spain" is almost an imprecation or a curse, not necessarily cynical but rather human. The poet has had enough of all this, and perhaps a little meditation induced by foul weather might do this shallow woman some good. Durrell is never so totally self-involved as to take himself and his romantic interludes completely seriously. A pox on her, and let us get on with it. The center of the poem is what has transpired within the speaker, and, when all is said and done, the woman and their affair have become virtually superfluous. The events of the past have been transformed into grist for the mill of spiritual progression.

Thus, the voice in the poem is actually a plethora of voices, ranging from the almost sardonic to the sincere. Discussing the voices in Durrell's poetry, G. S. Fraser has observed that "one seems to hear the poet not muttering to himself, as Yeats and Frost sometimes mutter, but speaking in a fine ghostly tone to his own ingenuous mask" (43). Fraser goes on to invoke what T. S. Eliot has called the three voices of poetry—"the poet talking to himself, the poet talking to others, the poet assuming and imitating the voices of others"—and he finds that Durrell's voice is all three, but without drastic or harsh changes of modulation in passing from one to the others: the self, the anti-self, the multiplicity of possible selves" (43). In this poem, all three possibilities or stances are intertwined to transcend the past-present-future logicality or linearity of time which would trap the poet in a nonsensical here and now. This oneness is what Durrell has accomplished in "Rain, Rain, Go to Spain" and, as he says, "If art has any message it must be this: to remind us that we are dying without having properly lived" (*A Key to Modern British Poetry* 5).

If Durrell is a poet of what he calls the new space-time, it might be fair to say that, if the poem just discussed is about time, then "Avignon" is about space, and about place, and about time again:

> Come, meet me in some dead café—
> A puff of cognac or a sip of smoke
> Will grant a more prolific light,
> Say there is nothing to revoke.
>
> A veteran with no arm will press
> A phantom sorrow in his sleeve;
> The aching stump may well insist
> On memories it can't relieve.
>
> Late cats, the city's thumbscrews twist.
> Night falls in its profane derision,
> Brings candle-power to younger lives,
> Cancels in me the primal vision.
>
> Come, random with me in the rain,
> In ghastly harness like a dream,
> In rainwashed streets of saddened dark
> Where nothing moves that does not seem.

(Collected Poems 316)

In these four quatrains, the poet invites the reader on a journey late at night through Avignon, where Durrell still lives today. Yet the Avignon we explore is not a sunny city of aqueducts and monuments. Instead, the sense of place we receive here is that time and space are out of joint, as Hamlet realized, that the dead spirits have displaced the living. The café in which we are to meet the speaker is itself "dead," and through a semantic disturbance we will partake of "A puff of cognac or a sip of smoke." As Durrell has insisted, "language at its most 'affective' seems to contain, not a logic, but a new kind of logic. The poetry which rises above categories is not nonsense, but a different kind of sense—sense without the help of standard logic, if you like" (*A Key to Modern British Poetry* 174). The semantic confusion of the senses in these images reflects the disruption in the spirit of the speaker. The light they will bring may be "prolific," but it will obviously not be illuminating. Here, the more the speaker invokes the light, the more he is plunged into the darkness of himself. The prolific light of the café can only show him that here is nothing left to see, like the old soldier who seeks to press his missing arm. All is surrounded by the pain of what is not.

Though the night brings avidity to the young, brings them "candle-power," the speaker can no longer perceive what he has called "the primal vision," an insight which seems to have been discovered in the poem which we just examined. Again enunciating a paradox, the evening comes for the young in "profuse derision," though who is being derided is not completely clear. Perhaps the young, the poet, and even the reader are to be included, but for the speaker this is only a "saddened dark." In essence, the space we move through here is no longer the city of Avignon, but rather the empty plots of a ruined cemetery. Ian MacNiven comments succinctly that "the three big words of Durrell's poetic vocabulary are art, love, and death" (101). A sense of space or place has thus become transformed into a sense of self, a psychological landscape which truly reflects what lies within, rather than without.

Here time and space have been equated with death, at least the death of the spirit, and memory brings pain along with it instead of the healing which was implied in "Rain, Rain, Go to Spain." Durrell is able to deal with both ends of the spectrum, picturing for us in "Avignon" a soul in disarray. The rain now allows no relief, and there is no fire to warm us. The speaker himself is a veteran with no arm, and the ache in the flesh is magnified by the ache in the mind which is the legacy of memory. The sexual implications embodied in the cries of late-night cats is denied in the poet, and is but another ironic form of torture. No matter how long he may wander through the city in search of some form of companionship, it is quite clear that this seeker is totally alone.

It is important to note that, unlike "Rain, Rain, Go to Spain," in which the poet is involved in something of a personal or private meditation, "Avignon" goes a step further, drawing the reader into itself and including him or her in the journey. This is not simply a vision of individual despair, since the command to "Come" at the beginning of the first and the final stanzas imply that we are in the same spiritual position as the speaker. We must realize that we are as desolate as he is. When the screech of a late-night cat twists the city's thumbscrews, it is we, too, who feel the pain. In many of his other poems, Durrell has called on the spirit of place to revive a sense of grandeur and mystery, but in this poem it seems that things are rotten at the core. A sense of place or space has now become a sense of self, and apparently the center will not hold.

Like Hamlet's ghost, our party will roam the streets in "ghastly harness," and like the ghost nothing in the internal landscape of Avignon is palpable. Just as the veteran soldier confronts a "phantom sorrow and memories which cannot be undone, we move in a dream, where shapes that appear in the darkness may *seem,* but never *mean.* With no direction pointed out or agreed upon, we and the poet must wander at random with a feeling of helplessness. Durrell says that "We speak of 'understanding' poems as if they were built up in sections like a child's Meccano bridge; but the truth is that we can never fully understand a good poem until we can fully understand ourselves. Our job then is to make ourselves accessible to the poem and use both sensibility and intelligence to this end" (*A Key to Modern British Poetry* 148). In this sense, "Avignon" is a haunting vision which will not let itself be resolved. It challenges the reader to involve himself directly in the poem, to assess the condition of the contemporary psyche.

Examining Durrell's sense of place, G. S. Fraser states that "the landscape is not there for its own sake but for its complex expressiveness, its meaning for Durrell as something on to which he can project, and by means of which he can define, moods, elusive and obsessive recurrences of human feeling" (44). In both the poems under discussion we can see just this concentration on the recurrent nature of the situation, the ways in which time and space are transcended in order to arrive at the eternal now. If there is significant meaning to be found in poetry, Durrell seems to say, it must reside in the archetypal oneness of the basic human condition. The poem must lead the reader toward this end, toward a perspective which can lead him out of the maze which is the conventional view of space and time, of life and death. Hayden Carruth asserts that "Durrell's fragments are protests, yes, gentle and nostalgic and pity-full as they may be, denials, the essential 'NO' shouted into the face of the future in the full knowledge that no consciousness may be there to hear it" (128).

To this end, Durrell synthesizes time and space in his poetry, ultimately subsuming both concepts within the human condition. His work is an attempt to break away from rigid definitions, to combine opposites, to reach a timeless and spaceless now. Esoteric at one moment, he can be ruthlessly pragmatic at the next, all at the service of a muse which demands nothing but the truth. In the two poems just examined, we can see that Lawrence Durrell can move easily and effortlessly from the inner to the outer and back again, ensnaring the reader into a dialogue or meditation with himself. For the poet, this is the crux of the question posed by the twentieth century that art alone can answer. Perhaps the essence of the situation has already been clearly laid out by Durrell himself: "The poet unlike the computer answers an unasked question in his work. Imprints the soft flesh of language with his love bites" (*Red Limbo Lingo* 13).

Works Cited

Carruth, Hayden. "Nougat for the Old Bitch." *The World of Lawrence Durrell*. Ed. Harry T. Moore. New York: Dutton, 1964.

Conze, Edward. *Buddhist Thought in India*. Ann Arbor: University of Michigan, 1967.

Durrell, Lawrence. *Collected Poems. 1931–1974*. Ed. James A. Brigham. London: Faber, 1980.

———. *A Key to Modern British Poetry*. Norman: University of Oklahoma, 1952.

———. *The Red Limbo Lingo: A Poetry Notebook*. New York: Dutton, 1971.

Fraser, G. S. *Lawrence Durrell: A Critical Study*. London: Faber, 1973.

MacNiven, Ian. "Mirror of Crises: The Poetry of Lawrence Durrell." *Critical Essays on Lawrence Durrell*. Ed. Alan W. Friedman. Boston: Hall, 1987.

Stanford, Derek. "Lawrence Durrell: An Early View of His Poetry." *The World of Lawrence Durrell*. Ed. Harry T. Moore. New York: Dutton, 1964.

5

Joan and Juan: Christ and Eros

Gordon K. Thomas

Among the literary productions of Lawrence Durrell, *Pope Joan* holds a distinctive and I think undeservedly subordinate place. Partly, I suppose, that may be
due to its being, as the title page says, "translated and adapted from the Greek
of Emmanuel Royidis"—that is, it is not even an original work. But the whole
question of what constitutes originality in fiction is interesting and complex; it
is a question which deserves the kind of fresh and unspoiled consideration that
Durrell always demands of his readers. I shall return to this matter of originality.

But first a bit of critical history to clarify what I mean by the different and
secondary position of *Pope Joan* among Durrell's productions. When the novel
was first published in Durrell's translation in 1954, it apparently generated only
the smallest of ripples in the literary sea. I have been unable to find any reviews
of the novel in that first appearance. But that was, after all, 1954; and Durrell
was just another good writer who had never received much attention. And then
within a few years came the popular and critical successes of *Justine* and *Bitter
Lemons,* followed by other installments of *The Alexandria Quartet,* and world-
wide fame. And in 1960 *Pope Joan* reappeared in what was called a *revised
edition.* There is no significant internal reason for calling this second outing a
revised edition; what was really revised was the receptiveness of the reading and
critical audience. This time around the novel was not ignored. The reviewer for
The Times Literary Supplement, which had ignored the novel in 1954, in 1961
hailed *Pope Joan* as "a brilliant piece of work," a really wonderful translation
"which exuberantly recaptures the curious scholarship and earthy humours of its
original" (76). *The Saturday Review* critic, six weeks later, obviously very
much aware by then of Durrell's growing reputation, exclaimed of *Pope Joan*
that in it "subject, author, and translator are ideally matched." And taking note
of Durrell's claim in his preface that Royidis's Greek novel is "in its own way
a small masterpiece," the critic for *The Saturday Review* insisted that Durrell's

lending his talents and name to the project resulted in "a 'small masterpiece' not only of Greek but also of English literature" (19). In the same vein, and in the same week, Dudley Fitts was writing in *The New York Times* his praises not just of the novel but particularly of Durrell's achievement: "Mr. Durrell's translation reads delightfully, of course; indeed it triumphs" (6). In the next month, writing in *The Library Journal,* J. A. Braswell topped them all in praising not the Greek original but the English translator: "A better translation probably could not be made." But at the same time, Braswell felt the need to warn nervous librarians, "It probably will offend the very pious" (1622).

What seems clear amid all this praise for a novel which is a "masterpiece" and a "triumph" and a "brilliant piece of work" is that *Pope Joan* began to get favorable attention only after its translator had become a big name in current literature. My British paperback edition, published by Hamlyn in 1982, prints the name of Lawrence Durrell in inch-high letters on the cover, with the title in letters only three-eighths of an inch high, and the name of Emmanuel Royidis only three-sixteenths of an inch high. The considerable renewal of Durrell's popularity occasioned by the gradual appearance of the novels of *The Avignon Quintet* in recent years has, predictably, resulted in wider interest again in *Pope Joan.* An American paperback edition was published in 1984 in New York by the perhaps aptly named Overlook Press, an edition with not even a mention of Emmanuel Royidis on the front cover and a note on the back asserting that "Durrell has done much more than translate" the book.

I have gone into these details of critical and publication history because I agree with that assertion: Durrell in *Pope Joan* is indeed much more than only a translator. There is a considerable point to be made here, a point bigger than publishers' type. If the nineteenth-century Greek novel by Royidis can be called, as cited from *The San Francisco Chronicle* on the back cover of the Overlook Press edition, "a classic of modern Greek literature," it still seems to be important to recognize what limited authority and influence such a work must have. What Durrell has done, besides providing a delightfully fluent English rendering of the novel, is to lend the very great authority of his name and reputation to a book meriting the kind of attention which Durrell's name provokes. To say on the title page of *Pope Joan* that it is "translated and adapted" by Lawrence Durrell is to say no small thing. The translation is superbly readable English, thus made available, as without it the book would not be, to the vast educated English-reading public of the whole world. I'm not very clear on what "adapted" means here, for the translation seems straightforward and unadulterated, though Durrell's brief preface is a valuable guide for the modern non-Greek reader. What Durrell has really accomplished here is to *transmit,* using his language and his art and reputation, a work which he obviously approves of and does not want neglected. This transmission, involving all the power and authority of the artist who performs it, is a very considerable accomplishment, even though at first glance it seems lacking in a quality we have somehow come to prize so greatly in our arts and artists, originality. But art far outweighs novelty. Truth is far more significant than originality, and the transmission of artistic truth is always a hugely commendable act—as it is in Durrell's transmission of *Pope Joan* to the huge audience of the English-reading world.

Such a transmission is also perfectly appropriate for this book; for the original Greek novel of Royidis was itself, in a related sense, a transmission. Geoffrey Grigson, writing in *The Spectator* in 1960, observed somewhat vaguely that *"Pope Joan* has a Don Juan quality of worldliness" (860). But there is no need to be vague about this "Don Juan quality." What *Pope Joan* has is a reassessing, an adapting—a transmission—of the masterpiece of the most popular poet of the nineteenth century, namely Lord Byron's *Don Juan*. Note the appropriateness of this transmission: Byron, who died in Greece in 1824 in the Greek war for independence just a month after the last two completed cantos of *Don Juan* were published, was transmitted through Royidis's novel to the Greeks in 1886 but only gained real acceptance in Greece in this century, and now the gift is returned through Durrell's translation into English. Clearly at the root of all this international exchange and transmission is a sharp awareness: Byron, in our time and in ways transcending nationality and time, we have need of thee!

Byron's poem depicts the misadventures of a picaro and anti-hero who is pursued back and forth across Europe, beginning at age sixteen, by mostly female predators of all ages, types, and classes, from a Turkish slave to a Russian empress, from his own mother's dear friend, half again his age, to the competing advances of a bevy of English socialites. The original Don Juan of Spanish story and legend finally encounters a ghost in the form of a walking statue, and the ghost drags him off to hell. The last encounter of Don Juan recorded in Byron's poem is with a ghost, too, a fake ghost, of course, the Duchess of Fitz-Fulke, who masquerades as the ghost of a monk, the fabled "sable Friar in his solemn hood" (*Don Juan* 16.117.8). This encounter, with its parody of the Don Juan tradition, fulfills the promise Byron made at the beginning of the poem: "I mean to show / The very place where wicked people go" (1.207.7–8). Wicked people go to hell, of course, as in the Spanish tale; or else, same thing, they fall into the scheming clutches of ladies of polite society in England.

Byron's hero awaits his ghastly fate:

> The night was as before: he was undrest,
>   Saving his night-gown, which is an undress;
> Completely *sans culotte,* and without vest;
>   In short, he hardly could be clothed with less:

> But apprehensive of his spectral guest,
>   He sate with feelings awkward to express
> (By those who have not had such visitations),
> Expectant of the Ghost's fresh operations.

(16.111)

The mood as Byron creates and manipulates it alternates between horror and comedy:

> Again—what is't? The wind? No, no,—this time
>   It is the sable Friar as before,
> With awful footsteps regular as rhyme,
>   Or (as rhymes may be in these days) much more.
> Again through shadows of the night sublime,
>   When deep sleep fell on men, and the world wore
> The starry darkness round her like a girdle
> Spangled with gems—the Monk made his blood curdle.

(16.113)

And then in a moment or two more comes the final revelation of identity and deception:

> The Ghost, if Ghost it were, seemed a sweet soul
>   As ever lurked beneath a holy hood:
> A dimpled chin, a neck of ivory, stole
>   Forth into something much like flesh and blood;
> Back fell the sable frock and dreary cowl,
>   And they revealed—alas! that e'er they should!
> In full, voluptuous, but *not o'ergrown* bulk,
> The phantom of her frolic Grace—Fitz-Fulke.

(16.123)

This culminating scene in Byron's poem, with its wonderful juxtaposing of damnation and sexual delight, of the disastrous and the ridiculous, of the spiritual fantasy and the very physical reality—such a scene deserves reexamining. And Royidis and Durrell in the culmination of *Pope Joan,* transmitting to a further reading audience, reexamine it in all its details:

All was still in the papal household [of the adventurous Joanna, who has managed to ascend the papal throne and take for herself the keys of the kingdom, while keeping her eye on a young man named Florus who looks as if he would make a good lover] with the exception of the owls, and the clocks, when his [Florus's] ears caught a low rustle of sound, like the flight of some nocturnal bird, or the movement of some young girl hurrying to her first assignation and fearful that the sound of her footsteps might be overheard. The door opened as softly as if by a light wind and once more that apparition approached the bed, walking on tiptoe. Florus felt his nightshirt grow moist with sweat as cold as the waters of the Styx, I mean, of course, the

Arcadian river and not the infernal one which was hot. The gloom increased his terror. The vision appeared to be self-illuminated and, like a ghost, carried no lamp in its hand. He could only dimly make out its shape in light of the smoldering fire but it seemed like some white and lowering cloud as it approached the bed. At last it stood by the bed, cloud, phantom, vampire, Joanna. Encouraged by the absolute immobility of the sleeper she began very softly to nibble the soft skin of the forbidden fruit with her lips. She did not dare to bite it.

This warm contact immediately dissipated the chilly fear which had settled on the blood of the boy; as he came to himself he stretched out both arms to seize the phantom but it just succeeded in evading him and escaping. It left in his hands a torn chemise and some yellow hairs. By now the good Florus was not satisfied with these spoils. His blood was up, and so was his curiosity. He pursued the apparition which fled swiftly into the bedroom, where it proceeded to go round in a circle until at last it caught its foot in a corner of its gown and fell full length on the floor beneath the open window. Florus stretched out his arms. Instead of encountering bones, maggots, corruption, or any other classical attribute of vampirism his hands found themselves upon a smooth warm skin which seemed to cover a living and beating heart. As he did so the moon came out from behind the clouds and shone full upon the face and the bare breasts of the Most Serene and Holy Pontiff, John VIII. (*Pope Joan* 141–42)

Not content with borrowing this whole scene in every detail from *Don Juan,* the novelist pauses to make an acknowledgment, and a comparison. The revelation that the pursuing ghost is human, and aggressively female, puts the author in a delicate quandary; but the quandary reminds both author and reader of Byron in a similar moment:

I do not feel that I have the right to pollute either my hands or your ears. The creator of *Don Juan* found himself in roughly the same predicament when, after a long pursuit, his hero's hand actually rested upon the white bosom of the third or fourth of his heroines—lulled as softly as the Ark on Ararat. And not being at all clear how to go on and remain his usual modest self, Byron abandoned the poem and poetry, and became in despair a misanthropist and philhellene, and took himself off to be buried in a swamp at Missolonghi. (*Pope Joan* 142–43)

But *Pope Joan* and *Don Juan* share even more—much more—than these culminating scenes, and their authors have much more in common than their mocking yet half-serious concerns for sexual modesty in art. Byronism is evident in the novel. Byron is repeatedly quoted, alluded to, paralleled, and praised. He is called at one point in the novel "by far the greatest poet" of the century, and much of the spirit, tone, and even details of plot can be traced right back to their sources in Byron. Examples abound, of which I shall cite only a few.

There is, for one, the famous description in canto 2 of *Don Juan* of the aftermath of a storm at sea and the resulting shipwreck, a scene which in Byron is itself a kind of parody of passages in Coleridge's *Ancient Mariner,* as well as an evocation of the difficult but heroic Mediterranean voyages of Odysseus and St. Paul. Note how little originality matters here. We have, instead, a writer who builds upon another who parodies another who evokes another, and another, so that literary works become akin to a series of nesting dolls, each looking a good deal like its predecessor but enclosing that and all other predecessors. In Byron, the few survivors of the shipwreck jam themselves into a perilous lifeboat only to find after a few days of drifting that cannibalism seems an invitingly easy double solution to the problems of both overcrowding and impending starvation. When the heroine of *Pope Joan* takes to the sea, author and translator need not tell the details of her adventures. A simple reminder of Byron's telling of the incidents of Juan's seafaring, coupled with that Byronic mocking tone, suffices to bring to mind the whole collection of poetic, scriptural, and epic components of the structure of a literary tradition, while emphasizing Byron's mock-epic contributions to that tradition. All this comes reduced in *Pope Joan* to a single allusion: "Nautical descriptions of the waves, the rigging, the pitch, the shipwreck and so on, are liable to induce nausea in the reader, so often has it been done before; except when a pleasant episode about starvation or anthropophagy is steathily introduced into the text" (*Pope Joan* 93–94).

A more important presence of Byronism in *Pope Joan* is in the very structure and organization of the novel. Both *Pope Joan* and *Don Juan* are constructed of a series of seemingly constant intrusions by the narrator, the apparent abandoning of plot at almost any turn to indulge in a lengthy digression by way of an aside to the "dear reader," and the denial amid all this that there is any deviation from the straight narrative track. "The regularity of my design / Forbids all wandering as the worst of sinning," Byron playfully announces near the beginning of *Don Juan* (1.7.3–4). But what may well be called the *irregularity* of his design is both evoked and transmitted in *Pope Joan,* and it has a clear and intentional Byronic stamp put on it. Part 3 of the novel, which begins in a typically casual aside—"Do you, my dear reader, like good wine?" (75)—has as its introductory refrain these telling lines from the opening passage of canto 4 of *Don Juan:* "But the fact is that I have nothing planned, / Unless it were to be a moment merry" (4.5.5–6).

These cited lines come in Byron's poem at a point when he is, once again, disclaiming any attack on religion and morality in *Don Juan.* The stanza from which the quoted lines are taken begins:

> Some have accused me of a strange design
>   Against the creed and morals of the land,
> And trace it in this poem in every line:
>   I don't pretend that I quite understand.

(4.5.1–4)

And the allusion to Byron in *Pope Joan* from this context leads into a discussion which is not a digression in fact at all from the *real* subject of the novel, which goes far beyond the picaresque adventures of Joan on her way to Rome and papal power. After quoting Byron and asking the "dear reader" about tastes in wine, the novelist comes to his real concern:

> As the true wine-drinker loathes adulterators of the article, so indeed should good Christians loathe those who mix religion, for the sake of profit, with the various inventions of their shaven or sprouting heads; the miracles of ikons, pagan gods disguised as saints, genuflections, tickets for Paradise, holy relics, rosaries—and the rest of the monkish truck which has rendered the profession of the Apostles as suspect as those of medical practitioners and the interpreters of dreams. From childhood I have always been fond of chemistry; and this book of mine is only a chemical analysis of the religious wine which the habited tavern-keepers of the Middle Ages gave the people of the West to drink. (75)

The fact is, as becomes clear in this last resemblance noted, that there is much more to all these elements of Byronism in *Pope Joan* than just admiration and evocation. There is, indeed, a very serious system of philosophy and art which underlies the close relationship between *Don Juan* and *Pope Joan*. Durrell, in his preface to the novel, writes that the purpose of telling or transmitting the story of Pope Joan is to provide "a sort of brief record of the history and misfortunes of Eros after his transformation by Christianity from a God to an underground resistance movement" (7). That certainly sounds like the kind of intention which should attract the interest of Durrell and inspire him to make the novel available to readers in English. What is equally obvious, and reinforced every step of the way by frequent references in the novel to Byron and his poetry and ideas, is the importance of Byron's *Don Juan* as a starting point for any pursuit of such an intention in modern literature.

George Bernard Shaw, in the "Epistle Dedicatory" to his play *Man and Superman*, briefly summarizes in his intentionally contrary way the development of the Don Juan tradition in European literature and art, and comments, almost by the way, that Byron's poem does not have much to contribute to the development of this tradition, "does not count for much philosophically," and that we can well "leave Byron's Don Juan out of account" (241). Clearly, this view of Byron as unthinking, unphilosophical, though a rather common view, is as ungracious as it is faulty, for Shaw himself owed much more to Byron than he ever acknowledged. And clearly, too, *Pope Joan*, among its other intentions, aims at settling the debt to Byron owed by many modern writers who have made the relationship of Christ and Eros a matter of contemplation.

Byron, in partial justification of Shaw's accusations against him, was surely as capable as any of his early nineteenth-century contemporaries of indulging, especially in his early poetry, in the sentimentalizing of sex, of trying to *combine* Christ and Eros. The Romantic notion of blending the effects of Christ's Passion with sexual passion finds an uneasy but willing expression in some of Byron's more sentimental and self-pitying works. The "Stanzas to Augusta," written to his half-sister just before Byron left England for permanent exile, are an extreme example, but in a sense they are a standard rendition of the theme. Amid darkness and despair and treachery, the one hint of salvation and of heaven's care in the poet's life is said there to be his sexual affair with Augusta:

> Oh! blest be thine unbroken light.
> That watch'd me as a seraph's eye,
> And stood between me and the night.
> For ever shining sweetly nigh.

(13–16)

What makes these lines an extreme example of a commonplace nineteenth-century sentimentalism is, of course, that the affair thus praised as providing such heavenly light was, in fact, incest, and the angelic lady-love was a sister who was, from much evidence, heartlessly manipulative and amazingly amoral.

But Byron resembled Durrell in that at his best and most mature he was much too wary of cant to convince himself for very long that incest and adultery are the surest paths to spiritual salvation. The poet was too honest to try to cling to such sentimental sludge. He was also too reverent, like Durrell, about genuinely holy things. Despite the warning expressed by *The Library Journal* critic mentioned earlier on behalf of "the very pious," *Pope Joan* resembles *Don Juan* also in the ability it demonstrates to sort through religious hypocrisy and cant and dead custom while leaving intact the basis and core of religious reverence. Such is clearly an important consideration for Durrell, who argues hard and well that his book deals with "innocence" pitted "against the real world with its bigotries and penalties" and that there is nothing in his telling of the story of Pope Joan "likely to disturb any serious faith worth the name" (8–9). Again I hear Byron's voice in the background:

> If any person should presume to assert
> This story is not moral, first, I pray,
> That they will not cry out before they're hurt,
> Then that they'll read it o'er again.

(*Don Juan* 1.207.1–4)

"I never could understand what they mean by accusing me of irreligion," Byron wrote his publisher John Murray from Ravenna in 1820 shortly after sending the third and fourth cantos of *Don Juan* to the press (*Byron's Letters and Journals* 7:47).

Besides this shared reverence for the genuinely sacred, Durrell and Byron share the view that one of the worst forms of irreligion is the hypocrisy of sexual cant spoken in the name of Christ. Byron writes of the lack of any real sense of moral responsibility in the various societies, especially the Christian societies, depicted in *Don Juan*. The Russia of the Empress Catherine—and Juan's encounter with this society is alluded to in several places in *Pope Joan* (e.g. 128, 140)—for example, is representative of the corrupt Christian world in that *love* and *lust,* two such different terms, are there commonly used interchangeably. The Empress herself sets the example, one which is followed on all social levels. Neither she nor her court nor the commoners nor even the narrator can distinguish between love and lust:

> The sovereign was smitten,
> Juan much flatter'd by her love, or lust—
>   I cannot stop to alter words once written,
> And the two are so mix'd with human dust,
>   That he who *names one,* both perchance may hit on;
> But in such matters Russia's mighty empress
> Behaved no better than a common sempstress.
>
> (9.77.2–8)

And somehow it always is in the name of noble-sounding philosophy and etiquette and refinement—and religion—that the sexual cant finds its widest employment. Writes Byron mockingly:

> The noblest kind of love is love Platonical
>   To end or to begin with; the next grand
> Is that which may be christen'd love canonical,
>   Because the clergy take the thing in hand;
> The third sort to be noted in our chronicle
>   As flourishing in every Christian land,
> Is when chaste matrons to their other ties
> Add what may be call'd *marriage in disguise.*
>
> (9.76.1–8)

Religion is, of course, especially susceptible to cant, and religious talk of love is almost invariably suspect:

> Ecclesiastes said, "that all is vanity"—
>   Most modern preachers say the same, or show it
> By their examples of true Christianity.
>
> (*Don Juan* 7.6.1–3)

Denounced in both *Pope Joan* and *Don Juan* are poets who allow their sublime and spiritual feelings and meditations about love to lead them and their readers astray, to wander into falsehood and unreality—for Byron, as for Durrell, among the worst of sins for an author. There is a long tradition of such writers; one who is cited as such in both *Pope Joan* and *Don Juan* is, in Byron's words, "Saint Augustine in his fine Confessions, / Which make the reader envy his transgressions" (*Don Juan* 1.47.7–8)—a work which, at his mother's insistence, "was a sealed book to little Juan" (1.48.1) and which is mentioned in *Pope Joan* because the young monk Frementius, later to become Joanna's first lover, "having [never] read . . . St. Augustine's confessions . . . was as spotless as the driven snow" (49). Both works take repeated shots at not only traditional poets of cant but moderns as well. There are repeated aspersions cast upon P. Soutos throughout *Pope Joan,* identified in one of Durrell's notes as a nineteenth-century "milk-and-water poet of Athens" (159, n18). Among contemporaries referred to in *Don Juan,* Byron cites Campbell, for writing such lines as "oh Love! . . . thou art a god indeed divine" (1.88.1–5); Wordsworth, who, like the sixteen-year-old Juan "wander'd by the glassy brooks / Thinking unutterable things," but finally in poetic expression of these high feelings proved "unintelligible" (1.90.1–8); and Coleridge, who again, adolescentlike, "so pursued / His self-communion with his own high soul" that he became not prophet nor poet nor truth-teller but "a metaphysician" (1.91.1–8). Byron's own view, like Durrell's, does not lose sight of the romantic sublimity possible in young love but insists on other elements of realism too:

> In thoughts like these true wisdom may discern
>   Longings sublime, and aspirations high
> Which some are born with, but the most part learn
>   To plague themselves withal, they know not why:
> 'Twas strange that one so young should thus concern
>   His brain about the action of the sky;
> If *you* think 'twas philosophy that this did,
>   I can't help thinking puberty assisted.

(1.93.1–8)

Worse for Byron, as for Durrell, than sexual error, whether in the flesh or in poetry, is *sexlessness.* No one receives more abuse from Byron than "the intellectual eunuch" who can commit no sexual transgression but is equally incapable of the softening and possibly saving influences of love: "cold-blooded, smooth-faced placid miscreant" (*Don Juan* Ded. 11.8–12.1). Incapacity is never innocence. "The mind / Emasculated," Byron observes, "hath but two objects, how to serve and bind" (Ded. 15.1–3). Where no feeling dwells, especially in art and religion, only evil can result. Similarly, in *Pope Joan,* sexlessness, the sin, at least in precept, of the monastery and the convent, is a greater sin than licentiousness. The heroine, Joanna, is a product of convent education. But it is only when she is granted a vision of the sensuality possible within the monastic life that her road is made clear. St. Ida appears first and offers Joanna the pleasures of the world. But St. Lioba then appears and offers the added pleasures of freedom of sexual expression in monastic disguise and respectability—the pleasure of having nothing forbidden: "As in the Song of Songs we give ourselves," promises St. Lioba, "to delicious dreams until at last, down the corridors, we hear the sandals of the coming one who will incarnate those dreams in flesh" (30). And it is the pursuit of this incarnation, this turning of sexual fantasy into flesh, which becomes Joanna's religion and purpose.

This sounds like the vocabulary of Christianity, of course: the incarnation, the hope made flesh, the devotion to the truth which makes one free. But Christ and Eros are not to be confused or melted down into a single amorphous lump. Such a confusion is "sickness," as it is called in *Pope Joan*. The sickness can affect anyone, but it must always be seen for what it is. Byron himself, the novel tells us, knew the power and pain of the sick confusion, but he knew too—it was the evidence of his greatness as a poet and thinker—that the condition *was* sickness, not truth. Writes Durrell:

> Sickness can transform lions into hares, and even the most skeptical man into a Christian. Byron, by far the greatest poet of this century, whose brain weighed 638 grams, has freely confessed that when he fell ill after his first phlebotomy, he felt himself capable of believing in the miracles of Moses; after the second, in the incarnation; after the third, in the immaculate conception. After the fourth phlebotomy he had reached such a pitch that he found himself grieving because there were no other beliefs of this kind to accept. (*Pope Joan* 130–31)

There is no honest resolution to this opposition between Christ and Eros. Having confronted it squarely in *Don Juan,* Byron, in the words of Durrell in *Pope Joan,* "abandoned the poem and the poetry," having nothing left to say on the subject (143). And in Durrell's transmission of the Greek novel which offers the same confrontation, Joanna, now Pope of Rome, dies in the end on the steps of the papal throne from the impossibility of reconciling the pangs of labor and childbirth, through which she is at that moment passing, with the superstitious expectations of the adoring throng around her.

"I am no enemy to religion, but the contrary," wrote Byron to Tom Moore from Pisa in 1822, in a letter filled with references and self-comparisons to Goethe's Faust, Milton's Satan, and Shelley's alleged atheism. "I think people can never have enough of religion, if they are ever to have any," he continued (*Byron's Letters and Journals* 9:119). But the search for religious truth is never an easy one. Especially difficult and elusive, indeed, perhaps impossible, as both Byron and Durrell show, is the permanent and total harmonizing of Christ and Eros.

Byron and Durrell—two great writers—are separated by over a century and a half in time, but united by their genuinely international and urbane perspectives, by their shared mission. As is quoted above, from the preface to *Pope Joan*, Durrell considers that he and Byron are significantly concerned with tracing the effects of the repression of Eros by Christianity (7). The regard, even reverence, felt by the later writer for his great predecessor shows up frequently—in Durrell's comic poems, certainly (Durrell's poetic treatment of Admiral Nelson's column in Trafalgar Square in his delicious "Ballad of the Good Lord Nelson" is an example, a comic sexual image which Byron himself would likely envy), and in Durrell's frequent Byronic technique in his novels of undercutting purple passages with ironic and often comic effect. Nowhere, though, is the relationship of these two writers, and that certain kind of reverence of Durrell for Byron, better demonstrated than in the transmission in *Pope Joan* of the whole donjuanesque tone and conviction: the conviction shared by the two writers that there can be something inherently right after all about what has happened to Eros under Christianity and about the lively tension which can result from that "transformation." Both Byron and Durrell know, above all, that a resistance movement *must* have something to resist.

Works Cited

Braswell, J. A. Rev. of *Pope Joan,* trans. Lawrence Durrell. *The Library Journal.* 15 April 1961, 86:1622.

Byron, George Gordon, Lord. *Byron's Letters and Journals.* Ed. Leslie A. Marchand. 12 vols. Cambridge, Mass.: Harvard/Belnap Press, 1974–82.

———. *Don Juan.* Ed. Leslie A. Marchand. Boston: Houghton Mifflin, 1958.

Durrell, Lawrence, trans. *Pope Joan,* by Emmanuel Royidis. Feltham: Hamlyn, 1982.

Fitts, Dudley. Rev. of *Pope Joan,* trans. Lawrence Durrell. *The New York Times Book Review.* 19 March 1961:6.

Grigson, Geoffrey. Rev. of *Pope Joan,* trans. Lawrence Durrell. *The Spectator.* 25 November 1960: 860.

Rev. of *Pope Joan,* trans. Lawrence Durrell. *Saturday Review.* 18 March 1961: 19.

Rev. of *Pope Joan,* trans. Lawrence Durrell. *The Times Literary Supplement.* 3 February 1961: 76.

Shaw, George Bernard. *Man and Superman.* In *Plays by George Bernard Shaw.* Ed. Eric Bentley. New York: Signet, 1960.

6

Durrell's Diplomats:
Inertia Where Is Thy Sting?

Frank L. Kersnowski

The biographical note to an early collection of Lawrence Durrell's short stories about life in the British diplomatic corps tells the reader that Durrell served in "various official and diplomatic capacities" (*Esprit de Corps and Stiff Upper Lip* 4). In fact, he was a Foreign Press Service officer in Cairo and Press Attaché in Alexandria during World War II and was transferred to Rhodes as Press Attaché in 1945. After an unpleasant stint lecturing in Argentina for the British Council, he returned to Europe as Press Attaché to the Embassy in Belgrade, Yugoslavia. Early collections of the stories contained this dedication: "Inscribed to the Members of the Chancery, H. M. Embassy Belgrade, 1951." The tone and accomplishment of the stories reflect the sincerity of the dedication, for there is not an ill-tempered word in them, though they are accurate characterizations of the diplomatic corps, as reviews have consistently mentioned.

Lawrence Durrell's diplomatic sketches, now gathered as *Antrobus Complete*, have been dismissed by him as pieces he could knock off in twenty minutes for easy money to buy baby shoes (Wickes 227–28). Baby must have been very well shod since all the magazines to publish these stories paid very well: *Argosy, Atlantic, Harper's, Mademoiselle, New Statesman and Nation, Playboy*, and *Vogue*.

> *F. K.: Clearly, these are not major fiction, but I really enjoy the Antrobus sketches.*
> *L. D.: Well, they'd have been great if P. G. Wodehouse had never lived. He was the master of this kind of humor.*
> *F. K.: How do the English receive these stories?*
> *L. D.: Very well. They've always been well reviewed and are even given as*

> *Christmas presents in the FO. They know what I'm about and recognize
> the accuracy of the characterizations.*

Perhaps, we should leave them, then, as Durrell has encouraged us to leave
them: magazine pieces to read in a dentist's office, a collection to pick up on a
rainy day during one's holiday. Yet not even Durrell has been content to let
them be simply somnolent prose. His tireless and attentive narrator, so like
Coleridge's wedding guest, is more than accidentally similar to the narrators of
The Alexandria Quartet and *The Avignon Quintet,* who record their irritation
and expectation without discretion or respect for confidence. And then, too,
what there is of evil in the sketches reappears in the last novel Durrell wrote,
Quinx, or the Ripper's Tale.

Antrobus, the endearing, never becomes an irritation to us, never achieves
diplomatic rank that would tempt him to make a decision more troubling than
the choice of a canape at a circumcision or an embassy party. Throughout a life
filled with the threats of such serious *faux pas* as seeing the ambassador, Polk-
Mowbray, choke on a pellet of bread, Antrobus shines with the last rays of the
Empire. He describes himself in reflecting on that age:

> In the Old Days (said Antrobus) before Time Was—I think it was the year Mrs. Gaskell won
> the Nobel for England—diplomacy was a quiet and restful trade carried on in soothing inanity
> among a hundred shady legations and embassies all over the globe. It was hardly more taxing
> than Divinity for a Scotchman. A fond bland light shone from the old dip's eyes—and why
> not? Minted at Eton, moulded by Balliol, and mellowed to the sunset tone of old brick by a
> Grand Tour, the fellow was in clover, and he knew it. Handpicked, packaged, dusted over
> lightly with male hormone, he was delivered to his post without a bally scratch. Then he had
> pride: he shaved with nothing but Yardley and scented his beard with Imperial Saddle. Look
> at the change now: fellows dashed over with cheap and perhaps combustible shaving lotions
> and industrial talc. (158)

Antrobus continues to indicate the ultimate degradation of the diplomatic corps:
female dips. They are for him, however, merely symptomatic of change.

On changes brought about by "Americanism," Antrobus finds himself in
company he would clearly not invite to his club. While Antrobus is cut to his
Latin-tag quick by Polk-Mowbray's chummy "Hiya" and by being referred to
as "my sidekick," he would clearly be equally displeased if Carl Jung sat down
to discuss the corruption of Americanism, to delineate the dangers of a spread-
ing uniformity and repressed awareness of the unconscious (94). Antrobus,
mercifully unaware of these problems or the enormity of their importance,
would smile with the professional diplomat's condescension and leave as soon
as possible.

Perhaps the seasoned dip and his upstart American counterpart did, in fact,
have an exchange, not simply a corruption of the former by the latter. In *The
Alexandria Quartet,* Durrell's premier diplomat appears. And David Mountolive

discovers the diplomat's role is to keep the cellar decent and act only on majority decisions. Never support the minority. Antrobus never makes such a mistake, but then he is never in a position to do so. Mountolive presumes a power to act no one in his position should. However, the clear directions of FO training have been altered by his cultural concerns, aroused and nurtured by sexual passion. Of course, Mountolive finds himself head of a mission, a role, thankfully, that never fell to Antrobus. Mountolive, too, would probably have enjoyed an exchange of theories with Jung. Not so Antrobus.

With a glance askance at life east of Calais, Antrobus tells his ideal guest (retentive and not likely to talk with anyone in the FO) of the dangers to the steady course introduced into life by the French:

> If there is anything really questionable about the French character it must be its passion for *culture*. I might not dare say this in the FO old man, but I know you will respect my confidence. You see, we are all supposed to be pro rather than anti in the Old Firm—but as for me, frankly I hate the stuff. It rattles me. It gives me the plain untitivated pip, I don't mind confessing. (100)

True, the introduction of *culture* into the round of embassy parties does release unknown potentials of an otherwise benign nature, such as the French Ambassadress who turned into a heavily bearded man and left the corps for the music hall. Such an event Antrobus accepts with a pronounced *sang froid* (only a French tag can suitably indicate the shallowness of the dip's concern) since only the French were concerned (105–6). When the French sent a somewhat less hirsute ambassadress to Vulgaria (Durrell's essential Eastern-bloc country), she brought with her the expected fondness for sopranos, pianos, and wind instruments. Quite unexpectedly, she also elicited a hitherto unrevealed masculinity from De Mandeville, a third secretary, "Eton and Caius," who seemed content with folkdancing on the lawn with his chauffeur. Yet the Ambassadress brought him to compete with his Italian counterpart, Bonzo di Porco, in matters of lineage, conferred privilege, and skill with the flute. The inevitable occurred:

> One evening, at a cultural soirée in the Froggish Embassy, they came to an open breech as to who should turn over the lady's music. Pull followed pull, push, push. I ask you to believe me when I say there was a mild scuffle. They pulled each other's ties and stamped. The lady fainted, and leaving her like a fallen ninepin, they stormed out into the night in different directions. (160)

In spite of all plots by the nefarious Dovebasket and all the prayers of Antrobus, De Mandeville survives "this fearful ordeal" (165). Clearly, such a scene is intended as burlesque, as is Drage the butler turning into a werewolf when embassy wags experiment on him with a potion intended to cure the PM's gout.

> *F. K.: In the Antrobus stories you don't treat the dangers of diplomatic*
> *relations between countries.*
> *L. D.: Of course not. That would spoil the fun. If you want that, go to*
> Mountolive.

Members of the diplomatic corps who stray from protocol into independent thought are a major concern of Durrell's in *The Alexandria Quartet*. Mountolive rescinds his objectivity when dealing with Nessim Hosnani, son of his former lover whose correspondence had given Mountolive an education unusual among diplomats (according to Durrell): an understanding of modern art and literature and a fondness for both. Indeed, this fondness contributed to his keeping on Pursewarden at the embassy in Egypt, even though to do so caused notice in the Home Office and in Egypt. His respect for Pursewarden's talent, fondness for his company, and attraction to his sister caused the new ambassador to act out of keeping with the essential model of the diplomat, as stated by the narrator of *Mountolive:*

> His profession which valued only judgment, coolness and reserve, taught him the hardest
> lesson of all and the most crippling—never to utter the pejorative thought aloud. It offered him
> too something like a long Jesuitical training in self-deception which enabled him to present
> an ever more polished surface to the world without deepening his human experience. (54–55)

In retaining Pursewarden, Mountolive turned from the comfortable example of Antrobus: never to be led so far into making a decision that a decorous recantation is impossible and never to allow his "real life" to emerge from the psyche into "that artificial world in which the diplomat lives" (55). Ideas and emotions are not to tempt the diplomat to solve any *real* problems. Instead he is simply to "propose" viable answers (87). This view, given to Mountolive by the last ambassador under whom he served, differs slightly from that of Polk-Mowbray, who advises his subordinates to keep "a stiff upper lip" (114). The diplomat's understanding of self and role need not be consciously sought in the museums and libraries of the world, for his character will be fashioned for him as his ideals and behavior are limited to norms provided by protocol.

Albeit ironically, Durrell presents Antrobus as the ideal member of the diplomatic corps. Almost ideal, he was not inhuman. Though he found no temptress with the wiles of Mountolive's Leila to lead him into the underworld of culture, Antrobus did have his skirmishes with passion:

> As for the Fair Sex (said Antrobus), I am no expert, old boy. I've always steered clear.
> Mind you, I've admired through binoculars as one might admire a fine pair of antlers. Nearest
> I ever came to being enmeshed was in the *Folies Bergères* one night. Fortunately, Sidney
> Trampelvis was there and got me out into the night air and fanned me with his cape until my

head cleared and I realized the Full Enormity of what I'd done. Without realizing it, I had proposed to a delightful little pair of antlers called Fifi and was proposing to take her back to the Embassy and force the Chaplain to gum us together. (107)

Though Antrobus casually admits to voyeurism, his embarrassment is that he almost left the neutral life of the diplomat who need not justify a wife by professional or social reasons. And of more importance, he had let passion direct him, as had Sidney, who had proposed to a contortionist. Both fled, Antrobus to his embassy and Sidney over to Dover with his hair dyed green "to escape identification."

In Antrobus's reflections indiscretions and outright violations of taboos are generally treated as harmless—as long as they do not incline the diplomat to hurried, or emotional, decisions involving actual relations between countries. True, within the embassy (at times even within the whole diplomatic corps) tempers might flare. Polk-Mowbray once flew into a rage at De Mandeville, who had instructed that garlic be added to all food prepared in the embassy: "Wretch!" he cried in a shaking voice. "Could you not see the harm that might come from such reckless and criminal cookery?" (65). Quite likely, simple childish pique or curiosity led De Mandeville down the fragrant path, as happened on other occasions when he caused distress, even havoc.

Always in a foreign country (long enough to be strangers to their own), the diplomats acquire a sense of difference from all around them. Even family life is never subject to the same demand for predictability that would be true of a native of the country; for dips, in most respects, live as exiles: with privilege and without the restrictions of societal norms. In the stories Antrobus tells, vagaries such as voyeurism and drunkenness never interfere with the profession—though generally the vagaries seem to demand full attention. In *The Avignon Quintet,* the unholy trio of Peirs, Bruce, and Sylvie devote their lives to refining the possibilities of sexual love and psychological dependency: incest, homosexuality, madness, and suicide. Never do the lives of Peirs and Bruce in the respective diplomatic corps of France and England appear as other than ways to finance and facilitate their elegant redundancy. Even in death Peirs avoids belonging, since his will rejects the Christian burial demanded by his ancestors and by his own relative, a priest. Peirs has an identity based on Gnostic conviction that what the God of his fathers offers is corrosive to the spirit. Thus, he has chosen to alienate himself from all that should have been natural to his life and death as a citizen of France and a member of the ancient family of de Nogaret. Whether separation of his beliefs from those of his Christian ancestors occurred to accommodate his incestuous love for his sister or simply added another dimension to his separation, his variance from the norm is less important than the effect of his Gnostic stance: he is freed from all obligation to follow the demands and practices of past and present. He lives only to control his death, to enter an objection to the force that has made excess enjoyable and sinful.

Clearly, neither Peirs nor Bruce is promoted to the point of needing a presentable and visible wife. The marriage of Sylvie and Bruce exists simply to sanction, or disguise, the intimacies of their lives. Neither of them needs or wants to be part of any society other than the one they create for themselves.

Mountolive, however, does not find a cul-de-sac of fulfillment that scotches ambition, nor does he remain within the limitations expected of him. His knowledge of their language and culture endears Mountolive to the Egyptians, yet he is surprisingly innocent. Having lived within the closed parameters of diplomatic expectations, even what he learns of cultural ways never touches his identity. His donning tarbush and sunglasses in the native quarter of Alexandria delights him when he is accepted as belonging but leads to horror as he is left in a child brothel. Though he may know the language and the manner, he does not belong, cannot accept as normal the practices of another culture that would conflict with those of his own.

Nor is he able to acquire a wife simply as part of his official pose, like wearing full dress. Instead, he once again lets his passion direct his needs. Lisa Pursewarden entrances him. If Lisa had been simply part of the ambassadorial role, her brother could, most likely, have accepted her marriage. But Pursewarden could never have shared his love for Lisa. He has separated himself from any experience that could induce him to accept such compromise. The incestuous obsession of brother for sister is the seed of all his other interests and obsessions that separate him from all others. Exiled from any country by his profession, separated from all around him by the septic eye of the writer, and removed from ordinary emotions by incest, Pursewarden shrinks in his own psyche to a divinity, a being lacking human credibility. As Lisa explains to Darley, her brother justifies their incest with mythological precedent: "He was pleased to come here to Egypt, because he felt, he said, an interior poetic link with Osiris and Isis, with Ptolemy and Arsinoë—the race of the sun and the moon" (*Clea* 191). Even in death, suicide, Pursewarden exists apart from the most normal of human emotions, fear of death. Instead, he welcomes the release his death gives Lisa, freeing her to marry; and death becomes, like life, a gift from a divinity. Mountolive is quite right as he uncovers Pursewarden's excuse for death in his knowledge of Nessim's plot: "Nobody kills himself for an official reason!" (*Mountolive* 185). No official dictum could direct Pursewarden's life, much less his death.

F. K.: The humor in the Antrobus stories is always so straightforward. Was there ever any real danger in the lives of the diplomats in Yugoslavia?
L. D.: Yes. Of course. The Yugoslavs suddenly found themselves with

complex equipment to run, equipment they knew nothing about. You might
pick up a glass of slivovitza *and be electrocuted.*

Lest we assume that Antrobus just dallies at his club with a glass in his hand, telling of lives spent knotting a tie, Durrell takes even that collection of supernumeraries into the very jaws of danger. Death itself has walked among the corps to tell jokes that always escape being macabre. When the entire corps rides the Yugoslav train named the Liberation-Celebration Machine to celebrate Yugoslav liberation, their lives are endangered by technological incompetence that is nearly malevolent. With love of life replaced by the fear of losing it, the corps travels through a night Dante would have avoided:

> At two in the morning there was a ghastly rending noise as we entered the station of Slopsy Blob, named after the famous independence fighter. The Hanging Coach somehow got itself engaged with the tin dado which ran along the roof of the station and ripped it off as clean as a whistle, by the same token almost decapitating one of the drivers. The noise was appalling and the whole Corps let out a unified shriek of terror. I have never heard diplomats scream like that before or since—and I never want to. (18)

That the most intense emotions in the stories come from a situation made ridiculous by exaggeration adds to the humor. The diplomats are anachronisms, and their fears trivial. But how delightful to know that no diplomat will die in such a comic manner—even though Armaggedon may be heard in the growls of large national interests that circle one another.

Bound by tradition to look at the position and not the person, the diplomat sees the societies and cultures left to his care reflect the personality of new leaders and players. He remains outside the experience of his task. Protocol, however, will be maintained as the limitations of the diplomat are told to us by narrators, created by Durrell with an expectedly high level of knowledge of the works and days of the diplomatic corps. The narrators encompass the corps but are neither limited nor protected by it. We are told in "The Ghost Train," the first of the Antrobus stories, virtually all we know about the life of the man who will break every confidence Antrobus entrusts to him:

> We've served together in a number of foreign capitals, he as a regular of the career, I as a contract officer: which explains why he is now a heavily padded senior in Southern while I am an impoverished writer. Nevertheless, whenever I'm in London he gives me lunch at his club and we talk about the past—those happy days passed in foreign capitals "lying abroad" for our country. (13)

We will not be given such concrete facts about the lives of the narrators of *Mountolive* and *Quinx,* the novels of what Durrell considers his oeuvre that most resemble the fictional mode of the diplomatic sketches.

F. K.: You know, there's been quite a lot of talk about who is the real narrator of Mountolive. *I think it's Durrell, just as in the Antrobus stories. Someone who understands the diplomatic corps but is not in it.*
L. D.: Well, of course.

All three narrators are conversant with the lives of the characters, have access even to their files, and both know and tell of the predelictions of their realities. We may, quite safely, assume that Durrell's own existence is reflected at the time he wrote the respective books. In the reflections we may trace the development of the writer from one who entertains to one who investigates the curious world of good and evil to a writer in very complete understanding of the quest for the nature of reality that he has entered with his readers. At each stage, this narrator provides us with what moral information he can. Often, he cannot guide but only help us see the ambiguity of life. Yet Durrell as narrator does not absent himself. We find him speaking against all structures that would destroy and limit individual freedom.

Limited as they are to Vulgaria (with an occasional uncorrected slip reading "Yugoslavia"), the stories of Antrobus express detestation for Slavic life and culture and for the Communist ideology. In the sketches, though, peremptory strikes are limited to deprecating the appearance and manner of the residents.

F. K.: Did anything like the story of the Central Balkan Herald *happen?*
L. D.: There was a Central Balkan Herald, *and all of the misprints actually occurred there.*

In "Frying the Flag," the narrator takes the role of storyteller from Antrobus, who is apparently too irritated to recount the history of "the *Central Balkan Herald* (circulation 500)." Edited by the sisters Grope, the remnants of an English diplomatic family, the newspaper provided anguish for the dedicated diplomat but delight for our narrator with such misprints as: "MINISTER FINED FOR KISSING IN PUBIC. WEDDING BULLS RING OUT FOR PRINCESS. QUEEN OF HOLLAND GIVES PANTY FOR EX-SERVICE MEN. MORE DOGS HAVE BABIES THIS SUMMER IN BELGRADE. BRITAINS NEW FLYING-GOAT" (34) and of course the culinary oddity in the title.

So far, the story has presented some unseemly misprints, but has not broached any great impropriety. However, the narrator indicates two objects of his displeasure, the first being the printers responsible for the printing:

The reason for a marked disposition towards misprints was not far to seek; the composition room, where the paper was hand-set daily, was staffed by half a dozen hirsute Serbian peasants with greasy elf-locks and hands like shovels. Bowed and drooling and uttering weird eldritch cries from time to time they went up and down the type-boxes with the air of half-emancipated baboons hunting for fleas. (34)

In such circumstances, the sisters Grope never had time to read proof. Yet they always published a paper—until World War II, when they left the country. The narrator is also displeased with the government of post-World War II Yugoslavia. The new Communist regime ignored their requests to begin publishing again. Polk-Mowbray, for once, found no reason to object to a decision made by the new government.

The story turns upon the old device of the malaprop, and differs in tone from other stories only in Durrell's own involvement. He clearly disapproves of the Slavs for their genetic stock, parochial politics, and unstinted grimness. Yet Polk-Mowbray and Antrobus, in their lack of delight in the unpredictable language of the *Central Balkan Herald,* indicate their difference from the narrator. He delights in all the oddities that distress the real diplomat, for only there does he find a trace of life other than what is prescribed by protocol. It is the narrator who structures and manipulates Antrobus and his colleagues for our pleasure. Antrobus, himself, never sees the humor in the situations which interrupt the steady course of the corps, the ridiculous and inconsequential acts and poses which in the story of David Mountolive will occur to a mind educated beyond its need.

Mountolive is handsome and clever. And like Polk-Mowbray's contingent, he has liaisons with the likes of ballet dancers, whom he drolly excludes from his life if they become troublesome and have expectations of emotional commitment beyond that of the casual affair. He, too, adopts the affectation of cordiality by calling subordinates "old boy." He had told himself he would never repeat that offense, but finds himself uncontrollably copying his last ambassador. Polk-Mowbray and Antrobus are untroubled by such weighing of the niceties of address. The FO is the rod of leadership, the staff of life; and they have no desire to exceed its limits. Mountolive must achieve their acceptance of protocol, of inertia, if he is to continue to be of use to diplomacy as well as to those about whom he cares.

The narrator, who tells all, indicates that Mountolive must accept as accurate the taunt of his former lover, the dancer Grishkin: "You are only a diplomat. You have no politics and no religion!" (*Mountolive* 54). The toll is considerable as Mountolive learns: the destruction of the Hosnani family, the deaths of Narouz and Pursewarden, the tangential shaking of his own career. But never does the narrator condemn. He simply lets Mountolive withdraw from personal involvement as the plot (of *The Alexandria Quartet* and of the Copts) careens to the end, scattering destruction. The novel begins with Mountolive very self-composed and at the mid-point of a promising career; but it ends with Nessim Hosnani in the desert where he has just buried his brother, who was killed in his stead. As Mountolive has learned earlier, Narouz has been chosen by Egyptian officials as the scapegoat. Nessim will live and continue to pay bribes to the officials who manipulated his existence from material Mountolive has been forced by his profession to turn over. Mountolive learns of his manipulation by the Egyptians, as well as by protocol, and disappears as a character upon being told that Nessim is innocent and Narouz guilty of leading the Coptic plot. His attempt to chart an independent course is over. If his career is to continue, he will have to accept the terms of the "artificial life" the narrator cannot, will have to let his pursuit of culture and passion be replaced with less volatile avocations.

We should not assume, however, that culture is a complete anathema to the diplomat. We have seen the shattering of De Mandeville and Mountolive by its arousing simply idiosyncratic behavior. Yet it is a strangely evil book, indeed, that brings no one to a calm port, though such a lesson was not the one Antrobus meant to teach in the story of "little Carter":

> Americans are notoriously Romance prone. He went off to Egypt on leave with the *ALEXAN-DRIA QUARTET* under his arm. Next thing we knew, he had become a Moslem—bang! Just like that. Gone over to them bodily. He came back from leave looking pale but jaunty in a ghastly sort of way and towing a string of little new black wives. "Durrell's right," he is alleged to have announced to his Chief with an airy wave. "Down there almost everything goes." Well, of course, he went too; but he had brought us a headache. (172)

Expectedly, Antrobus uses the story to illustrate the resiliency and forebearance of the corps:

> I felt for him. Yes, Carter cost us a great deal of extra legislation. After all, what was to prevent the whole State Department filling up one night with Mormons. Well, the waters closed over little Carter. I was sorry for him. Two of the wives were quite pretty, they said, with well-placed Advantages. But it was useless crying over spilt milk. We reformed our ranks and marched on, ever on. (173)

Considering the examples Durrell has provided, one must agree with Antrobus. For only once was the life of the embassy totally disrupted by an outside force, one determined to destroy protocol—perhaps even destroy the diplomat's *raison d'être,* the preservation of protocol.

> *F. K.: Did you write "Smoke, the Embassy Cat" specifically for inclusion in* Antrobus Complete?
> *L. D.: Yes.*
> *F. K.: And did it precede* Quinx *in composition?*
> *L. D.: I don't know really. Must have come out of my notes.*

In the last of the stories of Antrobus, "Smoke, the Embassy Cat," Durrell writes of disorder; but only in *Quinx* will he have an appropriate occasion to present the significance of Smoke, the intruder.

The story told by Antrobus begins, as might one of Eliot's, with the appearance at the embassy of a charismatic feline, one which reduces Polk-Mowbray's diction, previously weakened by Americanism, to drivel: *"Didums wazums drinkums pussums milkums"* (193). Appalling, yes, but hardly more so than the sight of the ambassador at an outdoor café drinking a Coca-Cola. Even the reasons Smoke had to be forcibly removed from the embassy would cause little trouble to anyone other than the rigidly humorless: she began to write memos and make telephone calls, all of a most disruptive nature. She seems hardly to deserve to be referred to as "Old Nick" by Antrobus, nor does declining to write a cat-ode about her because "she smelt disturbingly of brimstone" seem justified by her behavior (201–2).

The stories of Antrobus, with burlesque and parody, take what might be sad, even tragic, and turn it to comedy. No one is ever seriously hurt, all careers continue, and the corps wraps itself in inertia. Such is not the setting for a discussion of evil, and the story of Smoke was to remain an uneasy and unsatisfying ending to Antrobus until Durrell published *Quinx* in 1985. There, in evoking Smoke, the narrator allows us to view the workings of a reality in which evil and the recognition of it appear without disguise or apology:

> The poetic substance detached from the narrative line, the sullen monorail of story and person. Rather to leave the undeveloped germs of anecdote to dissolve in the mind. Like the accident, the death in a snowdrift near Zagreb. The huge car buried in a snowy mountain. She was in full evening dress with her fur cape, and the little cat Smoke asleep in her sleeve. The headlights made a blaze of crystal so it seemed the snow was lit from within. But they forgot to turn the heaters off. A white Mercedes with buried lights. Why go on? They suffocated slowly waiting for help which could not reach them much before dawn. Only Smoke remained. Her loud purring seemed to fill the car. (32)

Place and cat are repeated from the stories—with different intent: to look once again, seriously this time, into the nature of life and death, perhaps into the source of evil.

Throughout *The Avignon Quintet,* Durrell has woven plots of death and life, all of which add information to the continuing study of evil. The answers are as individual as perversion, as topical as conquest, and as eternal as a malevolent deity. Always, Durrell suggests that what seems to be accidental may well tell us much more than can excursions into biography and history. The desire to make the independent act or being conform to purposeful structures such as plot and character development, even in factual writing, can diminish the intensity of intrusion by a destructive force. We may call the manifestation of that force Smoke, Monsieur, or Nazi Germany, whatever our experience provides. But like the psychopathic killer Mnendis, who kills Affad in *Sebastian,* destruction needs neither introduction nor explanation. It simply is.

Such concerns with good and evil would be inappropriately addressed in the stories told by Antrobus. Remaining on the surface, he has no adequate measure of the significance of his experience. Food with too much garlic, a member of the corps who may be feeding his compatriots to the wolves, or the appearance of evil are all on the same plane for Antrobus. They disturb the peace of inconsequence. And so the stories of Antrobus, like the character himself, stay within the realm of manners, seldom consider morals, and never philosophic anxieties. Yet the anecdotes of Antrobus stay in the mind and when put into a different atmosphere lead to the disturbing inquiries that are the central concern of Lawrence Durrell's greatest writing.

Durrell's comments are from an interview I conducted with him in Languedoc, November 8–10, 1986.

Works Cited

Durrell, Lawrence. *Antrobus Complete*. London: Faber, 1985.
———— . *Clea*. New York: Dutton, 1961.
———— . *Esprit de Corps and Stiff Upper Lip*. New York: Dutton, 1961.
———— . *Mountolive*. New York: Dutton, 1958.
———— . *Quinx, or the Ripper's Tale*. London: Faber, 1985.
Durrell, Lawrence, and Henry Miller. *Lawrence Durrell–Henry Miller: A Private Correspondence.* Ed. George Wickes. New York: Dutton, 1963.
Jung, C. G. "The Spiritual Problem of Modern Man." *Civilization in Transition. Collected Works of C. G. Jung.* Vol. 10. New York: Pantheon, 1964.

7

The Narrator in *The Dark Labyrinth*

Gregory Dickson

In 1947 Lawrence Durrell published *The Dark Labyrinth* (originally *Cefalû*); in 1938 he had published his first major fiction, *The Black Book;* and in 1957 he was to publish the first volume of *The Alexandria Quartet.* Chronologically, at least, *The Dark Labyrinth* is a link between the time when Durrell first heard his "own voice" and the time when he showed the world that he had developed not only a very strong voice but a unique and fascinating one. But is *The Dark Labyrinth,* a work so often glossed over by the critics, nothing more than a good example of an author developing his skills on his way to writing four of the most praised novels of our time? I believe we can forgive the critics who see *The Dark Labyrinth* only in that perspective, but I also believe that we can see the book as an example of good fiction unto itself, and also as an example of Durrell's maturation as a stylist, particularly in the area of narration.

Durrell's first two novels, *Pied Piper of Lovers* and *Panic Spring,* were straightforward accounts of a group of young people attempting to find their own artistic voices in the period between the two world wars. *The Black Book* could be seen in that same general light, but the point of view—the perspective of the narrator—is so much more complex than that in the first two works. In it we find at least two narrators, Lawrence Lucifer and Death Gregory, the latter's diary becoming the narrative for pages at a time. In *The Alexandria Quartet* there are at least three: Darley, who is responsible for *Justine* and *Clea;* Balthazar, who, through his "interlinear," is responsible for much of the book bearing his name; and the anonymous third-person narrator of *Mountolive.* While the style of *The Dark Labyrinth* might harken back to the simplicity of the first two novels, and ahead to *White Eagles over Serbia* (1957) and *Mountolive,* the narrative complexity is closely allied with that of *The Alexandria Quartet* and *The Avignon Quintet.*

Critics have had trouble classifying the work: John Unterecker calls it "adventures . . . in caves" (248); John Weigel calls it an "allegory," and concludes that "it deals with knowledge beyond the systematically knowable. Despite its derivative qualities, it is authentic Durrell and rings true" (53–54); G. S. Fraser understands why the book was not a success and why it was not republished until *The Alexandria Quartet* had made Durrell famous (100); James A. Brigham finds that "the allegory is based on the traditional association of the labyrinth with the womb and with rebirth" but also links it to the "worlds of psychoanalysis and art" and to the questions postwar Europe was asking itself (19). But Durrell was self-effacing when he wrote to Henry Miller that *The Dark Labyrinth* "is a queer cosmological tale" which is "really an extended morality, but written artlessly in the style of a detective story." He concludes, "I have deliberately chosen that most exasperating of forms, the situation novel, in which to write it" (Wickes 201). Here again I wish to emphasize that I do not see *The Dark Labyrinth* as one of Durrell's exercises on the way to establishing the complex and intertwining narrative of his famous works, but rather believe that Durrell had taken an oft-used and relatively simple third-person-omniscient narrator and explored all the possibilities of such an approach.

Take, for example, the first page of the novel where the reader finds a very brief and very straightforward account of the events to be treated at depth in the remainder of the work. In four sentences we have what we could call "the newspaper facts" of the tragedy in the labyrinth. But who is giving us these facts? Is it Durrell himself, supplying us with just enough background to get into the novel immediately? Is it a reproduction of some news account? If so, who is reading it to us? Perhaps there is some explanation in the first line of the second paragraph: "Where a novelist might find it necessary to excuse himself for the choice of so formal a theme, the journalist feels no such inhibition" (11). Perhaps, we now think, this is not going to be a novel at all, but something on the lines of fictive "new journalism." To lend more credence to this theory, the narrator then describes how the newspapers in England, America, and Greece treated the story, and introduces us to an American reporter who has gone to the scene. This reporter, a certain Mr. Howe who makes his only appearance in the novel on these first pages, is ill at ease: he was "still a little awed"; he formed a sentence in his mind "but he somehow could not get it out" (12); he admits of the story that "it's very confusing"; and finally "the young American felt the vague irritation that always came over him when he had dealings with the English" (13). Clearly, this journalist, and journalism itself by extension, is not going to be capable of completing this tale of the labyrinth for us. But through Howe and his falterings, the reader knows the basics of the events and knows too that there is more, much more, to be explained.

All of this is contained in the first section of the novel, "The Argument," which is nothing more than the narrator (whoever he is and how he will treat the narrative are still undetermined) posing questions, establishing contradictions, and generally confusing the reader as well as Mr. Howe. The narrator continues this pattern in the second part of "The Argument," which consists of a conversation between Lord Graecen, the only known survivor of the labyrinth rockslide, and Sir Juan Axelos, who lives in Cefalû and who had discovered certain sculptures in a grotto in the labyrinth. Part of the reason Graecen had gone to the labyrinth was to look at these newly discovered works of art. He found them beautiful and authentic, and now Axelos tells Graecen that they are fakes planted by Axelos himself. Whether they are or not is another one of those questions—mysteries—posed to the reader, and for now the narrator is assuming no sides, lending weight to the statements of neither party.

The third section of "The Argument" shows Durrell at his complex best, for we find people and events occupying three levels of time and three levels of narration. The present consists of the crew of the ship going through the remains of the victims of the labyrinth cave-in; the near past is made up of the crew's evaluations of the passengers as well as remembered snatches of conversation with the deceased; and the past is apparently the narrator's own description of the characters, as he briefly tells us of the passengers' reasons for being on the ship and how they behaved once aboard. "As she turned over Miss Dombey's effects, which, apart from the bundles of tracts, were few, the stewardess remembered another incident which had surprised her. She had recounted it later in the voyage to the purser who seemed to find it very droll" (21). Here the narrator takes us from the simple past tense of an event already accomplished, through another event remembered in the simple past but which occurred in the far past, to yet another time from the past when this second event was recounted to the purser. To Durrell's credit, this juxtaposition of time frames is not confusing to the reader—the above passage is easily understood—but it is an example of how the narrator is manipulating time (not events) to demonstrate that a complex theme—time and our perception of it—must be dealt with in a complex narrative form.

In the next section of *The Dark Labyrinth*, "Ariadne's Thread," we find three methods of narration: third-person omniscience (within a character), limited third-person omniscience (again within a character), and the inclusion of conclusions apparently reached by the narrator himself. Graecen, for example, feels "a little empty and negative" (28) upon quitting his post at the museum, and the narrator adds to this observation by confirming that "in truth he felt" this way. Immediately after learning of Graecen's feelings on leaving the museum for the last time, we read that "Museum Street looked drab. So did Great Russell Street. Drabness multiplied by drabness. The last suds of light were running down behind St. Pancras. London was drawing up the darkness like a blotter" (29). Is this the narrator's description of the scene? It certainly does not sound like any of Graecen's prose (or his poetry), yet it is sandwiched between two examples of the narrator listening in to Graecen's mind for us. These two examples are set in quotation marks, though, as if Graecen were speaking directly to the narrator, while the observation is not. Durrell presents us with two possibilities then: one a formula reading Graecen/narrator/Graecen, and the second adding up to Greacen's conscious/Graecen's subconscious/Graecen's conscious. If it is true, as some theories hold, that the subconscious mind is capable of only deductive reasoning while the conscious is capable of both inductive and deductive, then the differences in these connections are vast. And when we add the *possibility* of the narrator supplying the subconscious rather than merely overhearing it, we are left with nothing but the ultimate in unreliable narration.

Is it incumbent upon the narrator to inform us who is thinking particular thoughts, who is speaking at all times? In a simple and straightforward exposition it probably is; but in a novel about complex motives, complex personalities, and complex resolutions, a complex narrative not only points out the difficulties of multiple perspectives but emphasizes the necessity for them. Again, the narrator in *The Dark Labyrinth* is either adding his own impressions to the scene or demonstrating that Graecen and some of the other characters are capable of thinking on more than one level at a time. This combination of narrator and character becomes more pronounced as the novel progresses.

Through all of "Ariadne's Thread," the narrator employs the Jamesian technique of limited omniscience. In Graecen's conversations with the psychiatrist Hogarth, for example, the reader can find only external description of Hogarth: "His face was like one of those carved Austrian pipe-heads—large bony features which were only kept alive by the small pointed eagerness of his eyes" (34). The reader rarely knows what Hogarth is thinking or feeling. The narrator informs us through this exclusion that only the members of the cast who take the trip to Cefalû are worthy of our in-depth consideration. He does the same much later in "At the Monastery" when Baird encounters his old friend Abbot John. We know, or rather the narrator gives us the impression that we know, precisely what Baird is thinking and feeling, but only twice do we eavesdrop on the abbot's mind.

"Portraits," the next section of *The Dark Labyrinth,* is a series of short sketches dealing with only a few of the passengers on the *Europa.* Here, on the first few days of the voyage, the characters are meeting one another for the first time, and their discussions with one another are halting, limited, and guarded. People on board reveal some of themselves to others, but, as usual in a first meeting, not all. Baird meets his old neighbor, the evangelistic missionary Miss Dombey, and tells her of "his little Moorish house in Fez," but omits "any mention of the kohl-painted pair of dark eyes that watched the dusty road by the cypresses so anxiously for him" (60). The narrator fills in little bits and pieces of the background for us, but for the most part takes his cue from the ambience of the "chapter" and refuses to supply much more detail to the readers than the characters are willing to supply to one another. Even when the narrative is devoted, for a number of pages, solely to Baird and his war experiences on Crete, we learn little more than we would from a newspaper account. Baird found "exhilaration" in the "freedom . . . and remoteness of control over his own actions" (67), but do not terms such as *exhilaration, freedom,* and *control* deserve more than a single sentence of explanation? The narrator is, of course, a pawn of the author, and the author of this tightly controlled narrative has dictated that the circumstances surrounding both Baird's experiences and the circumstances of first meetings in "Portraits" should limit the characters' relationships with one another as well as the narrator's relationship with the reader.

In "The Voyage Out," the next section of the novel, the characters have much more time to spend with each other—they are together for a longer time than ever before and they know the journey will take longer yet. Thus, they begin to relate more of their lives to their fellow passengers, broaching topics not discussed before. The narrator, as usual, follows their lead and the dictates of a logical narrative structure, extending the range of his omniscience and the amount of information he is willing to divulge to the reader. Once again, Graecen is the focal point of the section, and his relationship with both Miss Dombey and Virginia Dale are explored in embarrassing (I am sure that is the word Graecen would have used) detail.

He meets Virginia Dale, having "looked up her name on the passenger list" (100), and supposes she is an admirer of him. He becomes, therefore, an admirer of her. Graecen imagines that

> they would be spark to flint. On Majorca they would go for long walks together in that perfect scenery, and she would ask him to help her with a book on Keats she was going to write. They would not be able to part from each other. He would tell her that he was . . . (Her anguish at this Keatsian repetition of things gave him great pleasures to imagine). Quixotically, madly, they would marry in Naples and visit Keats' grave together. Then . . . Then . . . It all becomes a little misty. (101)

The narrator here has let us into Graecen's mind at the deepest level; not only can we find extrapolations into the future based on Graecen's thoughts, but the narrator affords us a third-person view that first-person Graecen would never express or acknowledge. In short, this is another example of the narrative the reader finds in the first section—Graecen revealed through his actions, thoughts, and either his subconscious mind or the opinion of the narrator. The combination affords the reader as complete a portrait as possible, even if some of the facts might be narrative speculation.

In the next part of the novel, Durrell continues with this same pattern for two reasons. One is that because the shipmates are so intimate by now that they reveal much more of themselves to one another, and the narrator, therefore, does not feel he is overreaching his narrative privileges to do the same. And the second reason, obviously related to the first, is that the narrator continues to sandwich his own comments between the quoted comments of the characters, indicating, again, either that the narrator is thinking along with the characters or that the character is being revealed to us in layers—thoughts transmitted directly through the narrator and thoughts on a different level which nevertheless become part of the narrative. The medium of "The Medium" is Olaf Fearmax, and his tale begins when Campion, the painter, strikes up a conversation. For a while the conversation is two-sided enough for us to learn of Fearmax and Campion both: "Campion went on like a river in spate almost unconscious that he had an audience" (114). The audience, of course, consists not only of Fearmax but, through the narrator, the reader as well. The key to the chapter comes when Fearmax tells Campion, "I will tell you about my own life. You can compare the experience, not the events, with your own" (115). The invitation extends to the reader as well as Campion, and Fearmax launches into a detailed first-person account of how he came to be on the Europa, and in the shape he is in.

Here the narrative shifts from the third-person mode of quotation to the direct narrative of the story being told for Fearmax. It is as if Fearmax had told his tale to Campion and the narrator, who relays it to the reader at some later date. There are brief interruptions of third-person quotations, but they come from conversations Fearmax holds within the context of the narrator telling his story for him, and Fearmax becomes "he," not "I."

It is only approximately halfway through the novel that the narrative actually comes to the labyrinth itself. In "The Labyrinth," the characters learn of the proposed side trip to the caves and "The Cefalû Road," and they leave the ship to set off, on land now, for the labyrinth. Graecen, Baird, Campion, Miss Dombey, Fearmax, Virginia Dale, and the Trumans all sign on for the excursion. This part of the novel is very direct narrative, describing the beauty of the island and the characters' reaction to it and reinforcing the character traits which the narrative has been building all along: Graecen is gracious and formal when saying goodbye to his companions; Miss Dombey is strident and confused; Baird acts like a man on a military mission.

As the excursion continues, the reader receives what seems a superficial view of the characters. We are told how they look and what they say, but rarely do we know what they think, and this last information is couched, again as always, in the terms of the narrator—the reader is never sure whether the character or the narrator is making judgments or expressing facts. Included in a description of Graecen's reactions to the cave and his observations of Virginia Dale is the phrase "the poor girl was afraid" (161), indicating, once again, either that Graecen is concerned for the woman (on a subverbal level) or that the narrator is using his omniscience to alert the reader to Virginia's state of mind.

On the same page, Truman's whistling is "consoling" and the guide's manner is "obvious," but is this clear to the narrator, the characters, the reader? The further the characters proceed into the cave, however, the more the narrator relates their thoughts to the reader, returning again to the familiar pattern of external observation, eavesdropping on conversations, and including unquoted material as either extensions of the characters' minds or conclusions drawn by the narrator.

These shifts in point of view are not always ambiguous for there are times the omniscient narrator is the only possible source for some comments. When we learn that the guide was crushed, for example, we know that the other characters in the cave were pushed away from the central cave before they were able to determine who had lived or died in the avalanche, but the guide's death, callous as this might sound, is not important to the narrative or to the other characters. Durrell has not allowed him to become important—has not developed his character sufficiently for the reader to know or care about the man. There is only enough room in this "morality" for the fates of the main characters to be examined. This chapter, "The City in the Rock," is tied chronologically to a subsequent section, "In the Darkness," wherein the narrator describes how each of the trapped characters deals with the circumstance of being imprisoned in the labyrinth. Durrell writes in *The Greek Islands* that both the minotaur and the maze are "full of enigma. . . . Myself, I think that a man sentenced to death was given an outside chance of redeeming his life by crossing the labyrinth and avoiding the Minotaur if he could" (63). Or perhaps it was "a place where initiates had to find a way through the muddled penetralia of their own fears and desires?" (65).

Graecen, of course, is not trapped, and almost immediately finds his way out of the darkness and into Axelos's backyard. The others, though, have a great deal of soul-searching and coming-to-terms-with-their-pasts to accomplish before their fates are determined. Miss Dombey is first, and her doubts and fears of not just being stranded in the labyrinth but of her failure as a saver-of-souls, including her own, cause her to take an overdose of sleeping pills. Virginia Dale and Campion find their way to an outcropping of rock, and their fate is revealed by the narrator later. Baird, of course, never entered the labyrinth, which leaves only the Trumans and Fearmax; and the tale of Olaf's experiences in the labyrinth is the beginning of another, divergent, startling perspective of the narrator's role in the novel.

It is here, for the first time, that we find that the narrator has apparently been truly nothing more than a reporter, that the incidents of interpretation which we suspected to be a product of the narrator's omniscience are exactly what the characters said and thought, simply with different punctuation. For it is first with Fearmax, then with the Trumans, and finally with Campion, that the reader discovers that perhaps he or she has been seeing into the characters' minds all along, and whatever interjections the narrator supplied he supplied from the subconscious of the character. We see the narrator as reliable, but reliable only to the point of being true to his sources, not necessarily true to the reader. Durrell, with the accounts of these four, takes us into another world.

Lost in the labyrinth, Fearmax thinks to himself: "To deal with evidence that cannot be reconciled to the body and canons of everyday science has been the task of all independent minds since the beginning of history," and he concludes that "madness, therefore, must be a conditional term in our judgment of [men with independent minds]" (191). As he goes deeper into the labyrinth he remembers Hogarth telling him: "We act our inner symbolism outward into the world. In a very real sense we do create to the world around us since we get it to reflect back our inner symbolism at us" (192–93). As he follows the smoke from his cigar, and the batteries in his flashlight begin to weaken, he again hears the "voice of the minotaur." Then he asks himself the most revealing question asked by or of anyone in the novel, one which explains much of what is to follow concerning the fate of the other characters: "Was this whole place merely a mad exteriorization of his inner confusion; his feet walking slowly down metaphoric corridors of his own subconscious—in which only the roar of the sleeping monster gave him a clue to his primal guilt?" (193). The answer to this question, and a clue to the narrator's bifurcated reliability, comes when we see and hear the last of Olaf Fearmax: "He felt himself picked up at last in a soft wet mouth of enormous dimensions and carried, half-senseless, down the long damp corridors of the labyrinth" (197). Fearmax, according to Fearmax and the narrator, is eaten by the minotaur.

The Trumans, of course, become the most important members of this group of people whose fate tests the limits of reliable narrative because Durrell devotes an entire chapter, "The Roof of the World," to them. They stumble up through the labyrinth into a fertile and verdant valley, and Elsie Truman remarks: "It's like being reborn" (226). And when she stuffs her husband's mouth with ripe cherries he asks: "Where do you think you are? The Garden of Eden?" (229). This garden, though, soon becomes more than just a haven from a dark and inhospitable cave, and here again the narrator reveals his ability (propensity? obligation?) to go beyond the "real" facts of the rational world and depend on the psyche of the characters.

After a long introduction concerning the Trumans' adjustment to their new life, we find that the only other resident of the place, the American Ruth Adams, never sleeps, and the ax she uses to cut firewood never becomes dull. We also learn that the Trumans are stranded in this place—there is no way out except back through the now-plugged labyrinth. After reading of Fearmax's fate and now being confronted with less than believable facts from the roof of the world, the reader has, it seems to me, two choices: he or she can accept the narrator as reliable and therefore read the narrative as a morality, or accept the narrator as unreliable and thus capable of spinning a tale, of taking "the newspaper facts" and embellishing them into an ending much more psychologically important than "falls of rock separated several members of the party from the main body" (11). This chapter concludes with Elsie Truman's not-surprising thought: "She had realized that the roof of the world did not really exist, except in their own imaginations!" (256). Durrell, in his description of Crete in *The Greek Islands,* states that "the mountains are high enough to be snow-tipped throughout the dour winter," and the visitor's eye is halted, "not by the sea-line as in the smaller islands, but by a land skyline, often massive and forbidding. . . . The verdant and bounteous valleys that open everywhere offer no lack of water or shade or greenery" (58). Durrell has obviously given the narrative a natural and "real" location in which the characters can play out their allegorical morality.

The final episode of the narrator asking us for a willing suspension of disbelief occurs when, in the last chapter of *The Dark Labyrinth,* he describes the fate of Campion and Virginia Dale. Baird appears at Cefalû and reports that Virginia is safe, but he adds some interesting detail to the account of her rescue. We recall that at the end of "Campion," Campion and Virginia had jumped, hand-in-hand, into the sea. However, when Virginia is rescued from the sea by the same monks who were entertaining Baird, the one who saw her fall into the sea stated that "we had just started off, the Abbot and I, when the mad novice jumped in the air and said he'd seen a woman falling out of the sky" (261). One might, as did Baird and the Abbot, distrust such a vision, yet they did find a woman—Virginia—floating in the ocean. But where was Campion? They searched for him, but Virginia Dale "said she wasn't sure whether he jumped with her or not" (262). The last time the two appeared in the narrative, however, the narrator assured us that they had, indeed, leaped from the cliff together.

This episode is the climax to the confusing and contradictory narrative. The narrator has, in the first three-fourths of the novel, led us to believe that he was capable not only of reading the minds of the characters and listening in to their private conversations and relaying their attitudes and thoughts on a different (not technically quotable) level but also of interpreting actions, thoughts, and events on his own and inserting them into the narrative as a part of the overall portrait of the characters. However, when, in the labyrinth, the supernatural receives as much credence as the rational, the reader begins to believe that *The Dark Labyrinth* is truly a morality and not an attempt at a novel rendered without true psychological insight.

Stephen Spender writes that "the modern aim [in literature] was essentially the re-invention of reality: re-presentation of the shapes and forces of a new world, and also of a modern kind of sensibility" (133). Spender argues that the modernist tried to do this through the use of the first-person-singular narrator who acts "as it were, on behalf of both poet and reader" (134). Through his skillful use of the third-person narrator in *The Dark Labyrinth,* Durrell has distanced himself from both Spender's modernist author and from the text, but has included the reader by bringing the worlds of modern Europe and ancient Greece together, using, as Brigham says, "the worlds of psychoanalysis and art" (19) to entertain, educate, and amaze. *The Dark Labyrinth* is indeed a step for Durrell from his often-simplistic early work to the wonderful complexity of *The Alexandria Quartet* and *The Avignon Quintet.* It is also a masterful attempt at creatively dealing with the near-endless possibilities of an imaginative and perceptive third-person narrator in a traditional form. This is, simply, a modern psychological novel dealing with the complex problems of modern life; and through the author and the narrator, the narrative itself reflects these complexities.

Works Cited

Brigham, James A. "Initiatory Experience in *The Dark Labyrinth." On Miracle Ground II: Second International Lawrence Durrell Conference Proceedings.* Eds. Lawrence W. Markert and Carol Peirce. *Deus Loci* 7:5 (1984) and University of Baltimore Monograph Series, pp. 19–29.

Durrell, Lawrence. *The Dark Labyrinth.* New York: Dutton, 1962.

———. *The Greek Islands.* New York: Viking, 1978.

Durrell, Lawrence, and Henry Miller. *Lawrence Durrell–Henry Miller: A Private Correspondence.* Ed. George Wickes. New York: Dutton, 1963.

Fraser, G. S. *Lawrence Durrell: A Critical Study.* New York: Dutton, 1968.

Graves, Robert. *The Greek Myths.* 2 vols. Baltimore: Penguin, 1955.

Rose, H. J. *A Handbook of Greek Mythology. Including its Extension to Rome.* New York: Dutton, 1959.

Spender, Stephen. *The Struggle of the Modern.* Berkeley: University of California Press, 1963.

Unterecker, John. "Lawrence Durrell." *Six Contemporary British Novelists.* Ed. George Stade. New York: Columbia, 1976.

Weigel, John. *Lawrence Durrell.* New York: Twayne, 1965.

8

Lawrence Durrell's Plays: A Reevaluation

Peter G. Christensen

Lawrence Durrell's plays suffer from both critical neglect and lack of public visibility. Indeed, Durrell is so well known for *The Alexandria Quartet* that almost none of his other writings, both flawed and successful ones, have received the attention they deserve. Consequently, in 1989, we can still ask profitably: Can Durrell's apparently disparate plays be seen as a whole, both in terms of theme and stagecraft? Such a question has yet to be answered.

The critical material on Durrell's plays can be summarized fairly quickly. In 1962 Lander MacClintock contributed an essay, "Durrell's Plays," to Harry T. Moore's collection *The World of Lawrence Durrell*. He discusses *Sappho,* completed in 1947 and published in 1950, and *Acte,* which had not yet appeared in *Show*. MacClintock lavishes praise on both plays. He believes that *Sappho* is "primarily and essentially a *poem,* conceived as such, written as such" (76). He doubts that it would do well on the stage, but praises it for its "free verse of extraordinary litheness and flexibility" (77). Sappho emerges as a "damned soul, a truly tragic figure" who has misjudged her own nature (73). For Mac-Clintock, the play is clearly Racinian, whereas *Acte* is Cornelian. Both seem "more Shakespearean than Ibsenite" (85). *Acte* encompasses tragedy because there is no possible reconciliation between the claims of love and duty (81). Despite his enthusiasm, MacClintock fails to see the dramatic quality of *Sappho* and underestimates the importance of Petronius in *Acte*. Nevertheless, his discussion of the plays in the light of tragedy is a fruitful first step that deserves to be pursued.

In John Weigel's 1965 monograph on Durrell, the plays are treated less sympathetically, and the author thinks of *An Irish Faustus* as a far lesser work than the earlier dramas. By the time he was writing, *Acte* had been performed in Hamburg in a German translation by Robert Schnorr and published in *Theatre Heute* along with some correspondence between Durrell and Gustaf Gruendgens, the director. A third version was issued in hardcover by Faber in 1963, two years after the appearance of *An Irish Faustus*.

Weigel has no overall interpretation of the plays, and he does not like Durrell's stagecraft. On *Sappho* he writes: "The story is properly predictable from the premises and promises, and it unfolds as it must" (132). *Acte* "tells much of what is coming; and when it ends, it tells what came" (135). He criticizes *An Irish Faustus* for being "half-way out of the theatre and on its way to the cinema" (142). None of these statements holds water, for there is little attempt to understand Durrell's use of genre.

G. S. Fraser in his 1968 *Lawrence Durrell: A Critical Study* positions himself between admirers and detractors of Durrell's theatre, for he prefers *An Irish Faustus* to the other two plays and finds it the one that gives "the most coherent expression" of his concerns (114). Fraser believes that the play represents Jung's thoughts on quaternities and compares Faustus to Shakespeare's Prospero. In contrast, he misses the anguish at the heart of *Sappho,* where, for him, the characters are artworks conversing in a "period of human history when the simple, the primitive, the perennial seem to have existed in a wonderful poise" (107). *Acte,* following MacClintock, is categorized as Cornelian, but unfortunately without the clear structure of a neo-classic play. Its three versions are not compared.

A few articles devoted entirely to *An Irish Faustus* have followed these overall assessments. Hans-Peter Gerhardt's 1976 "Durrells *An Irish Faustus* als Beispiel einer modernen angelsaeschsischen Auspraegung der Faustfigur" benefits from the author's correspondence with Durrell. Gerhardt stresses the importance of Goethe's drama (and even Valéry's *Mon Faust*) rather than Marlowe's tragedy to Durrell's conception of the play, and he reads *An Irish Faustus* by comparing the ring of magic power to nuclear energy. Michael Cartwright's "The Playwright as Miracle Worker: *An Irish Faustus*" (1981) points out the comic elements in the play with reference to Durrell's heraldic universe and Northrop Frye's and Wylie Sypher's views on comedy. Robert F. Fleissner in "Faustus's Wearing of Faust's 'Green'" (1981) connects the color scheme of the play with Goethe's famous work. Additional brief comments on the play can be found in several of the many surveys of the Faust theme in world literature.

All Durrell's plays succeed because the conflicts of the characters engage our interest. They are neither allegories nor Manichean dramas. Most of the character interaction is handled by pointed dialogue between two or three figures. The background is always a world in which tyranny either rules the day or threatens to do so, as in our own time. Although it would be wrong to call each play a tragedy, the concept of tragedy, as MacClintock suggested, provides the best generic entry to the action.

Before elaborating on the idea of tragedy, I will expand my comments on conflict, power, and stagecraft. Sappho, in contrast with both Phaon, the poet who withdraws from the world, and his twin, Pittakos, who tries to gain military control over it, resists the idea (stated by both brothers) that we are all victims (54, 130, 140, 177). Rising from years of lethargy, she spiritually dies in deposing Pittakos and having him murdered. Acte leads a Scythian revolt against Rome out of her beliefs in human freedom, love, and duty to her country. Yet Nero and Petronius (the latter of whom she never meets) play with her like cats with a mouse, desiring a world in which art and life have blended to such a degree that her goals are meaningless. Faustus must first consider if he should be prodded by Mephisto to use the ring. Once he refuses, and destroys the power of the ring, he must decide if he should listen to the call of Peter the Hermit, embrace a passive existence, and retire from the world.

In each play the protagonist is thwarted by a tyranny. Sappho's uneventful married life with Kreon is ruined by Pittakos's return to Lesbos as tyrant. Fifteen years later, she herself burns her city, returning as an enemy ruler. Acte's dream of an independent Scythia is destroyed not just by the superior military power of the Roman Empire but by the demented, all-powerful Nero. Faustus is forced into exile by Queen Katherine once his triumph over her vampire husband has restored her to her senses. The tyrants, however, are not cardboard figures of evil. Pittakos does not rule in an evil way once in power, if we are to believe his words, and in his final reunion with his brother, Phaon, he seems brave and noble. A desire on Nero's part for the union of life and art shows him to have an idealistic side. Queen Katherine's mad love for her husband gives her a gruesome grandeur.

In *Sappho* the shape of the dramatic conflict may at first seem unclear because of the length of the speeches. Here, Durrell uses a type of scene structure which is similar to Wagner's in the *Ring* cycle. The big action is kept for the climax of the scene. Also, the stress on the groups of one, two, and three characters, which Wagner developed from his reading of Aeschylus, is evident. In *Sappho,* except for the poetry contest (five characters), there really is no large ensemble number. The audience, however, does not get cheated on action. A messenger arrives with a severed arm; Sappho tries to kill Pittakos; Diomedes expires after taking poison; and Minos and Kreon consult an oracle supervised by a masked woman. A chorus is employed in the poetry contest, and the arrival of Pittakos from Athens is treated as a spectacle.

The nine scenes move in a logical progression. The play opens with a monologue by Minos, who introduces both the island of Lesbos and his pupil Sappho. In scene 2, Phaon returns to Lesbos after years away in order to dive for the tablets which Sappho's husband, Kreon, hopes will gain him control of all the land he lost before an earthquake led to property redistribution. Then we learn that Phaon has found the tablets and that Pittakos will return from successful military engagements in the Aegean (scene 3). Pittakos returns and Phaon rejects his offer to give him a position in the new order. Pittakos's announcement of the death of Diomedes' son leads to news of Diomedes' suicide attempt (scene 4). Sappho tells the dying Diomedes that she functions as the voice of the God at the oracle (scene 5). She serves as the oracle when Kreon asks the god about the possibility of his having committed incest with the daughter of his first wife—the baby who grew up to his second wife, Sappho (scene 6). Sappho and Kreon are voted into exile because the oracle requires their facing the charge of incest (scene 7). Pittakos flees Sappho fifteen years later as she amasses power from Corinth. He arrives on Phaon's island and is reconciled with him (scene 8). Sappho, back on Lesbos, learns that Phaon, as well as Pittakos, has been murdered by her men and she is reunited with her daughter, Kleis, who had been held hostage by Pittakos.

Although Sappho is the central character, she is not always onstage. Twice she has major confrontations with Phaon and twice with Pittakos. Similarly, the two brothers face each other twice. Minor characters such as Diomedes are clearly needed to hold the plot together. Durrell unfortunately helped spread the idea that his play was not well constructed by adding a note in the back of the 1950 Faber edition, stating that Diomedes' part could be eliminated to shorten the playing time.

The play as published gives us a Sappho whom we see before and after but not in the process of her emotional transformation. The plot is structured around an ellipsis, one in which the rapprochement of the poetic and the action-oriented brothers represents their finest moment—while offstage the heroine falls apart morally.

Acte, unlike *Sappho,* does not move with the same clear narrative bridges from scene to scene. Acte is not introduced until the third of the eleven scenes of the 1965 version. She dominates the action for six straight scenes (1.3–5, 2.1–3) and the penultimate scenes (3.1), but she remains offstage in 1.1–2, 2.4, and 3.2. Petronius, the uncle of Fabius's wife, Flavia, holds our attention in 1.1, 2.4, and 3.2. The first scene introduces the revolt in Scythia, Nero's summons to Petronius to appear in Rome, and Flavia's anxiety over her husband in Scythia. When Petronius appears with Nero six scenes later, Fabius and Acte have already become lovers, and Acte has begun to think of murdering Nero on one of his next visits to her. Petronius (2.4) persuades the Emperor to let Fabius and Acte go free to allow them to construct their own disaster. Then he is encouraged by Flavia to work for Acte's death. In the last scene, he uses his dying moments (he has committed suicide in the wake of his wife's death) to discuss the outcome of the story (Fabius's killing of Acte, his ensuing drunkenness, and the madness of the son he has with Flavia) and the happier outcome he had written for the lovers in a novel about their lives. Although Acte has confrontations with Nero (2.2) and Flavia (2.3), she never meets Petronius, which dramatically establishes that she fights an unseen force over which she has no control. As in *Sappho,* Durrell employs a major narrative ellipse. We do not see Acte in her final meeting with Fabius—that is, just before he cuts off her head.

The 1961 version of *Acte* is less tight in its dramatic structure. First, a larger group of minor characters (first and second jailors, the Scythian leader Amar, and Myrko the dwarf) diffuse the dramatic center. Second, two major dialogic confrontations are given to Fabius each time with Amar. The 1961 *Acte* opens in Scythia, rather than in Italy with Petronius and Flavia. Thus when Petronius is brought onstage in the middle of the play, the audience feels an intrusion. The 1965 version also has dramatic superiority over the 1962 version in which Acte's father, Corvinus, is brought onstage with her to debate the benefits of revolution against Rome. Recently, Durrell has expressed a desire to work on the play once again.

An Irish Faustus at first glance appears to be dramatically simple compared to the earlier plays. It is the most dramatic, for it includes the impalement of a vampire and a descent into the fiery pit. Faustus holds the stage through almost all of the play's nine scenes. He is offstage only when Katherine confronts and blackmails her niece, Margaret, to work against Faustus at the end of scene 1 and when Martin and Bubo are together selling indulgences at the beginning of scene 2. The climax, the destruction of the ring of power (scene 6), comes earlier than in the other two plays; and once Faustus is done facing his external adversaries, Mephisto and Katherine, he has to deal with his inner self and try to find his own path to salvation. This change of direction makes the play's ending problematical, for the audience must decide whether his decision to retire to Matthew's hermitage represents a step toward his personal enlightenment. Instead of using an ellipsis, Durrell leaves the play more ambiguous and open-ended than in his earlier plays.

In each play Durrell relies on references to the tradition of tragic drama. *Sappho* echoes *Oedipus Rex* with its use of oracle and incest motifs. The conflicting ties of love and duty in *Acte* remind us of the Roman plays of Corneille and Racine. The Faustus legend has hundreds of treatments in addition to those of Marlowe and Goethe.

In his preface to the 1961 version of *Acte* (the only play with a preface) Durrell points us toward the consideration of tragedy in this play. He writes:

> Meanwhile, at the heart of the Roman cobweb the two spider shapes are also provoking destiny: Nero and Arbiter struggle like unsuccessful artists to discover the meaning of history. Behind their intellectual maneuvers lies the question: Can history ever be harnessed and molded by the artist? Or is it always to be a succession of tragic errors which must engulf the individual and destroy him? Is there such a thing as the tragedy in the Greek sense—the irremediable fate which lies in store for man? Or is this extreme view too fatalistic? (47)

In this statement Durrell mentions both "tragic errors" and "irremediable fate," two ideas which have haunted discussions of tragedy, but which do not mesh very well. The former suggests free will and the latter does not. A discussion which avoids this problem is given by Oscar Mandel in his well-argued study, *A Definition of Tragedy:*

> A work of art is tragic if it substantiates the following situations: *A protagonist who commands our earnest good will is impelled in a given world by a purpose, or undertakes an action, of a certain seriousness and magnitude; and by that very purpose of action, subject to that same given world, necessarily and inevitably meets with grave spiritual or physical suffering.* (20)

Mandel does not think that free will is a necessary part of tragedy, and he claims that "in the Greek drama absolute freedom existed side by side with the most severe necessity" (133). He finds that it is only since the writings of the German Romantics that it "became fashionable to think of tragedy as a freely willed action struggling against an external necessity" (177).

Sappho most closely approaches Mandel's paradigm for tragedy. Sappho seeks revenge on Pittakos after her son, held hostage in her custody, is accidentally killed in a freak accident. Not only is Pittakos killed by her men, but also Phaon, whom she could easily have loved. She destroys her home city of Eresos as well. In *Acte* the heroine's decision to join Amar, the tribal chieftain, and wage war against the Roman forces under Fabius, her ex-lover, leads to her death at his hand. Here the suffering is more physical than spiritual. The situation is also tragic for Fabius, who kills his lover and then becomes a drunkard.

In *An Irish Faustus* the anticlimactic ending of Faustus sitting down to a game of cards with his earlier antagonists (Mephisto, Martin, and Matthew) may be seen as tragic; for Faustus is losing his independent spirit. But if it is tragic, the spiritual decline is known only to the audience and not Faustus. Irony dominates here, and one is eerily reminded of the conclusion of Luis Buñuel's 1961 film *Viridiana,* in which the eponymous heroine's sitting down to cards in the last scene of the film announces her capitulation to the forces of evil, ignorance, and indifference. The other possible way of reading the ending is to believe that Faustus has readily found the *via negativa* in his retreat from the world. There is no character who challenges Faustus on this point; but on the other hand, the card game looks suspiciously inadequate as a symbol of a new attainment on the order of destroying the vampire, seizing the ring of power, and descending into the fiery pit to destroy it.

In short, as a series, Durrell's dramas move from tragedy closer to irony. In *Sappho,* as we shall see, the issue of human freedom is much discussed, and we are to take it into consideration in analyzing Sappho's suffering. In *Acte* life and art do not remain the opposites that Petronius believes. Instead, they are ironically united in his political influence on the Emperor. In *An Irish Faustus* the chief irony is not that we have a Faust figure who has no interest in action, for this idea is part of a burlesque tradition of adaptation. Rather the irony lies in the possibility that "the dance of pure forms" (86) has not really begun for Faustus.

Unlike Acte and Faustus, Sappho has a major flaw. She cannot control her ennui, her discontent with life. It was out of boredom, when she was conscious and not ruled by a drug, that Sappho as oracle had sent away Pittakos, her lover, years before. Although people everywhere think of her as a goddess (46), she remains prosaically chained to her husband, Kreon, a vulgar mercantile type, whom she does not love. Only when she meets Phaon does she really begin to understand the extent of her bitterness. For Phaon, they are two people who as lovers would be "two bankrupt states / Combining empty treasuries against a famine" (74). It is uncertain whether taking Phaon as her lover will save Sappho from herself. Durrell grants them a love duet (spoken in unison) which suggests that even if Phaon had remained on Lesbos and not decided to leave shortly after his brother's arrival, misery would still have followed them:

> Damned in effect and still neglecting cause,
> Soft brief and awkward as the kisses which combine
> To intersect with death till time follows us, time
> Finds and details us here in time,
> In this eternal pause,
> Fumbling outside immortality's immobile doors.

(78)

Sappho's attitude here, as before, is that death makes life absurd and renders human strivings grotesque.

The issue of freedom and responsibility, so essential to Sappho's relations with all about her, had early been introduced in the poetry contest, which occurs just before her tête-à-tête with Phaon. Diomedes, Sappho, and Minos all compose poems on the topic of freedom, with Diomedes and Sappho singularly concerned with the limitations on the individual's gratification of desire. Sappho concludes that freedom is the "prison of the free" (69). Here, freedom imprisons the wise more than other mortals because the imaginary ideal ruins those who are smart enough to see it as illusion.

Only Minos discusses freedom in terms of politics, and his poem remains incomplete since he is continually interrupted. He recites the following fragments:

> Who guessed what freedom was or e'er could be
> Until our Pittakos discovered she?

And who until our island banner rose
In Attic air knew freedom would disclose
So grave a rapture, so sublime a law.

(69–70)

Diomedes does, however, end the poetry contest by questioning whether any personal freedom is possible without political freedom or whether political freedom is a ruse which distracts people from personal freedom.

Pittakos feels no obligation to believe in political freedom since he does not think there is any personal freedom either. And the conflict between his views and those of Sappho introduces the significance of religion. Pittakos has no idea that Sappho speaks for the God at the oracle. For him the "Gods are bound / As men are, neither more nor less, / But in a frame of reference something similar" (129). Because of the part she plays in the oracle, Sappho has less faith in the gods and more in human beings. Here Durrell implicitly links organized religion with a predetermined world order and the possibility of dictatorship. Such a combination of beliefs has continued to haunt our own era.

Sappho, losing her confrontation with Pittakos, is exiled and separated from her children for fifteen years, until the death of Pittakos. After her son dies, she hopes that some action, no matter how extreme, can balance it out; but she discovers that even the death of Pittakos is "not enough" (185) for everything she has endured. Action no more leads to happiness than had her earlier indifference or will her later torpor. For Sappho, there is an inadequate catharsis as she is reunited with her daughter, Kleis. She tells her to weep so that the moment may be invested with the pathos she thinks it deserves but which she cannot experience:

Weep, little Kleis. You shall weep for both of us,
For the whole world if you have tears enough,
And for yourself long after you imagine
There are no tears left in the world to weep with.

(186)

Sappho requires someone to whom she can communicate this drama of waste and futility. Her only triumph is to plant in her child her own bleak vision of life. The same appeal is also made to the audience—to accept her as a tragic heroine who has gone through unbearable spiritual suffering.

The 1961 version of *Acte* comes closer in spirit to *Sappho* than the 1965 version, as the conflict between love and duty is stressed through Fabius's two encounters with Amar and the idea of political freedom is more openly discussed. Gustav Gruendgens, as we can see from his correspondence with Durrell, encouraged him to tighten up the play (1962:2). As a result, the relationship between art and freedom is given more prominence than the Cornelian theme of love versus duty. In the first scene between Fabius and Amar, the Scythian leader who marries Acte, Fabius, wears the ring of a friend named Basil, who once saved his life. Amar challenges Fabius to throw the ring into the fire (a similar motif occurs in *An Irish Faustus*) as an indication that he is not really a Scythian, despite his repeated references to the happy childhood he spent there:

> *Amar:*   About Scythia! About freedom! It is very simple.
>   We are easygoing people, as you know,
>   But people provoke us, make us angry.
>   But we are also easily pleased. O yes!
>   And if you please us, we are your men for life.
> *Fabius:* Rome cannot give you freedom.
> *Amar:*   But doesn't Rome want to please us?
> *Fabius:* Not in that way.
>
> (1961:54)

Fabius wants to convince Amar that Rome offers Scythia neither freedom nor slavery as part of the Empire. Amar taunts Fabius, jeering "What does [freedom] mean / To people who are happy" (54). Fabius does not deign to answer the question.

The second scene between Fabius and Amar is more melodramatic, and it once again shows Fabius in an unpleasant light. A child will soon be born to Acte and Amar, and when Amar tells Fabius this news, Fabius feels betrayed and shouts: "Bring me her head—and save your own, Amar" (104). In the 1965 version, we go from the last meeting of Acte and Fabius, a tender parting, directly to Petronius's talk with Flavia. Acte's final big speech to Fabius is very moving, but she is unaware of both her own errors and the actions of Petronius behind the scenes. She cries out:

> Yes, we can oppose history, bend history,
> But only human duty dare stare history in the face!
> Love by it we must, live by it we must;
> There are no options taken out with fate.
>
> (1965:67)

Despite her attempt to preserve an independent Scythia, Acte has made mistakes which have ruined her cause. She has confided in the tattletale Galba, missed her opportunity to kill Nero, and failed to anticipate that Amar might revolt. In her personal drama, she is fighting with external events to a greater extent than is Sappho.

Acte never meets Petronius, the novelist who decides her fate. It is Petronius who persuades Nero not to have Acte and Fabius killed in a straightforward manner. Instead, he proposes that they be allowed to work out their own doom. Petronius's cynical and detached attitude blinds him to the reality that the outcome of the Scythian independence struggle will be altered because of Nero's allowing Acte to go free. It could be that Petronius hopes the lovers will escape or will find a fate imposed on them from their own interaction. More likely, he sympathizes with Flavia in her desire to have Acte humiliated.

When Durrell asks in his preface, "Can history ever be harnessed and molded by the artist?" (47), he is only looking at one side of the problem posed by the play. Although Acte and Fabius each has a free will the artist cannot control, Petronius refuses to acknowledge his amorality in tinkering with their lives. Abnegating the moral sphere, Petronius tells Nero that he is merely an artist:

> I write books, that is all; but when they are
> Good books, it is because they follow the outlines
> Traced by life itself, of the complex truth of reality.
>
> Of course, you could kill your characters on the first
> Page and finish with them; but where's the book then?
> Where's your art, my duck? Where's your bloody art?
>
> (1965:57)

Petronius's interest in life exists primarily on the level of narrative curiosity. Life is aestheticized to the point that a long life full of successes and failures has more innate interest than one which is shorter and perhaps more morally responsible. When Durrell wrote *Acte,* the similarity of history to fictional stories had already been noted by R. G. Collingwood in *The Idea of History* (1945), and it would be taken up again later in terms of Northrop Frye's classification of genres in Hayden White's *Metahistory* (1973). For the audience Acte's story is a tragedy, but Petronius is able to turn it to romance with the reconciliation of the lovers.

In *An Irish Faustus,* as in *Acte* and *Sappho,* Durrell presents us with a basically noble-minded character. He makes Faustus, who has often been treated as a tragic figure, the leading character in a play designated a "morality." This is a surprising title since we normally associate a morality with allegorically personified virtues and vices. This strategy is not used in the play. Even if we use "morality" in the looser sense of "a story that points a moral," it seems like a useless designation, since the ending, as has been pointed out, is ambiguous.

Faustus's spiritual progress can be charted by comparing his ideas over three major scenes: his conversation with his pupil Margaret about the *via negativa* (scene 1), his summary of his experiences in the fiery pit (scene 7), and his conversation with Matthew the Hermit about retreat from the world (scene 9). Whereas it appears that the knowledge Faustus gains by his descent into the pit coincides with the ideas that he had originally held, it is not evident from his conversation with Matthew that he has found the right path of action or inaction.

In the first scene, Margaret conveniently summarizes Faustus's teachings:

> So that somehow one must turn oneself
> Into a place of visitation, refining by negatives
> Until the void, abhorred by nature, is filled by it
> Rushing in to expel the categories of the mind?
> But this field of grace, then, can only be discovered
> By the act of dreaming!
>
> (10)

There is a dreamlike quality to Faustus's experience of the underworld, as well. The qualities of space and time are defamiliarized, as he tells Anselm:

> I . . . felt the very heart of process beating;
> All time, the annals of our history were spread
> As if in section on a huge chart before me. . . .
> It sounds mad no? Luxuriant panoramas of human destiny
> The contingency of human desires and wills. . . .
> Like all time smouldering away in the dark glare
> Of furnaces such as no alchemist has seen or dreamed of!
> There all matter is undifferentiated, burns itself away
> In an ecstasy of disappointment.
>
> (69)

Faustus believes that now he can see the world with entirely new eyes. He wants to take a trip to recover what he has glimpsed. Since Queen Katherine, restored to her right mind, will not allow him to stay in the kingdom, he can immediately begin his journey. It has two stages: his meeting with Martin the Pardoner and his settling in for the winter in Matthew the Hermit's log hut.

Matthew's defense of the virtues of his retreat from the world either have to be taken on faith or questioned, as there is no further revelation to support it. He sees an open passivity as the way to personal salvation: "for when nothing begins to happen / . . . at long last Everything / Begins to cohere, the dance of the pure forms begins" (86). The benefits of contemplation or letting go are not manifested through the last action of the play, a four-handed game of cards (which may last the whole winter) between Faustus, Matthew, Martin, and Mephisto. Rather than achieving fulfillment, Faustus, it seems, has swerved from the *via negativa*.

Both Michael Cartwright and G. S. Fraser, as well as John Unterecker in his review of the play, find Faustus more successful on his quest than this reading allows. In Cartwright's view Faustus initially refuses "to face the dark, irrational aspects of the reality that constituted his own psychic illness" (185).

The hero is only interested in white, not black, magic. Once he says the Great Formula in the fiery pit, he is reintegrated into a psychic whole:

> When this reintegration and acceptance [are] accomplished the observer has stepped into the amoral, systemless whole that Durrell calls the heraldic universe. When Faustus descends into hell he takes with him a cross, the symbol, in this case, of white magic and the gold ring, the symbol of black magic. *Both* are burned to ashes. Both fictions or conventions are symbolically destroyed, and Faustus returns with full knowledge of the heraldic universe. (186)

For Cartwright, Faustus's return from the pit is that of the comic hero, and his encounter with Martin the Pardoner teaches him the secrets of artistic endeavor. However, I think we can see Martin as another example of the aestheticization of politics. Behind his false indulgences the spiritual power of the Pope is never questioned. The status quo remains the same; and authority is not challenged at all, as it was to be, historically, during the Reformation. Faustus's retreat allows Queen Katherine to continue to rule without any respect for human life. Whereas once Durrell's Faustus had delivered the kingdom from many scourges (14), now the powerless are left to fend for themselves. "Leaving human wrongs to right themselves" is part and parcel of Faustus's refusal of the world.

G. S. Fraser recognizes more ambiguity in the play's ending than does Cartwright; but he uses Jung's ideas of the quaternity to interpret it to Faustus's benefit:

> One should note, however, that the happy ending of *An Irish Faustus* is not quite unequivocal. The three friends at their game of cards, Matthew the Hermit, Martin the Pardoner, Dr. Faustus the Magician, are joined by a fourth figure, the masked Mephisto. Mephisto is something like Jung's shadow, the un-spoken element of darkness called into consciousness, for completeness, by all bright trinities. Martin the Pardoner perhaps also is a Jungian figure. He lies, he knows he is a liar, he says he is a liar, and yet his forged relics perform miracles; for Jung the myths and rituals of traditional religion can never be superseded by a purely rational view of reality since they body forth a pattern built into the human psyche. They are a game which *homo ludens* must continue to play. Mephisto, it should be noted, has in this play not been deliberately conjured up by Faustus but, at a moment of crisis, has emerged as the dark side of Faustus of which he has suddenly to become palpably aware. (115–16)

This interpretation also poses a problem because of what Mephisto represents in the play. He has goaded Faust to use the power of the ring—even for good. He stands for the principle of striving. Thus, the reintegration of Mephisto into Faust's psyche is unlikely to take place at a card game in a hermitage. Such a retreat indicates that Mephisto is more expelled from than reunited with Faust. Thus, neither Fraser nor Cartwright is completely convincing that the ending is other than what I have suggested, an ironic conclusion to traditionally tragic material.

After having praised all three of Durrell's plays, it may seem hard to understand why they are so seldom performed. Part of the answer is that critical comment has not stressed their topicality and their exploration of ideas. If *Sappho* is primarily seen as the decline of a woman who fails to find love and becomes a tyrant, *Acte* as a seventeenth-century play about love and duty, and *An Irish Faustus* as a presentation of Durrell's views on the heraldic universe, then the dramatic conflicts relating to the conceptualization and exercise of human freedom in a world of tyranny are obscured. Such living issues indicate the potential of these plays to appeal to and inform a new audience.

Works Cited

Cartwright, Michael. "The Playwright as Miracle Worker: *An Irish Faustus.*" *Deus Loci* special issue 5.1 (1981): 178–89.

Durrell, Lawrence. *Acte.* London: Faber, 1965.

––––––– . "Acte." *Show* 1.2 (Dec. 1961): 47–55, 96–105.

––––––– . "Actis." *Theatre Heute* 3.1 (Jan. 1962): 3–20.

––––––– . *An Irish Faustus: A Morality in Nine Scenes.* New York: Dutton, 1963.

––––––– . *Sappho.* London: Faber, 1950.

Durrell, Lawrence, and Gustaf Gruendgens. "Briefwechsel uber 'Actis.'" *Theatre Heute* 3.1 (Jan. 1962): 1–2.

Fleissner, Robert R. "Faustus's Wearing of Faust's 'Green.'" *Germanic Notes* 15.3–4 (1984): 57.

Fraser, G. S. *Lawrence Durrell: A Critical Study.* New York: Dutton, 1968.

Gerhardt, Hans-Peter. "Durrells *An Irish Faustus* als Beispiel einer modernen angelsaechsischen Auspraegung der Faustfigur." *Faust Blaetter* 31 (1976): 1150–63.

MacClintock, Lander. "Durrell's Plays." *The World of Lawrence Durrell.* Ed. Harry T. Moore. Carbondale: Southern Illinois University, 1964.

Mandel, Oscar. *A Definition of Tragedy.* New York: New York University, 1973.

Unterecker, John. "Learning to Live with the Devil." *The Saturday Review of Literature* (21 March 1964), 42–43.

Weigel, John A. *Lawrence Durrell.* New York: Twayne, 1965.

9

A Letter to Lawrence Durrell

Vincent Gille

*An Unpublished and Somewhat Caricatural Text
on a Young French Writer's Fascination
with Lawrence Durrell*

I was born pure and innocent right in the middle of a bewildering and icy museum gallery. Old paintings, carefully arranged, lined the walls: respectable and respected personages, grand and noble literary figures, whom the French, contemplating their navels, took to be the only true writers in the world. Proust, Gide, Balzac, Zola, Céline, from within their gold frames, threw dark and haughty glances down upon the infrequent visitors. In a corner, Rimbaud dipped his right leg into his formaldehyde bath, beside the erect organs of Baudelaire, Maupassant, and a few others. From the nearby toilets could be faintly heard the virulent echoes of a dispute among neo-surrealist *lycée* students, while a small group of long-limbed individuals, awkward in their vast raincoats, scrutinized the backs of mirrors, hoping to find there some hypothetical "new novel." I was born pure and innocent in a country with a strong literary tradition, Nobelized and Gallimardized to death; and hardly lifting my nose out of the cradle, I saw over its edge the tall and hideous silhouette of the French-made writer, his face misshapen by a grimace of pain, his body stiffened by the weight of a laborious task, his shoulders bent by the lifelong combat, waged behind illusory barricades on both sides of the Boulevard Saint-Germain, between the champions of literature and the defenders of literature. Each man was summoned to choose his camp and remain there.

I came of age cautiously in the midst of this glaucous hodgepodge that was presented to me as the pinnacle of intelligence and civilization, a country surrounded by impenetrable walls. We had invented camembert, champagne, revolution, cinema, the automobile, and *boules;* we possessed the French language, one and indivisible, as well as so many valorous knights fallen on the honor field of poetry. I believed I was doing the right thing: I crammed all this into my skull, persuaded that with such an illustrious host behind me I could understand and achieve anything. As the years went by, I paled. From too much reading, my eyes took on the color of paper and print, my body grew heavy, my ideas fell neatly into little pigeonholes and carefully labeled drawers, my knowledge of the world was perfect and locked shut. I wanted to write? The royal road lay traced before me. I was in the land of literature. I shut myself up in a dark room in the sixth *arrondissement* of Paris and got down to work.

I almost kept at it. All of a sudden, on page 2576, a ray of sunlight caressed the sentence which I had, with great difficulty, just finished: "The duchess went out at. . . ."[1] I lifted my eyes, put down my pen, my heart skipped a beat, and suddenly I vomited all: my 2576 pages, my pen, my knowledge, and my entire library. I abandoned literature to take a little trip to the seashore. For years I kept away; and from all the books which fleetingly passed through my hands, I read only a few lines, quickly tiring of the cold and dusty wind blowing from them. Yes, indeed, they all said just about the same thing. They all delighted in a more or less sinister and slow mortification and in a quite sterile debate which in the end left me dissatisfied. None of that resonated within me. It seemed to me confusedly that creation had to be, above all, sunlike; that literature should produce something other than this endless lamentation, that in writing we might again find hope, jubilation, and a will stronger than all the horror that the world, during those same years, offered to us as ruthlessly as a spectacle. And so I knew nothing more about it.

Until the day, that is, when my idle steps led me into a large bookstore in the Latin Quarter. I ferreted mechanically through the displays and almost by chance came upon a huge book with a soiled orange cover that must have been through a thousand boxrooms and other unlikely places before ending up here. It was second-hand and modestly priced. Indecisive, I turned the volume over and over in my hands. The title, *The Alexandria Quartet*, was vaguely familiar to me, as was the author, of whom Henry Miller and Anaïs Nin had spoken glowingly. With a commercial end in mind, the editor had placed on the back cover this sentence by Pierre Dumayet: "If you had lost the desire to read, Lawrence Durrell would give it back to you." That made me smile and convinced me.

Now let's get serious. Lawrence Durrell is a writer so essential, a man so respected that I cannot reasonably envisage presenting a thorough judgment of him or attempting to analyze, even succinctly, his eminent work. Others will demonstrate far better than I what an incomparable poet, what a brilliant novelist he is. What I simply want to indicate here is the immense respect that I feel for him. For here is a man who has managed to present a view of the world that is new, lucid, and all things considered, kind; a man who has constantly sought within himself the greatest openness, the sincerest generosity; a man who, going beyond the most legitimate despair, has set off on a quest for a vaster tenderness; a man, therefore, who thanks to and through his creation, has become more *human,* wiser—and not more knowledgeable, or more "literary." That is to say, he rebelled against what seemed revolting to him—the dictatorship of stupidity and repression, wherever they come from—without forgetting for one moment that all this might be no more than yet another illusion. The road was narrow and travelled only by the courageous: yet he transformed these heaps of absurdities into a serious, tender, and funny game; recreating hope by using all the resources of humor, exultation, sun, and poetry, all the humanity within him. Yes, Lawrence Durrell sings of life, of faith in the harmony between people and their world, of polite despair, or perhaps of a joyous, powerful, and alert serenity. As you like it.

And all the rest is literature.[2]

Translated by Alan Astro

Notes

1. The allusion here is to the French poet Paul Valéry's contention that he could never write a novel because of the arbitrariness involved in a sentence such as "La marquise sortit à cinq heures"— The marquise went out at five o'clock.

2. The allusion here is to the last verse of Paul Verlaine's poem *Art Poétique:* "Et tout le reste est littérature"—And all the rest is literature.

10

Lawrence Durrell and *Two Cities*

Jean Fanchette

To begin at the beginning: April 1957. I walked into Blackwell's in Oxford intending to buy Caitlin Thomas's *Leftover Life to Kill*. I did not know this was to be a first step toward a friendship which I rate among the best things that ever happened to me, an encounter with one of the two or three major figures to have emerged on the English literary scene since D. H. Lawrence and James Joyce: Lawrence Durrell. I walked out of Blackwell's with *Justine* which had just been published, the *Selected Poems*, and *Bitter Lemons*. Of Lawrence Durrell, I knew only what Henry Miller had written about him in *Colossus of Maroussi* and the Famous Katsimbalis letter. Larry came out in sharp relief in the book, clean-cut and disturbing at the same time, with the existential depth of a character in a novel. Back in Paris where I lived and studied medicine I read *Justine* and realized immediately it was a major work, something new and vigorous in the bloodless English novel of the late fifties.

Some time later I was offered the editorship of a literary supplement to a medical students' monthly magazine supported by corporate funds. That kind of thing could only happen in Paris. Thus, *Lettres Suivent* was born and most of the first issue was devoted to a long article I had nursed for weeks in my mind: "Lawrence Durrell ou La Démesure de la lumière." *Justine* had just come out in Paris. Not without pain. As it was, I happened to write the first (or second) article to be published in French on Durrell's major work.

Two years later *Lettres Suivent* (with a circulation of 12,000 copies) was wrenched from me when those subsidizing it realized that their original magazine had become a "medical supplement" to my own venture. But by then, I had had time to publish the French and English writers I admired, the same ones I was to publish later in *Two Cities,* to boost my painter friends, Milshtein, Neuhaus, and Coutelle, for example. Meanwhile Larry's address had been given me by the beautiful publicity girl at his French publishing house, and I sent him the first issue of *Lettres Suivent*. There came the following warm note of thanks:

Sommières, Gard, March 4 (1958)

Dear Monsieur Fanchette,
    A brief note to thank you for the splendid review of "Justine." It was quite overwhelming and I am deeply grateful to you.
    "Balthazar" is not out yet. It will appear in April. I shall ask Faber to send you the English text—you seem to be another of these amazing Frenchmen who speak perfect English. The third volume "Mountolive" is finished and will appear in November. By then I hope that the form I have chosen will be clear (I hope it won't seem mechanical and dead).
    With many thanks for your warm-hearted review,
    I am very sincerely,

Lawrence Durrell

So, that was the first letter. I still read it and read it again as I did then. Really, everything could have stopped there. Nice letter from well-bred writer to young, enthusiastic would-be critic. As it turned out, it was the first of the hundred and fifty or so letters and postcards I received, mostly during the late fifties and early sixties, a very interesting period indeed in Larry's creative life, before the celebrity and the legend, which he took with a mixture of coolness and elation, bulged round him.

Back to chronology. I wrote to Durrell in Sommières (I was to visit him there a few months later), and letters started winging between Paris and Languedoc. Letters about the elaboration of *Clea,* about his difficult and active life down South, about the warm reception the first volume of *The Alexandria Quartet* was encountering. He wrote, for example:

Many thanks for your friendly letter and the note on the second volume which appears April 11th and should reach you around that time. Yes, I saw a bit of the *Justine* press and was delighted. Never really thought the French would like it (critics); you have such a magnificent tradition for novels of passion and such experience that I didn't think a wretched Anglo-Saxon could carry any weight in such a full and exploited field. I am so damned romantic about the French and their culture that I felt as if I had won half a dozen Nobel prizes!

The correspondence had been going on for a few months when Larry wrote that he was coming to Paris in mid-spring: "It will be great fun to meet you; I shall be coming to Paris in May for a meeting with Anaïs Nin when I hope to be able to stay a little longer. But France is so expensive and I'm rather broke and working like hell—to pay my daughter's school bills! The old problem!"

That was in May 1958. Paris was living through a dangerous pre-Revolution period once again and there was grim talk of barricades and a military coup: "Every time I settle somewhere, in Alexandria or in Cyprus," wrote Larry, "there is a riot or a revolution. Ouf!" Did he not say about the bizarre punctuation of *Bitter Lemons* that it was the unexpected blast of machineguns or bombs that made him nervous while drafting the final script of the book on his too responsive typewriter?

However close I came to Larry because of our regular correspondence, I was somewhat apprehensive of that *a posteriori* meeting. And the more so as Durrell's voice on the Royal Raspail hotel phone, suggesting a drink at the Dôme, sounded terribly FO. I was naturally wrong. Larry was up to his letters in warmth, generosity, and humor; and Claude, the unforgettable Claude, contributed her particular brand of Alexandrine-Midi gaiety to this first encounter. We sat for hours drinking Tavel on the terrace, walked a flight of steps for lunch, and came down for more *rosé*. I knew from the start that one needed a good drinking capacity in Durrell's company.

I saw Larry and Claude almost every day during their visit to Paris. I introduced my friends. Larry introduced his, including Sir Walter Smart (that delightful "Smartie" who is supposedly the original of David Mountolive) and his Oxford-educated Egyptian wife. The evening before they left (paratroopers from Algiers were planning to occupy Paris that night and trigger *La Révolution*), the Durrells plus children and all had drinks with my wife and myself at our very Bohemian bed-sitter in rue Scipion. I invited the whole party to a Chinese supper in rue Claude-Bernard a few blocks away. When we said goodbye, Larry with his usual tact and regard for others noticed that the reason I did not take a cab was that I had spent my last franc on that Chinese meal.

Back in Sommières he sent me as a gift the printer's copy of the *Mountolive* manuscript with its many decipherable erasures and handwritten additions. A little note accompanied the parcel: "Later on, if I become famous, you may be able to sell it to someone and take Martine to the movies—by taxi this time." As a matter of fact, a few years later this collector's piece got me over a hurdle; I sold it to Southern Illinois University in order to keep *Two Cities* going and placate irate members of the printing corporation.

Meanwhile Durrell arranged a meeting for me with Anaïs Nin. In June 1958 I received a *pneumatique* from Anaïs, written on posh Hotel Crillon stationary: "Dear Monsieur Fanchette, Lawrence Durrell suggested we meet and have a talk, etc." I immediately telephoned, and a rendezvous was arranged at Deux Magots. Anaïs has written at length about all this in the sixth volume of her *Diary*. She thanked Larry for having introduced me to her. Years later she wrote: "When Lawrence Durrell wrote to me in Paris to look up J. F. I did not know that he was giving me a link with France. . . . I helped the magazine. I was grateful for J. F.'s understanding. I count him my best friend in France. The magic link."

Ever since I met Larry and took the measure of his impressive talent, I had decided to start a literary magazine and take advantage of the impact *Lettres Suivent* had had. Bilingual, astride two cultures, with friends and literary friendships on both sides of the channel, Paris and London, Cambridge, and Oxford (and even Weymouth), I decided to do for Durrell, in my own modest way, what *Transition* had done for James Joyce and *Nimbus* for Samuel Beckett. And I gloated from afar on the princely fortunes of *Botteghe Oscure* and what it could achieve to promote writers and multilingual modernity.

I talked about all this to Anaïs Nin, about my admiration for her books (that strong underpull that was to be recognized as best-seller material twenty years later), for Durrell's and Miller's. I talked about the need to demystify, to despise fashion and go back to the very sources, to the very core of literary criticism. I quoted Leavis and Trilling, Sykes and Shapiro. I talked about my plans to Larry. I had no money at all. *Two Cities,* of which a reprint set by Kraus-Thompson, Inc., costs more than two hundred dollars today, started with fifty francs, the advance to the printer toward the cost of subscription slips!

The first issue was intended to carry an "Hommage à Lawrence Durrell." Larry was amazed by the precision of my objectives. I browse through the letters and find this, for example: "Dear Jean, Temple turned up yesterday with Richard Aldington and we talked a good deal about you; I must say the thought of people spending money to print homage to me is wonderful." I wrote to Anaïs, to Aldington. Larry wrote to Miller: "Never had a boost before except in *The Booster* and it would give me quite an old time feeling if you were there! In fact it wouldn't be quite the same without you."

Two Cities was due in early spring (1959). I sent the first copy the printer gave me to Larry, and he wrote back immediately: "My dear Jean, just a word of gratitude for Two Cities in its handsome blue cover; I was delighted and sent it to my mother at once. . . ." Most of the issue was devoted to the homage to our hero, with articles by Henry Miller and Alfred Perlès on the young Durrell of *The Black Book* days, a long and brilliant essay by Richard Aldington on the three volumes of *The Alexandria Quartet* already published, and another essay on *Mountolive* by Edwin Mullins, who had just come down from Oxford and had agreed to be the London editor of *Two Cities,* and who, with Anaïs Nin as New York editor, contributed in considerable measure to giving our magazine its international dimension.

Jacques Temple, our man in the South, wrote about Larry in his garrigue environment, building stone walls around his *mazet.* There was also an interview, "Lawrence Durrell Answers a Few Questions," which I conducted in some Montparnasse café with the help of a considerable amount of refreshment. But that first issue of *Two Cities* also carried work by some of the best living French poets, an interview with Aragon, notes on the London and Paris scenes, and a long piece, "Notes pour une préface," intended to be the introduction to the French edition of Anaïs Nin's novels. Anaïs refers to this "preface" in a very friendly way in volume 6 of the *Diary*. For the time being she had it translated by Louise Varese, printed, and widely distributed.

The publication of *Two Cities* coincided with Henry Miller's first visit to Paris in more than a decade. He had not seen Durrell for twenty years, since his hasty exit from Greece in 1940 as reported in *The Colossus of Maroussi*. Over breakfast with Edwin Mullins at Deux Magots we decided to celebrate both events worthily and to give a huge party for the launching of *Two Cities* and the reunion of the two *confrères*.

I did not have the first *billet de mille* to pay for the festivities, but I believed in my good star. An American friend offered her comfortable flat on the boulevard Saint-Germain and promised to get two bottles of Scotch at the PX of the American Embassy. I kept sending invitations and saw with some apprehension the list of prospective guests getting longer and longer. Fortunately, a few days before the party, I won the much-coveted Fénéon Prize for poetry, which carried with it a very handsome check. Everything was rushed, but the party was an enormous success. I remember Miller escaping from two middle-aged ladies who were gloating over him and shaking his hand as if to wrench it from him, and taking refuge in a room where I found him playing with my two-month-old daughter, Frédérique. I remember Larry hiding his shyness behind a special brand of what Jean Paulhan would have called "terrorist dialectics"; I remember Raja Rao, the Indian philosopher and writer, William Hayter, Gerald Sykes. Sinclair Beiles wrote about that memorable evening in *South African in Paris,* giving it a seasoned flavor of snobbishness it never had: "A cocktail party for Henry Miller and Lawrence Durrell, in an elegant flat on the Boulevard Saint-Germain, with the late afternoon sun setting jewels on fire, fine clothes, well-oiled faces, success, champagne glasses. . . ."

After the party (hurrah for the Fénéon Prize) I took Miller with his wife, Eve, and daughter Val, Larry and Claude Durrell, Gerald and Buffie Sykes, Raja Rao, and a few others to supper at *Chez Papille,* a fashionable new restaurant in rue Saint-Séverin, run by Madeleine, the wife of the great French poet Jean Follain.

I remember Miller looking out of the window at the policemen chasing Algerians in the Paris dusk; Raja Rao the Brahmin trying hard not to look at the first course, *queues de cochon grillées*, Eve and that premonitory light in her beautiful dark eyes. Later an old lady with a famous name edged over to Miller's table, told him rather embarrassingly that she had *known* him years (aeons?) before and offered Dom Perignon to celebrate the reunion. And while Larry looked on with that kind of smiling self-possession which he can assume after any amount of drink as if to reclaim his calm and lucidity, Miller in gratitude for the champagne talked away as was expected of him: a brilliant collection of reminscences of *Tropic of Cancer* and *Black Spring* laced with considerations on Lao Tzu, Keyserling, and Kropotkin.

Edwin Mullins, who had been quick to see the importance of the occasion, gave a remarkable account of that evening on the BBC under the title "Encounter in Paris."

Larry left a few days later and immediately wrote with his usual *savoir vivre:* "Safe back in my fox-earth! We are both dog-tired. I feel like a cake which has been cut into a million pieces. But I feel I must dash you off a line to thank you so much for the truly royal welcome in Paris, the gargantuan party and dinner. It was a double pleasure to have Henry there too, sharing it with me after twenty years."

There were other memorable parties for Larry—and parties without Larry. We took *Two Cities* and not *ourselves* seriously. I inscribe that venture among the lightest and most serious of my life, under the sign of *La Féte* (which was to be the rallying cry of the May 1958 furor) and even the weekly *comité de lecture* meetings were merry occasions in George Whitman's bookshop near Notre Dame, from which we operated. Many people called: pretty young ladies, usually with the offering of a bad poem, foreign writers, and one day André Malraux himself popped in with Gustav Regler, who had been his comrade in the Spanish Civil War.

I saw a lot of Larry when he was in town. I collected him at his hotel on the boulevard Raspail, and we would have lunch at the Dôme or the Chinese restaurant round the corner. Larry was surprised by my availability: "Young editor, young medical student, young father, where do you find the time to be all that at the same time?" I, in turn, was subdued by his warmth and generosity, fascinated by his culture and Elizabethan personality. This was not just a literary friendship—whatever that means—but something deeper, which lit my younger years and certainly left its mark on what I was to do later.

I also visited Durrell several times in his successive Languedoc abodes. The first visit in August 1958 stands out sharply in my memory. We had traveled all day, down from Cannes, Martine and I, and at last got to Sommières in the early evening. I remember the short compact figure in blue denim waiting for us on the platform, the jogging drive in Larry's decrepit Peugot 203 to the Villa Louis, where the Durrells lived on fifty pounds a month in still very comfortable conditions. At the end of the road stood that house of hospitality on the outskirts of the thyme-scented garrigue: the warmth, Claude's smile, enormous quantities of food and booze. We sang the songs of Georges Brassens far into the night: "Quand 'y a plus de vin dans mon tonneau," and so on. And Larry kept filling our glasses.

I also remember very vividly another visit, this time to the beautiful house in Engances, two years before Claude died. Claude probably counted more than anyone else in Larry's life and made him take the full measure of his Protean talents. I had taken along with me a small eight-millimeter movie camera. Strangely, I could not make it work properly, and the only scene that survived was that of Claude and Larry walking around their walled garden under the low, threatening November sky.

Back to the late fifties. Almost overnight, as with Byron, celebrity caught up with Durrell. He remained clearheaded. "Let us keep our fingers crossed," he kept saying. He seemed to have been taken by surprise by world-round celebrity. As late as April 1958 he was writing to me in the following vein:

> *Balthazar* comes out on the 11th and I shall probably get a severe caning from the self-elected sixth-formers of criticism! But so far Correa [his French publishers] haven't made a move to deal with it—probably waiting for the English press in case it's a flop. The Germans and Italians however seem quite excited and the former have bought the whole quartet for cash down! It remains for me to make a mess of it now.

And later, in March 1959:

> The American press on *Mountolive* is terrific. It is bad for one really this inflation of the ego; when I get my first really cruel review I shall probably faint with rage! Avanti! . . . If only I don't fuck up this last book. . . . Great expectations! I don't want to be stinking with money, just to have enough for a coup de rouge and a cigarette. Just to have got established in France is a big enough ambition satisfied.

And established in France he certainly was! His work was translated by the best writers, first-class poets in their own right such as Roger Girous and Alain Bosquet. The French had not recognized James Joyce while he was living in their midst. Apparently, they did not want to make the same mistake about Lawrence Durrell. They really took to Larry's Irish-Mediterranean personality. He was interviewed in the best daily and weekly highbrow papers. He quipped from the coverpage of *L'Express:* "I am an angry old camembert!" cocking a snook at the pompous "Declarations" of the Angry Young Men. He was whisked from cocktail parties to French cultural broadcasts and star television appearances. And though he took all this very coolly, his elation showed through at times (not without some Midi exaggeration), as in a letter to Alan G. Thomas quoted in his *Spirit of Place:*

> I am trying to avert further crowd scenes in Paris when *Mountolive* comes out; they offer me parties and television appearances and a formal signing of my own work at the biggest bookshop in Paris. Jean [yours truly] tells me that Gagliana [*sic:* he means the famous English bookshop in the rue de Rivoli] had a blown-up picture of me life-size in their window between Proust and Stendhal.

And in another letter to Thomas he wrote, "Just got back after 10 hectic Paris days—I am becoming quite a celebrity in Paris. It's surprising and pleasing to have young kids mobbing me at *cafés* in St. Germain."

Larry knew that the Brits, as he sometimes called them, would be somewhat surprised at the continental success of an English writer who had written about English Death, had sneered at them and their way of life, and had installed Greece and Egypt and Languedoc as landmarks of his sentimental journey rather than Finchley, or Bournemouth for that matter! He wrote to me that he knew the English would "cough a bit behind their fingers" at this overwhelming celebrity reaped in France, Germany, Italy, and elsewhere: "It will sound unpatriotic, but I don't really care *what* the English say. I refuse even to read the reviews and make Faber send them to my agent. They've turned literature into a branch of mental snobbery and one sighs with despair to see them turning their laborious cartwheels."

And when the *Times Literary Supplement* a few years later taunted Durrell, saying, "Mr Durrell and Miss Compton-Burnett meet with such praise in France as to raise many a lukewarm eyebrow," Larry hacked at them in savage Byronic vein with "Ode to a Lukewarm Eyebrow" which I published in the last issue of *Two Cities* (Autumn 1964).

Critics in England and America and elsewhere complained at first that *Two Cities* looked like a platform for the Miller-Durrell-Nin constellation. But what a constellation that was! Actually, during the four years *Two Cities* survived, we published ten articles by these three, our most famous contributors. But we also published very distinguished writers and poets from France, England, the United States, and elsewhere. Ecumenism was the hallmark of *Two Cities*. I shall mention a few names out of impressive tables of contents: William Golding, C. P. Snow, Ted Hughes, Colin Wilson, Aldous Huxley, Peter Levi, Brian Higgins, and Christopher Middleton from Britain; Yves Bonnefoy, Malcolm de Chazal, A. Pieyre de Mandiargues, Jean Follain, Pierre Emmanuel, André du Bouchet, Michel Deguy, and Joseph Delteilo from France; Karl Shapiro, William Burroughs, Gregory Corso, Richard Wright, and Gerald Sykes from the United States. Other contributors were Octavio Paz from Mexico and some of the best Indian writers. Fernando Pessoa, Dylan Thomas, and Rilke documents appeared also. And we paid homage to painters such as Jean Hélion, Paul Jenkins, Ruth Francken, and Manoucher Yektai, among others.

Larry helped *Two Cities:* by his faith in the magazine from the beginning, though he claimed that he did not understand how poor young poets could spend money printing homages to him; by his expert and absolutely unpaternalistic advice; once by a check that arrived in the nick of time to calm down a very angry and threatening printer. On that occasion he also gave me a piece of friendly advice: "Dear Jean, Glad the cheque arrived in time! But be a sensible man and do as real editors do—appoint a *comptable* and open a bona fide account in a bank. Then you can always borrow on future receipts. It is not good rambling along like old Tambimuttu of divine memory who used to keep all his contributions in one chamber pot and his spare cash in another."

With characteristic generosity he asked me once to publish the poems of a young American poet dying of cancer who believed deeply in literature: "I wonder if you would care to help over this tragic case—a dying poet, by carrying one or two of the enclosed poems? They are quite respectable I think, could do you no harm and him perhaps some good; anyway I imagine that nothing could please him more than a letter from Paris saying that *Two Cities* had accepted two poems for publication." I wrote, of course, with the exact amount of enthusiasm. But my letter came too late for Roger Bush III, of Dallas, Texas.

Some of the publishing choices I made (two or three) worried Larry somewhat, particularly the Tagore issue, to which Nehru contributed, and a book by a Swedish writer, Georg Stenmark, sponsored by the Arthur Lundkvist Foundation, which I published at Two Cities Editions, which had meanwhile sprouted and in which we published *Minutes to Go,* by William Burroughs, Corso, Gysin, and Beiles, and the first album of the paintings of Paul Jenkins. Larry wrote: "No more Tagore please and no more solipsistic Swedes." In retrospect I agree with Durrell's judgment. I still do not agree, however, with his "grave reservations" about *Minutes to Go,* the bible of the "cut-up" poetry. The book has become a very rare collectors' piece today, and no one has any doubt about the genius of William Burroughs. But all the same, Larry's critical advice about the contents of *Two Cities* was always given with discretion and wit. He never behaved patronizingly and never had big-brother attitudes.

Two Cities came out in sharp relief against the rather bleak literary landscape of the late fifties and early sixties. Malraux gave us a grant for one issue, but I rejected the offers of two well-known publishers—one French and one English. I had made up my mind that literary magazines should die young . . . like Keats (as I wrote in a Romantic vein). The last issue came out in Autumn 1964. It carried letters from Durrell to me bearing on the beginning of the venture and that famous "Hommage." It was time for the final curtain.

Of course the friendship did not grind to a halt after 1964. Claude died on the first day of 1967. The letters became a trickle. But we kept seeing each other whenever Larry came to Paris, checking in at the same hotel on Raspail, drinking or having meals (very often as second course "merlan en colère") at the same restaurants: La Coupole or Le Dôme.

I visit Larry often. Sommières is just ninety-nine kilometers *porte à porte* from the shack I own near the Lac de Salagou in the Haut-Hérault, my Innisfree. And in April 1981 he paid me a very great compliment indeed. He asked me to introduce him at the lecture he was to give at the Centre George Pompidou about his Indian childhood: "Du haut d'un éléphant." As if anyone had to be introduced to Lawrence Durrell. Centre Pompidou was crammed. Hundreds of people fought to get in. After the lecture, we had a big party in my *seizième arrondissement* flat. Times and circumstances had changed. The friendship and the warmth had not.

I met Lawrence Durrell nearly thirty years ago. I still admire, respect, and love him as I did then. I am proud to be his friend and to be able to feel the same buoyancy and intellectual *complicité* with him over a meal in an Indian restaurant in Shepherd's Bush in the London winter of 1986 as I did in the Paris spring of 1958 sipping Tavel with him and Claude at the Dôme.

Hallelujah!

11

"One other gaudy night": Lawrence Durrell's Elizabethan *Quartet*

Carol Peirce

Toward the end of the first volume of *The Alexandria Quartet,* Lawrence Durrell's young narrator, Darley, referring to the central character of that volume and, in many ways, of the whole *Quartet,* writes:

> I thought back along the iron chain of kisses which Justine had forged, steadily back into memory, hand over fist, like a mariner going down an anchor-chain into the darkest depths of some great stagnant harbour memory. (*Justine* 196)

And he adds a few pages later that Clea, the central character of the last volume, "told me many things about Justine's past which only she knew; and she spoke of her with a wonder and tenderness such as people might use in talking of a beloved yet infuriating queen" (228).

These two passages together lead toward an understanding of one important element of *The Alexandria Quartet.* For in it Durrell himself goes down, layer by layer, into the past of "Alexandria, the capital of Memory" (188), bringing back and imaginatively recreating much of its history, philosophy, and myth in what he calls the "historic present." As he explained in an interview:

> The thing was, I wanted to produce something that would be readable on a superficial level, while at the same time giving the reader—to the extent that he was touched by the more enigmatic aspects—the opportunity to attempt the second layer, and so on. (*Big Supposer* 66)

Although Durrell plunges deep into the history of Alexandria and beyond that even to the ancient myth of Isis and Osiris, his second layer reveals the story of Antony and Cleopatra. The whole of *The Alexandria Quartet* echoes its music: for it is this legend that he uses as a central symbolic strain in his great memory fugue. He moves back in time through literary tradition, as well, to view the story prismatically, now lighted by Eliot's *The Waste Land* or Shaw's *Caesar and Cleopatra,* now by Cavafy's poetry, but most consistently by Shakespeare's great play, as retold from Plutarch. In evolving this symbolic pattern he utilizes plot structure, character portrayal, and many methods of poetic technique from rich Elizabethan language to a running leitmotif, to create within the book a mighty metaphor of love and loss and time and memory.

The first scene of Shakespeare's *Antony and Cleopatra* sets the stage for the ancient love story:

> *Cleopatra:* If it be love indeed, tell me how much.
> *Antony:* There's beggary in the love that can be reckon'd.
> *Cleopatra:* I'll set a bourn how far to be belov'd.
> *Antony:* Then must thou needs find out new heaven, new earth.
>
> (I.i.14–17)

And Cleopatra later in the act gives her own phrasing to their love: "Eternity was in our lips, and eyes" (I.iii.35).

In the "Consequential Data" at the end of *Justine,* Durrell includes a workpoint that seems in essence to suggest and reflect Shakespeare in theme, mood, and pattern of language:

> *"Then how long will it last, this love?" (in jest).*
> *"I don't know."*
> *"Three weeks, three years, three decades . . . ?"*
> *"You are like all the others . . . trying to shorten eternity with numbers," spoken quietly, but with intense feeling.* (248)

Durrell's attraction to Shakespeare's world has a long history. In 1953, as he began finally to put *Justine* on paper after many years of planning, he wrote his friend Alan Thomas, "How wonderful now the winter is setting in to immerse in the Elizabethans. . . . Send my beloved Eliza's will you when you can?"[1] And in 1959, as he was completing *The Alexandria Quartet,* he lamented to Richard Aldington, "I am so downright sad not to have been an Elizabethan" (*Literary Lifelines* 114). Actually he comes near to being one; for his love of the Elizabethans and Shakespeare permeates his work. Names of characters and song titles refer to them. He creates a sonnet-sequence soliloquy for Hamlet. *Prospero's Cell* is filled with the presence of the enchanter, and quotations and echoes from *The Tempest* appear in *The Alexandria Quartet.* Asked in an interview which past poets he most admired, Durrell responded: "Shakespeare and Donne. . . . And then Ovid" (*Big Supposer* 90).

With this background one would expect *The Alexandria Quartet* to have many Elizabethan aspects, and a number of critics have noted them, especially in Durrell's use of language. George Steiner speaks of his "Shakespearean and Joycean delight in the sheer abundance and sensuous variety of speech" (16). In "Why English?" in comparing the Elizabethan approach to the modern American, as opposed to the British, Steiner again mentions Durrell. The likenesses he discusses—an appetite for new words and new meanings, a love for the special languages of music and science, a delight in metaphor and poetry, and the "spendthrift joy in the feel and multiplicity of words"—are all characteristic of Durrell's work (11). All language is taken to be the province of the writer, archaic as well as current, poetic as well as prosaic. This sort of vocabulary, alive with racing color and enchantment, marks Durrell's writing in *The Alexandria Quartet*. In the rush of his brilliant language, he returns from the spare realism of the mid-twentieth century to something of the mighty line of Marlowe, of the baroque prose of Donne, of the protean poetry of Shakespeare. He is, in a sense, a magus who transmutes the vitality and glory of sixteenth-century language into twentieth-century gold.

Durrell's integration of a world view into his writings may also be compared with that of the Elizabethans, for his construct is as many-leveled as was theirs. They considered love and personality within the wider circumference of the political and social order and that order itself within the still larger order of the cosmos. Durrell centers his investigation of modern love in a world of intricate political moves, which itself circles within the Einsteinian cosmos. And just as within works such as *The Faerie Queen* and *The Tempest* varied levels in both plot and characters coexist, so Durrell in *The Alexandria Quartet* creates a multilayered plot with characters that are not only twentieth-century people but are symbolic in several deeper senses.

Indeed, all Durrell's characters, whatever their other derivations and in spite of being thoroughly modern, seem somehow Elizabethan, as if he were seeing his fictional world through an Elizabethan imagination. When one thinks of the dark character Narouz, one turns to Webster and Ford. In the comic genius of his idiosyncratic secondary characters, such as Pombal, Mnemjian, and old Scobie, one feels oneself in the milieu of Sir Toby, of Falstaff, of Shakespeare's fools. And then there is Cleopatra, embodying, as Shakespeare sees her, the queen described by Plutarch, the goddess Isis, Passionate Woman, and the Elizabethan "lass unparallel'd" whom the boy actor is playing on the stage. Her spirit fills the *Quartet*.

Durrell uses the Cleopatra legend in many ways. Perhaps his most beautiful allusion is to the drifting music Antony hears in Plutarch, in Shakespeare, and in Cavafy. But it is in the characters and in the larger movement of the *Quartet* that Durrell draws most intrinsically on Shakespeare. All of them, although very immediate personalities in themselves, have symbolic shadows lying long behind them. And all his women are in some ways Cleopatras.

Melissa, Darley's fragile young prostitute love, is one of these. The only Greek woman among them all, she is only once compared directly to Cleopatra: "Together we staggered with her down the corridor and into the blessed privacy of my box-room where, like Cleopatra, we unrolled her and placed her on the bed" (*Justine* 57). But Melissa, fraily loved and loving, seems only slightly, as in her beautiful voice, to relate to that far-off world (perhaps the younger Cleopatra).

Leila and Liza, on the other hand, in very different ways, seem to possess more of her characteristics, while suggesting, as well, other Hellenistic figures of history or myth. Leila, "the dark swallow," who protects her son Nessim, the "prince" of Alexandrian finance, with a passionate devotion, is deeply involved in a Coptic plot to gain power in the Middle East. Brilliant and beautiful, with intellectual ambitions, she was married to unite two family fortunes and dynasties. But with her bright intelligence, "she subscribed to books and periodicals in the four languages which she knew as well as her own, perhaps better. . . ." (*Mountolive* 240). She seems to reflect that Cleopatra who "could pass from one language to another so that in her interviews with barbarians she seldom required an interpreter" (*Lives* 294). And like Cleopatra with Antony, she captured the love of Mountolive, the representative of empire, and turned all that intelligence to ways and means to hold it, so that, far away on other diplomatic missions, he could never forget her and always longed to return to her and to Egypt. Like Antony, he finally does return, only to disillusionment. Now old and pockmarked, Leila sits "like a dethroned Empress," with a veil masking all but her "youthful dark eyes," her pet cobra coiled beside her (*Balthazar* 78). Mountolive rejects her and Nessim but not before he dreams, in his own brief moment of nostalgia and Antonian identity, of sleeping in her arms, "as if he were Antony at Actium" (*Mountolive* 249). Later Leila speaks of their love as "immortal in its way" (*Clea* 267).

It is actually, however, in her aspect of mother that Leila most fascinatingly takes us back into the Alexandrian past. Here we find her leading us not to Cleopatra and Caesarion but to that older, darker story and relationship, from the very beginnings of the city and before, of Olympias and Alexander.[2]

And then there is Liza, the mysterious sister of Pursewarden, the last and deepest of Mountolive's loves. She has committed incest without ever feeling it morally wrong—feeling "the simple beauty of shamelessness" (*Mountolive* 66). She too can be seen as Cleopatra in her aspect of Hellenistic goddess as well as Ptolemaic queen, divinely by destiny, pragmatically for racial purity, married over and over again to her brother and reaching back through that race of queens and Cleopatras into even older Egyptian mythology.

Liza explains to Darley that as children they studied by heart a volume of Plutarch about Isis and Osiris: "That is why he was pleased to come there to Egypt, because he felt, he said, an interior poetic link with Osiris and Isis, with

Ptolemy and Arsinoë—the race of the sun and the moon!" (*Clea* 191). Liza and Pursewarden's story (and the volume of Plutarch they read) is but another retelling of the myth Shakespeare saw behind Antony and Cleopatra. Initially seeming to be Plutarch's *Lives,* it is actually his esoteric study of Egyptian myth, *De Iside et Osiride.*

Durrell's most powerful evocation of Cleopatra, however, lies in his portrayal of Justine. She naturally holds the central position in the first volume, and her romantic portrait as the queen of modern Alexandria exists at its very heart. Durrell once said in an interview, "I think Cleopatra was probably something like her" (Fanchette 158). She was, and is, in fact, Justine's mirror-image; in some ways it is as if one character has been superimposed on the other.

The first hint begins on the second page of *Justine* with the sound of Antony's music:

> A drunken whore walks in a dark street at night, shedding snatches of song like petals. Was it in this that Anthony heard the heart-numbing strains of the great music which persuaded him to surrender for ever to the city he loved? (*Justine* 14)

Just a little further along the reader first meets Justine: "She passes below my window, smiling as if at some private satisfaction, softly fanning her cheeks with the little reed fan" (19). Described by the narrator as seen in the great glass mirror of the Hotel Cecil, squired by her husband, "dressed in a sheath of silver drops, holding her magnificent fur at her back," "She could not help but remind me of that race of terrific queens which left behind them the ammoniac smell of their incestuous loves to hover like a cloud over the Alexandrian subconscious" (20). Compare this with the opening of *Antony and Cleopatra,* in which, after Philo complains that his general has given himself to "a tawny front" and "a gipsy's lust," Cleopatra enters, *"with Eunuchs fanning her,"* voicing the love theme of the play (I.i.14).

In Justine we clearly meet again this queen of Alexandria, though the exact complement of Shakespeare's scene is missing. But put together, all the elements are apparent, even to the charming "little reed fan" with which Justine cools her cheeks. Soon Antony says:

> Fie, wrangling queen!
> Whom every thing becomes, to chide, to laugh,
> To weep: how every passion fully strives
> To make itself, in thee, fair and admired!
> . . . all alone,
> Tonight we'll wander through the streets, and note
> The qualities of people.

(I.i.48–54)

And Durrell's Justine again, this time in the words of her first husband, Arnauti: "I have already described how we met—in the long mirror of the Cecil, before the open door of the ballroom, on a night of carnival" (*Justine* 70).

We see Justine swinging from the sexually passionate but never fulfilled woman to the magnificent, catlike queen with the strong, masculine mind:

> The cult of pleasure, small vanities, concern for the good opinion of her inferiors, arrogance. She could be tiresomely exigent when she chose. Yes. Yes. But all these weeds are watered by money. I will say only that in many things she thought as a man, while in her actions she enjoyed some of the free vertical independence of the masculine outlook. (26)

Compare this with two swift lines in Shakespeare:

> *Enobarbus:* Hush, here comes Antony.
> *Charmian:* Not he, the queen.
>
> (I.ii.76)

These lines move quietly but forcefully to establish role reversal and androgyny as an underlying theme in Shakespeare's play. Cleopatra, longing for Antony, reminisces about the time she "laugh'd him out of patience" and "into patience" and

> drunk him to his bed;
> Then put my tires and mantles on him, whilst
> I wore his sword Philippan.
>
> (II.v.21–23)

Again, this can be compared to Justine's coming to love her husband, as she came to desire to share his plans for political power. Suddenly, she desired him with a desire more powerful for its androgyny:

> For the first time she felt desire stir within her, in the loins of that discarded, pre-empted body which she regarded only as a pleasure-seeker, a mirror-reference to reality. There came over her an unexpected lust to sleep with him—no, with his plans, his dreams, his obsessions, his money, his death! (*Mountolive* 200)

On the second page of *Justine,* Durrell tells us that there is "something different, something subtly androgynous, inverted upon itself," in the very air of Alexandria—surely partly the living memory of the legendary queen.

Androgynous rather than masculine, both Cleopatra and Justine are changeable—and may be pliable and passionately feminine—in a moment. Indeed, changeableness is one of the most constant, most charming, of all Cleopatra's characteristics, as in her advice to Charmian on how to hold a man (I.iii.3–5).

And Justine: "yet how touching, how pliantly feminine this most masculine and resourceful of women could be" (*Justine* 20). Arnauti emphasizes the same characteristics in recounting his experience: "The more I knew her the less predictable she seemed" (68). Arnauti, incidentally, not a bad parallel to Julius Caesar, bears his own relationship to Antony. Balthazar says, "He is when all is said and done a sort of minor Antony, and she a Cleo. You can read all about it in Shakespeare" (96–97).

Like Cleopatra, too, the darkly beautiful Justine is of mixed background. For Cleopatra, almost pure Greek with perhaps a little Syrian blood, nonetheless came from a line steeped in Egypt and Egyptian life for three hundred years. Ernle Bradford in his *Cleopatra* biography used Gibbon's earlier statement that "the people of Alexandria, a various mixture of nations, united the vanity and inconstancy of the Greeks with the superstition of the Egyptians," and commented:

> It was not only the Egyptians themselves, nor the Greeks, but the Jews, Syrians and traders from all over North Africa, who made this city an uneasy one in which to live. Cleopatra, who knew most of their tongues, was—although Greek by blood—a compendium of this world. (52)

So Durrell writes,

> And hearing her speak his [Cavafy's] lines . . . I felt once more the strange equivocal power of the city . . . and knew her for a true child of Alexandria; which is neither Greek, Syrian nor Egyptian, but a hybrid: a joint. (*Justine* 27)

And finally Justine, like Cleopatra again in her aspects of both Aphrodite and Isis, takes on the mythical: "Like all amoral people she verges on the Goddess. If our world were a world there would be temples to accommodate her where she could find the peace she was seeking." (77). Beyond Cleopatra, here is "the austere mindless primeval face of Aphrodite" (*Mountolive* 205).

A fascinating and similar change of tone occurs early in both *Antony and Cleopatra* and the *Quartet*. Shakespeare turns from the Egyptian to the Roman view of Cleopatra in act 2. Pompey calls her "Salt Cleopatra"; Octavius Caesar, who spoke sarcastically of Antony tumbling "on the bed of Ptolemy" dominates this world; and we return to the gypsy lust and strumpet fame of Philo's first speech. In fact, act 2 moves into a Roman world of duty and realism as opposed to love and romance. Here is the opposite of lush, fertile, sensual Alexandria. Rome looks on Egypt as rotten with sensuality but shows itself, in Caesar's Machiavellianism, in the arranged marriage of Antony and Octavia, in the scene on Pompey's barge, as both cynical and corrupt.

Balthazar, the second book of the *Quartet,* turns full circle as well to attempt to show the "reality" of the story, as opposed to the first book's romance. We learn from Balthazar that Justine was only using Darley as a decoy to cover her tracks with yet another man, Pursewarden. Also, in moving toward realism, Balthazar emphasizes the comic as opposed to the tragic, and we find in it a more cynical vision. If Enobarbus can say of Antony, referring to Cleopatra, "He will to his Egyptian dish again" (II.vi.123), and Agrippa of Julius Caesar, "He plough'd her, and she cropp'd" (II.ii.228), Pursewarden, the ironic, cynical commentator-novelist of the *Quartet* (not unlike Enobarbus, including his twin qualities of irony and tenderness) can add: "I regard her as a tiresome old sexual turnstyle through which presumably we must all pass—a somewhat vulpine Alexandrian Venus" (*Balthazar* 115). Darley's romantic queen has become Pursewarden's earthy whore.

In addition to presenting the cynical version of the story and showing Justine using Darley as Antony cynically uses Octavia in *Antony and Cleopatra*, *Balthazar* and Shakespeare's act 2 move toward similar explosive endings in orgy and carnival. In each work the rich, prolific language, as well as the behavior of lovers unfulfilled, erupts into madness. *Balthazar* climaxes in a wild, masked carnival party, a photograph of which shows "a group of hooded figures, frenziedly swaying with linked arms" (216). In the concluding scene of act 2, a party also blows into orgy, and enemies dance together in Bacchanalian frenzy. Pompey cries that this is not yet an Alexandrian feast, but Antony responds, "It ripens toward it" (II.vii.95).

The rush of carnival and the description of Justine herself also recall Cleopatra's own last gaudy night. The opulence of her bedroom[3] and the troubling, haunting scent of her perfume remind one of the Cleopatra who lured Antony to her barge and on to many such a night: "The fullness of Justine's dark beauty in her dress (the color of hare's blood) glowed among the ikons, seeming to enjoy the semi-darkness of the candle-light—to feed upon it and give back the glitter of her barbaric jewelry" (*Balthazar* 195). All the richness of both the Alexandrian and the Elizabethan worlds colors *The Alexandria Quartet*. To quote Durrell quoting Shakespeare in another equally vivid context—the superb study of old Scobie—"Ripeness is all" (*Justine* 125).

Shakespeare's play reaches its crescendo in act 3 when Antony and Cleopatra, to whom he has returned, stake their world and all they have and are in an enormous battle against Octavius. Actium is the high-water mark of their power and the beginning of their downfall. Despairing and quarreling, the lovers reunite in an upsurge of the magnificent language of the first act. But Cleopatra now seems less the love goddess, more the empress, using all her power to achieve and hold power. Changeable as ever, her actions can be interpreted in tantalizingly different ways. Justine, in an important passage, suggests that people project many different mirror images of themselves; certainly Cleopatra did (*Justine* 27).

In Durrell's third book, *Mountolive,* the whole perspective changes. In another seemingly complete turn we find in this "objective account" that Justine's obsession from the beginning has been power and possession (*Mountolive* 102). In fact, her love and loyalty belong only to her husband—and the plot. Actually each lover was being used to protect the Coptic conspiracy, to regain power in Egypt, and to aid Palestine—perhaps finally to create a new Hellenistic third world in the Middle East.

Nessim too takes on a totally new aspect in *Mountolive:*

> His image had suddenly been metamorphosed. It was now lit with a new, a rather terrifying grandeur. As she smoked and watched him, she saw someone different in his place—an adventurer, a corsair, dealing with the lives and deaths of men; his power too, the power of his money, gave a sort of tragic backcloth to the design. (200)

Here, seen through Justine's eyes, this "very perfect, gentle knight" has been metamorphosed into Antony, both leader and lover, whose conspiracy is revealed as the active core of the *Quartet.* Nessim sums it up:

> We, the foreign communities, with all we have built up, are being gradually engulfed by the Arab tide, the Moslem tide. Some of us are trying to work against it; Armenians, Copts, Jews, and Greeks here in Egypt, while others elsewhere are organizing themselves. Much of this work I have undertaken here. (*Mountolive* 198)

Or, to repeat Cavafy's roll call of the Hellenistic world as it prepares for its last stand against the Roman empire:

> We the Alexandrians, the Antiochians,
> the Selefkians, and the countless
> other Greeks of Egypt and Syria,
> and those in Media, and Persia, and all the rest.
>
> (166)

The same movement, the same mood prevails. But the plot fails in modern Alexandria, as it did in old Alexandria; and in its discovery Pursewarden (like Enobarbus who loved Antony still but betrayed him and then died) kills himself, even as he informs on Nessim to the English ambassador.[4] Mountolive, torn by conflicting loyalties, comes almost to hate his old friend Nessim. As the representative of English law, power, and empire, Mountolive seems like a new Octavius, albeit a reluctant one, fighting for control of the Middle East—the British order versus the Copts and Palestine.[5] As in Shakespeare—and in history—the lovers lose and empire wins.

Finally, in Shakespeare's play death and rebirth and apotheosis through memory become the keynotes of the last two acts, as Antony, dying in Cleopatra's arms, grows into legend and Cleopatra turns to marble constant, the mythic goddess of immortal longings. In the fourth book of *The Alexandria Quartet, Clea,* Durrell also moves into myth and places the same emphasis on memory and rebirth. Darley returns from self-exile to Alexandria and early in the book, in a bitter, disillusioning meeting with Justine, finds her totally changed. Nessim, with an eye lost and a finger missing from the war, berates and is berated by Justine like Antony after Actium. Under house arrest at Karm Abu Girg, "a swarthy imperious queen," with a drooping eye, a voice of "contemptuous shrillness," the smell of liquor on her breath, and the cloying richness of spilt perfume upon her person, Justine seems the very Cleopatra of the scratched face and breasts, blubbering eyes, and streaming hair that Octavius Caesar saw before the end (*Clea* 15, 49). Darley concludes, in fascinatingly chosen words: "She had become a woman at last, lying there, soiled and tattered, like a dead bird in a gutter, her hands crumpled into claws. It was as if some huge iron door had closed forever in my heart" (*Clea* 62). So too Cleopatra, after Antony's death, with the great door of the monument locked tight, speaks similarly of her fate: "No more but e'en a woman" (IV.xv.73).

"A lass unparallel'd," mourns Charmian, as Cleopatra dies (v.ii.315). And Darley muses near the end of *The Alexandria Quartet:* "I feel it [Alexandria] fade inside me, in my thoughts, like some valedictory mirage—like the sad history of some great queen whose fortunes have foundered among the ruins of armies and the sands of time!" (*Clea* 276).

Though the play ends in death and *The Alexandria Quartet* in a memory of Cleopatra, both also end looking toward an "eternity" of love. As Antony and Cleopatra die, each speaks triumphantly of their imagined future life. Antony glories in the prospect of a reunion, "Where souls do couch on flowers" (IV.xiv.51); and Cleopatra gives up all other titles as she calls out, "Husband, I come" (V.ii.286). This victory of love seems echoed in the last pages of *The Alexandria Quartet:*

> Walking down Rue Fuad at ten o'clock on a bright Spring morning I saw her come towards me, radiant and beautifully turned out in a spring frock of eloquent design. . . . His [Nessim's] appearance staggered me, he looked so much younger, and so elegant and self-possessed. It gave me a queer pang, too, to see the passionate way they embraced, Nessim and Justine, as if oblivious to the rest of the world. (*Clea* 280–81)

Truly the dark lady of Durrell's poetic imagination can be seen as the modern reflection of the Egyptian queen in all her roles, as lover, whore, empress, and goddess out of myth: "And yet how magically she seemed to live—a mistress so full of wit and incantation that one wondered how one had ever managed to love before and be content in the quality of the loving" (*Justine* 166). One is drawn irresistibly back to Shakespeare:

> Age cannot wither her, nor custom stale
> Her infinite variety: other women cloy
> The appetites they feed, but she makes hungry,
> Where most she satisfies.

(II.ii.235–38)

Durrell has, however, in the fourth volume, one other—and last—Cleopatra for us to meet. Darley is finally moving toward some inevitable destiny with the most radiant of all Durrell's Cleopatras, the beautiful artist Clea, who in this book holds the central position that belonged to Justine in the first volume. Her personality, though, is different: "A whole new geography of Alexandria was born through Clea, reviving old meanings, renewing ambiences half forgotten, laying down like a rich wash of color a new history, a new biography to replace the old one" (*Clea* 229).

If in Justine can be seen the goddess Aphrodite in her most elemental and primitive aspects, Clea is a younger and fresher goddess, the Marine Venus of Rhodes, Botticelli's lady of the sea (*Clea* 152), a new vision and version of the queen. Her name is closely related, but her affinities lie more deeply with Plutarch in his philosophical guise. It is to Clea, a young priestess at Delphi, that Plutarch addresses *De Iside et Osiride,* and he continues to speak to her throughout the work as he seeks to learn the nature of the gods. Pursewarden says, "That brilliant glance exposed everything and forced me to take shelter from her" (*Clea* 152).

Clea, too, has a personal role to play, along with Darley, in the final unfolding of the Antony and Cleopatra story at the end of *The Alexandria Quartet*. The destiny they share lies in the folds of a small island with a natural underwater cave, whose aspects suggest a temple or chamber for ancient Dionysian or Orphic rites.[6] Dead sailors from a lost ship stand guard like caryatids. And as Darley and Clea play in the water, they imagine and half believe the island to be Antony's Timonium:

> They've never found the site, you know. I am sure this must be it. . . . And here he must have spent his leisure—*here,* Darley, going over the whole thing again and again in his mind. That woman with the extraordinary spells she was able to cast. His life in ruins! And then the passing of the God, and all that, bidding him to say goodbye to her, to Alexandria—a whole world! (*Clea* 227)

It is also the island of Narouz, Nessim's brother, who loved Clea without response and died calling her. She superstitiously continues to hear him calling her to death and is accidently shot with his harpoon and pinned by her hand to the wreckage deep in the underwater cave. Darley needs heroic strength, for he must cut off her hand to release her, carry her back, and breathe new life into her: "Yet we hit the sky with a concussion that knocked the breath from me—as if I had cracked my skull on the ceiling of the universe" (250). After vast effort, "softly we baled her up like Cleopatra" (253).

But Durrell knows that she is not only his last Cleopatra. She is also Plutarch's muse, Clea. And beyond that she is Clio, the muse of history. For her letters and love end each but the third volume of *The Alexandria Quartet,* and hers is the final story of Alexandria: "Time had rendered her up, whole and intact again—'natural as a city's grey-eyed Muse'—to quote the Greek poem" (245).

Part of the effectiveness of the conclusion with its return to Timonium and to Cleopatra's tomb of tragic inevitability lies in the surprise and delight of the ending. Because of the expectation of tragedy, the rebirth that cracks Darley's skull on the sky and marks the beginning of his realization of artistic maturity brings a catharsis to the reader as well.[7] The expectation of sorrow, the lilt of returning joy climax well a modern retelling of the play of "immortal longings."

Thus *The Alexandria Quartet* in the end focuses on Clea and Darley as Cleopatra and Antony. Just as each of its women has been a Cleopatra, so is each man in some ways Antony—Nessim, especially in his politics and love and Pursewarden in his laughing madness and in his guise of Osiris. Even Narouz hears his music, and Mountolive feels his fate. But it remains for Darley himself finally to become or at least to relive the last experiences of Antony.

As well as mirroring the characters and plot structure of *Antony and Cleopatra,* Durrell transforms one scene of Antony's last days like a drift of memory and old gods into a haunting leitmotif that echoes through *The Alexandria Quartet* to reach a crescendo at the end.[8] The strange episode comes from Plutarch, is transmuted by Shakespeare, and adapted by Cavafy. Its first strain comes in the opening pages of *Justine,* with the woman's singing, and its music swells again as Cavafy's poem, "The God Abandons Antony," concludes the volume.

The poem itself goes back to a small scene in *Antony and Cleopatra* in which, out of nowhere, soldiers appear to talk of Antony's defeat. They hear "music i' the air" and "under the earth" and decide that "'Tis the god Hercules, whom Antony lov'd" leaving him (IV.iii.12–15). Actually the scene has an even older history; for there is also a small and poignant moment in Plutarch, when, near midnight,

> suddenly a marvelous sound of music was heard, which seemed to come from a consort of instruments of every kind, and voices chanting in harmony, and at the same time the shouting of a crowd in which the cry of Bacchanals and the ecstatic leaping of satyrs were mingled, as if a troop of revellers were leaving the city, shouting and singing as they went. (*Lives* 340)

Plutarch concludes that the god Dionysus, "with whom Antony claimed kinship and whom he had sought above all to imitate," is now leaving him (*Lives* 340).

Durrell returns to this legend, with all its strange magic in each metamorphosis, and incorporates it, with as much power as those before him, into the very fabric of *The Alexandria Quartet*. "Listen to the music!" says Cohen, dying; and Darley adds, "I thought suddenly of the dying Antony in the poem of Cavafy.... How different from the great heart-sundering choir that Antony heard—the rich poignance of strings and voices which in the dark street welled up—Alexandria's last bequest to those who are her 'exemplars'" (*Justine* 111–12). For Durrell adds the thought, implied by Cavafy, that each true Alexandrian receives that last tribute of farewell. And though the reference here is to Cavafy, the emphasis on the word *music* particularly recalls Shakespeare's scene.

In *Balthazar* the leitmotif sounds again, especially in the festival Narouz attends, which includes a real procession coming on in marvelous cavalcade, led by leaping acrobats and dwarfs, followed by gonfalons, then dervishes; and still the flood pours on "in a tide of mystical light" to "its own wild music" (155–56). Again the implication extends far beyond Cavafy, to Plutarch's description this time; for the revellers and satyrs are there, "shouting and singing as they went" from Antony's Alexandria (340). One almost feels as if this were the same procession with the same figures two thousand years since.[9]

Durrell calls up this musical moment, not just as a memory strain but in actuality, at the climax of each volume, first in Cavafy's poem concluding *Justine* and again in the carnival-murder ending of *Balthazar*. In *Mountolive* the procession comes on even more powerfully. With Narouz's death at the tragic finale, the ritual dances are performed, "an orgiastic frenzy" in which women circle his body, "striking their breasts and howling, but dancing in the slow measured figures of a dance recaptured from long-forgotten friezes upon the tombs of the ancient world" (*Mountolive* 312). Here once more is a terrible recelebration of Plutarch's throng at the death of "some lost king, conscious of the body and breath dissolving within him" (*Mountolive* 310).

Finally in *Clea*, on the last pages of the whole of *The Alexandria Quartet*, Darley, preparing to leave Alexandria forever, is caught up with Balthazar in one last festival. And again the great processional approaches with acrobats and tumblers, chanters, and the order of the dervishes. But Durrell has added a different note to Darley's hearing of the music: "Somewhere far away I heard the siren of a ship boom in the harbour, recalling me to my senses" (*Clea* 270). For Darley has heard this siren call through the music before. It sounded early, when Cohen died and when he received Justine's letter of goodbye. Now, as the ship's siren calls him again, Darley is ready to leave. He has found at last his own proper self. He has, like Antony, suffered into truth.

Durrell confessed once in an interview, "I admit to having Elizabethanized" ("The Kneller Tape" 167). Much earlier in his life he had written, "Shakespeare is not a text but a festival, a rite, and there's no clue to give you the meaning of it" (*Spirit of Place* 54). But there is one final, delightful clue in *The Alexan-*

dria Quartet. The book has been laced with festivals and processional music, the lost music of Antony. In "Some Notes for Clea," Pursewarden as Durrell's alter ego writes, "As you get older and want to die more a strange kind of happiness seizes you; you suddenly realize that all art must end in a celebration" (*The Alexandria Quartet* 879). "Each man goes out to his own music," Darley reflects (*Justine* 112). Durrell's last festival celebrates the name day, the Mulid, of El Scob; for the memory of old Scobie has drifted into myth. That Scobie's birthday is on St. George's Day Durrell tells us (*Clea* 84). What he does not mention is that St. George's Day, April 23, is also Will Shakespeare's birthday. That the celebration and festival the *Quartet* "goes out to" is also Shakespeare's then is, perhaps, not coincidental at all but one more Elizabethan level for the reader who wills to plumb.

Notes

1. Lawrence Durrell, *Spirit of Place: Letters and Essays on Travel*, ed. Alan G. Thomas (New York: E. P. Dutton, 1969), pp. 120–21. The phrase "my beloved Eliza's" refers to Durrell's prized collection of Elizabethan works that he had left with Thomas temporarily.

2. That Nessim is connected to Alexander is established clearly in his "great cycle of historical dreams" (*Justine* 175–80) and in a brief reference in the "Consequential Data" to a coin portrait of Alexander (*Justine* 250). Leila relates to Olympias in her emotional nature, her obsessive love of her son, her long years of letter writing, and her symbolical affinity with the serpent.

3. Compare with the boudoir scene in T. S. Eliot, *The Waste Land and Other Poems* (New York: Harcourt, Brace and World, 1934), pp. 32–33.

4. In *Clea,* he dies for love, however.

5. Mountolive, however, in relationship to Leila, dreams that he is Antony. That in another context he becomes Pilate of Judea and in still another the charioteer of the tarot deck suggests the depths and complexity of Durrell's layers of imagery and symbols.

6. Darley calls it a "cathedral," but that involves another layer of symbol, the medieval grail quest.

7. J. R. R. Tolkien, discussing mythic symbolism, calls this sort of ending "Eucatastrophe" and writes that "it is a sudden and miraculous grace, never to be counted on to recur," denying final defeat and "giving a fleeting glimpse of Joy, Joy beyond the walls of the world, poignant as grief." "On Fairy-stories," rpt. in *The Tolkien Reader* (New York: Ballantine, 1966), pp. 68–69.

8. Victor Brombert writes perceptively that "his frequent references to the poignant music Antony hears before dying constantly evoke the world of Cleopatra—a world in which sexuality, far from being frivolous, is transformed into a quasi-mystical, transcendent experience." "Lawrence Durrell and His French Reputation," in *The World of Lawrence Durrell*, p. 178. Jane Lagoudis Pinchin also discussed this music at some length in relation to Cavafy's poem in *Alexandria Still: Forster, Durrell, and Cavafy* (Princeton: Princeton University Press, 1977), pp. 193–96.

9. In fact its origins may well lie in the great festival, the Ptolemaic, founded by Ptolemy II. Like the Olympics, it was held every four years, and people came to celebrate it from throughout the Hellenistic world. It took two days for the tremendous procession, of which the central figure

was Dionysus, to make its way through the city. Hans Volkmann, *Cleopatra: A Study in Politics and Propaganda*, pp. 28–32.

Works Cited

Bradford, Ernle. *Cleopatra*. London: Hodder and Stoughton, 1971.

Brombert, Victor. "Lawrence Durrell and His French Reputation." *The World of Lawrence Durrell*. Ed. Harry T. Moore. New York: Dutton, 1964.

Cavafy, C. P. *Collected Poems*. Trans. Edmund Keeley and Philip Sherrard. Ed. George Savidis. Princeton: Princeton University Press, 1975.

Durrell, Lawrence. *The Alexandria Quartet*. London: Faber, 1968.

———. *Balthazar*. New York: Dutton, 1958.

———. *The Big Supposer: A Dialogue with Marc Alyn*. Trans. Francine Barker. New York Grove, 1974.

———. *Clea*. New York: Dutton, 1960.

———. *Justine*. New York: Dutton, 1957.

———. "The Kneller Tape" (Hamburg). Rpt. in *The World of Lawrence Durrell*. Ed. Harry T. Moore. New York: Dutton, 1964.

———. "Lawrence Durrell Answers a Few Questions." (*Two Cities* 1959). Rpt. in *The World of Lawrence Durrell*. Ed. Harry T. Moore. New York: Dutton, 1964.

———. *Mountolive*. New York: Dutton, 1959.

———. *Spirit of Place: Letters and Essays on Travel*. Ed. Alan G. Thomas. New York: Dutton, 1969.

Durrell, Lawrence, and Richard Aldington. *Literary Lifelines: The Richard Aldington–Lawrence Durrell Correspondence*. Ed. Ian S. MacNiven and Harry T. Moore. London: Faber, 1981.

Eliot, Thomas Stearns. *The Waste Land and Other Poems*. New York: Harcourt, 1934.

Pinchin, Jane Lagoudis. *Alexandria Still: Forster, Durrell, and Cavafy*. Princeton: Princeton University Press, 1977.

Plutarch. *Plutarch's De Iside et Osiride*. Ed. and trans. John Gwyn Griffiths. Cardiff: University of Wales Press, 1970.

———. *Makers of Rome: Nine Lives by Plutarch*. Trans. Ian Scott-Kilvert. New York: Penguin, 1965.

Shakespeare, William. *Antony and Cleopatra*. Ed. M. R. Ridley. The Arden Edition of the Works of Shakespeare. London: Methuen, 1954.

Steiner, George. "Lawrence Durrell: The Baroque Novel." *The World of Lawrence Durrell*. Ed. Harry T. Moore. New York: Dutton, 1964.

———. "Why English?" *Contemporary Approaches to English Studies*. Ed. Hilda Schiff. London: Heinemann, 1977.

Tolkien, J. R. R. *The Tolkien Reader*. New York: Ballantine, 1966.

12

Sailing to Alexandria: The Reader in/of Durrell's Byzantine *Quartet*

Steven G. Kellman

Larry was designed by Providence to go through life like a small, blond firework, exploding ideas in other people's minds, and then curling up with catlike unctuousness and refusing to take any blame for the consequences.

Gerald Durrell

Buried within the ancient name Alexandria, site of the greatest library of antiquity, is the word *read*. Implied within Lawrence Durrell's *The Alexandria Quartet* is a reader with the eyes of Argus and the lenses of Leeuwenhoek. "I read you with a powerful magnifying glass," wrote Henry Miller to Durrell thirty-five pages from the end of an early copy of *Mountolive* (Wickes 351). Shortly after completing his tetralogy, Lawrence Durrell summarized *The Alexandria Quartet* as both *Künstlerroman* and *Bildungsroman:* "The whole business of the four books, apart from other things, shows the way an artist grows up" (Young 62). And many other critics have proceeded to note how thoroughly self-conscious the work is, in part because stocked with a large cast of invented writers whose own artistic preoccupations call attention to those of the fiction in which they appear.[1] Frequently, it seems harder to find a Durrell character who is *not* a writer, or at least an artist of some sort, than one who is.

There is, of course, L. G. Darley, narrator of three of the four volumes, *Justine, Balthazar,* and *Clea,* the nascent novelist who—like Durrell himself, whose initials he shares—aspires to give aesthetic form to Byzantine Alexandria. Darley's spiritual and artistic progress culminates in his inability to sit down and begin to recreate "the old story of an artist coming of age." His elliptical opening ("Once upon a time . . .") at the end of the final volume, *Clea,* provides whatever pause there is to Durrell's perpetual-motion machine (282).

Jacob Arnauti, Justine's first husband, is the author of *Moeurs,* a *roman à clef* that, if read astutely, provides useful information about their marriage. Ludwig Pursewarden is an eccentric English poet, aphorist, and novelist, author of a revealing and concealing trilogy called *God Is a Humorist.* Another potential novelist is the hack journalist whimsically named John Keats, who undergoes a conversion to art and exclaims in the final volume: "I've become a writer at last!" (*Clea* 181). Exactly one hundred pages later, Clea Montis, a painter, announces: "I wait, quite serene and happy, a real human being, an artist at last" (281). Other texts within Durrell's supremely self-conscious text include the "Great Interlinear," S. Balthazar's commentary on and emendation of Darley's version of events; the diary of Nessim Hosnani, Justine's second husband; and letters by Clea, Paul Capodistria, and Leila Hosnani. "The part that literature plays in our lives!" muses Balthazar (*Clea* 69), and it is a part that is almost equal to the whole of *The Quartet.*

The effect of the novel's pervasive references to writing is to foreground the process of creation, to make art its true, and heroic, subject. While his champions have thereby been able to present Durrell as the quintessential Modernist, his detractors dismiss him as an epigone of *fin-de-siècle* aestheticism, a plagiarist of Proust, and a misinterpreter of both Bergson and Einstein. Whether it makes the work derivative or sumptuous, *The Alexandria Quartet* clearly is heir to a rich tradition of writing about writing.

However, in turning the pages of Durrell's four volumes, we are also reading about reading. And while the books look back to earlier achievements, it is remarkable how they also anticipate developments in critical fashion three decades later. Not merely another *Künstlerroman, The Alexandria Quartet* is also a *Lektorroman,* a fable of the reading experience that almost seems designed to illustrate the theories of Wolfgang Iser, Walter J. Ong, and Stanley E. Fish. Darley, for example, is not merely, as everyone has noted, a surrogate for his author and for authors as a class; in trying to make sense of his puzzling experiences and relationships in Alexandria, he is also an earnest reader—not only of Balthazar's "Interlinear" and of other documents that fall into his hands but of a wide variety of cryptic and conflicting codes. "How then am I to manipulate this mass of crystallized data in order to work out the meaning of it and so give a coherent picture of this impossible city of love and obscenity?" (*Balthazar* 183), he asks. And much of the pathos in the question is due to the fact that each of us must pose the same question.

For Wolfgang Iser, one of the most influential of contemporary literary theorists, indeterminacy is a hallmark of the reading experience, "the fundamental precondition for reader participation" (14). For both aesthetic and ethical reasons, he considers reader participation crucial; a fully determinate text is tediously unreadable and a denial of imaginative freedom. Iser contends that "since the eighteenth century indeterminacy in literature—or at least an awareness of it—has tended toward a continual increase" (23). And, although he is a sympathetic and learned critic of eighteenth-century fiction, Iser's homiletic conclusion that "it is perhaps one of the chief values of literature that by its very indeterminacy it is able to transcend the restrictions of time and written word and to give to people of all ages and backgrounds the chance to enter other worlds and so enrich their own lives" (45) would make him a partisan of Modernism. I am not aware of any statements by Iser about Durrell, but *The Alexandria Quartet,* with its aim of defeating both time and text—"The object of writing is to grow a personality which in the end enables man to transcend art," says Pursewarden (*Balthazar* 141)—would seem to be just his cup of indeterminacy.

The word itself even appears in the tetralogy. In a signal passage that is frequently quoted because it is so manifestly a *mise en abîme* of Durrell's entire fictional apparatus, Pursewarden suggests the kind of work Darley might write:

> You might try a four-card trick in the form of a novel; passing a common axis through four stories, say, and dedicating each to one of the four winds of heaven. A continuum, forsooth, embodying not a *temps retrouvé* but a *temps délivré.* The curvature of space itself would give you a stereoscopic narrative, while human personality seen across a continuum would perhaps become prismatic. . . . I can imagine a form which, if satisfied, might raise in human terms the problems of causality or indeterminacy. (*Clea* 135–36)

The Alexandria Quartet is determinedly indeterminate. A continuum that lacks discrete beginning, middle, and end, it baffles our ability to attribute definitive meanings to statements and gestures. Why does Justine kiss Darley? Why does Pursewarden kill himself? No single hypothesis is entirely adequate, just as no single reading of the tetralogy suffices. But the indeterminacy elicts many.

In *A Key to Modern British Poetry,* an earlier book that Durrell had put together out of a series of lectures he gave in Argentina during 1948, he invokes "The Principle of Indeterminacy" and illustrates its increasing application to English poetry from Tennyson's "Ulysses" to Eliot's "Gerontion"; the progression from Fielding's *Joseph Andrews* to Joyce's *Ulysses* that Iser traces in English prose is remarkably similar. As explained by Durrell, the Principle of Indeterminacy "is founded upon the theory that we cannot observe the course of nature without disturbing it" (29). So, too, is *The Alexandria Quartet,* which makes of its multiple perspectives not only a technique but an unresolved drama that invites the reader to collaborate as playwright.

According to the author's "Note" at the outset of *Balthazar,* "the central topic of the book is an investigation of modern love" (4). As an investigation rather than a verdict, the work is forever *à la recherche,* and its sentences are interrogatory rather than periodic. In respect to the species, Durrell told an interviewer: "Human beings are really walking question marks, how's and why's and perhapses" ("The Kneller Tape" 164). The plot, the characters, and the setting of Durrell's best-known work are appropriately enigmatic. Of all punctuation, it is the question mark that places the greatest demands on a reader.

Palimpsests, prisms, kaleidoscopes, and sliding doors provide the figural equivalent of question marks throughout *The Quartet.* Darley, for example, writes of the characters' shared reality as "a palimpsest upon which each of us had left his or her individual traces, layer by layer" *(Balthazar* 21–22). Later, Balthazar recycles the image of overlapping texts as a metaphor for the kind of novel capable of embodying the multiple, unstable realities of Alexandria— "some medieval palimpsest where different sorts of truth are thrown down one upon the other, the one obliterating or perhaps supplementing another" (183). Like *The Alexandria Quartet* itself, a palimpsest confronts its readers with particular problems of deciphering and reconciling competing transcripts.

The analogy with "sliding panels," which Balthazar adapts from Purse-warden (183), suggests that, even if on paper, the object of our scrutiny is not stationary. Elsewhere, a persistent metaphor suggests that we must see through a glass all too brightly, as if through a prism that fragments our unified vision into numerous shimmering planes. Says Justine, with a metafictional wink at Durrell, "Now if I wrote I would try for a multi-dimensional effect in character, a sort of prism-sightedness" *(Justine* 27). And, declares Darley, "To every one we turn a different face of the prism" (119). It is remarkable how much Durrell's version of the literary experience as iridescent and polyscopic resembles Wolfgang Iser's account of the reading process: "As we have seen, the activity of reading can be characterized as a sort of kaleidoscope of perspectives, prein-tentions, recollections" (278).

The Alexandria Quartet, "a four-decker novel whose form," we are told by the author's "Note" to *Balthazar,* "is based on the relativity proposition," proceeds from the Gnostic premise that reality *as such* is unknowable. Durrell claims to derive from Einsteinian physics the premise that phenomena are a function of observation and the practice of focusing a multitude of perspectives on what could, imprecisely, be called the same phenomena. "No one thing can explain everything," says Pursewarden, "though everything can illuminate something" *(Justine* 140). The complete truth is a syncretic vision but, as Balthazar suggests, if we are limited to a few perspectives we ought not presume to it, "nor dare one make a claim for omniscience in interpreting people's actions" *(Balthazar* 98). When Darley concludes a chapter in *Clea* with the bald assertion "It is hard to know" (47), it echoes throughout the tetralogy—a four-volume monument to ignorance. The reader is its unknowing soldier.

An avatar of the Romantic femme fatale, as irresistible as she is irreducible,

Justine is probably the most obvious example of Durrell's Gnostic conception of human personality. But Pursewarden, too, is ascribed an "enigmatic character" (*Clea* 155), and in fact, as Pursewarden himself insists, he is no more baffling than anyone else in their cryptic world: "I must say, when you think that everyone is both polymorph and perverse here, it seems hard luck to be singled out like this as the main character in a *roman vache*" (*Mountolive* 110). Proteus seems the patron saint of the Alexandrians, who are partial to masked balls and even transvestism. It is many pages before we discover that it was someone other than Capodistria who was accidentally (?) killed at Nessim's annual duck shoot, but in Durrell's novel all identities are in a sense mistaken identities.

Durrell rejects the conventional psychology of human beings as stable clusters of discrete, categorical traits. As Arnauti explains, "For the writer people as psychologies are finished. The contemporary psyche has exploded like a soap-bubble under the investigations of mystagogues" (*Justine* 113). To ask what makes his elusive characters tick is to smuggle a horological metaphor into a universe that defies chronology, psychology, and epistemology. The reader attempting to get a fix on someone in *The Quartet* will soon discover that it is quick and brief at best.

To attempt to construe a coherent pattern to the tetralogy's varied events is to court frustration as well. There are many figures in Durrell's carpet, and interlopers like David Mountolive, trying to make sense of the Copts, must tread carefully. Amid the abundance of amorous, religious, political, and diplomatic intrigues in Alexandria, anyone attempting to read the significance of specific actions must learn to accept partial illiteracy. Ultimately, it is the exotic cosmopolis itself, a torrid cauldron of cabals, cults, nationalities, and emotions, that is Durrell's most compelling emblem of inscrutability. At the conclusion of a long letter to Mountolive, who is preparing to return as British ambassador to Egypt, Pursewarden describes the posting as "everything that is heteroclite, devious, polymorph, anfractuous, equivocal, opaque, ambiguous, many-branched, or just plain doty" (*Mountolive* 28). Durrell is often praised for his vivid sense of place, but his Alexandria, like his *Alexandria Quartet,* is a vivid place built on runes that are not fully decipherable.

Inscrutability is not only a quality of Alexandria, its characters, its happenings, and its quartet, but it is also, according to Durrell, a criterion for literary excellence. *Caveat scrutator* is the message not only of *The Quartet* but of Durrell's *A Key to Modern British Poetry*—"As for poetry: in the last analysis great poetry reflects an unknown in the interpretation and understanding of which all knowledge is refunded into ignorance" (164). With this Pyrrhonistic aesthetic, it was perfectly appropriate for Durrell a few years later to present his readers with a four-volume cryptogram devoid of a key.

If, as Pursewarden declares, "Art like life is an open secret" (*Balthazar*

246), Durrell does not see his task as divulging either. In practice and in principle, his art is difficult, demanding an active, assiduous reader. Says Pursewarden again: "I love the French edition with its uncut pages. I would not want a reader too lazy to use a knife on me" (*Balthazar* 246). Elsewhere, that oracular author insists: "We must learn to read between the lines, between the lives" (*Clea* 143). But how do we learn to read if the text was designed to be arcane?

If this is, as the "Author's Note" to *Balthazar* states, "a four-decker novel whose form is based on the relativity proposition" (5), then there is not in fact a text independent of the reader to read. Is anything *in fact* in a universe where, as Balthazar contends, "Fact is unstable by its very nature"? (*Balthazar* 102). Durrell rejects the ancient subject-object dichotomy and with it the certainty that an independent reality awaits interpretation by a constant reader. As Clea explains, "This idea of objectivity is really a flattering extension of our sense of humbug" (*Clea* 135). Without that idea, it becomes more useful to talk about reading as an open experience, a continuing process, rather than as a finite transaction between two autonomous entities.

Refusing to reify literature, Stanley E. Fish likewise approaches it as a collaborative activity and defines his method of studying it as *"an analysis of the developing responses of the reader in relation to the words as they succeed one another in time"* (73). Durrell is of the part of Fish, and of Heraclitus, in his emphasis on the dynamic qualities of the reading process and on the quickness of the text; you cannot dip into the same book twice.

However, he does part company with Fish in refusing to locate fiction *in time*. The principle behind the first three volumes of *The Quartet* is an evasion of time. *Clea* is a genuine chronological sequel—"The first three parts, however, are to be deployed spatially (hence the use of 'sibling,' not 'sequel') and are not linked in a serial form. They interlap, interweave, in a purely spatial relation. 'Time is stayed'" (*Balthazar* "Author's Note"). Durrell's chronoclastic ambitions recall Joseph Frank's influential thesis about modern fiction's aspiration toward spatial form as an attempt to subvert the temporal sequence inherent in narrative (221–40, 433–56, 643–53). It certainly does take time to read *Justine, Balthazar,* and *Mountolive,* but the illusion created by the multiple perspectives reverting to the same events is of liberation from chronology and even temporality. Far from eternity, the reader proceeds in the belief that *sub specie aeternitatis* all will be reconciled and known, that each partial view embraced in time will ultimately contribute to a synoptic vision out of time. Pursewarden, again, suggests the kind of timeless machine Durrell would construct: "A continuum, forsooth, embodying not a *temps retrouvé* but a *temps délivré*" (*Clea* 135).

The word *continuum* recurs continually throughout *The Quartet,* emphasizing Durrell's attempt to create a form that, lifted out of time and out of the conventions of linear reading, has no genuine beginning or end. There is no limit to the number of times a reader might pick up this kaleidoscopic work, but it is an experiment in translating eternity into infinity, boundless time into boundless space. In a 1958 letter to Henry Miller, Durrell likens his tetralogy to a Calder mobile (Wickes 338). As a work that can have no first or final reading, another analogy might be the Möbius strip.

In the manner of both generative and collaborative art, *Balthazar* and *Clea* close with lists of "Workpoints"—suggestions for additional perspectives on Alexandria we might extrapolate on. *The Alexandria Quartet,* thus, halts at a virtual ellipsis, leaving its *mobile perpetuum* to the reader's imagination. If it is expansive enough, the fiction need never end—"it should be possible to radiate in any direction without losing the strictness and congruity of the word continuum" (*Clea* "Author's Note").

"We live by selected fictions," notes Pursewarden (*Balthazar* 140), but the elaborate form of the fiction in which he appears invites the reader to expand Durrell's selection *ad infinitum.* Pursewarden dreams of an "n-dimensional novel" (*Justine* 248); and, with the collaboration of its readers, *The Alexandria Quartet* is just that. Durrell's novel will probably survive on its reputation as the paradigm of literary impressionism, a sort of *Rashomon* transported to Egypt. If it did not exist, it is the kind of novel that had to be invented in order to illustrate and justify post-Jamesian preoccupation with multiple perspective. But, as with its reader's indulgence, the life of Durrell's "word continuum" is more extensive. Its "Workpoints" invite a task that has no limits. It anticipates such collaborative creations as Marc Saporta's *Composition no. 1* (1962), whose readers are instructed to cut out its perforated pages, shuffle them, and create their own narrative combinations, and Julio Cortazar's *Rayuela* (1963), which offers us a choice of chapters to read. *The Alexandria Quartet* does not leave quite as much to reader discretions as Bruce Harris's *The Nothing Book* (1974), an edition of blank pages. But it is more solicitous and even more ambitious than conceptual artist On Kawara's *One Million Years* (1970), a ten-volume list of all the years humans have inhabited the earth. It is the story of *n* readers reading in *n* dimensions.

Notes

1. See, for example, discussion of *The Quartet* as a reflexive work whose central drama is its own creation in my own *The Self-Begetting Novel,* pp. 93–97.

Works Cited

Durrell, Gerald. *My Family and Other Animals.* New York: Viking, 1963.
Durrell, Lawrence. *Balthazar.* New York: Dutton, 1958.
_____ . *Clea.* New York: Dutton, 1960.
_____ . *Justine.* New York: Dutton, 1957.

―――― . *A Key to Modern British Poetry.* Norman: University of Oklahoma, 1952.

―――― . "The Kneller Tape" (Hamburg). Rpt. in *The World of Lawrence Durrell.* Ed. Harry T. Moore. Carbondale: University of Southern Illinois, 1962.

―――― . *Mountolive.* New York: Dutton, 1959.

Durrell, Lawrence, and Henry Miller. *Lawrence Durrell–Henry Miller: A Private Correspondence.* Ed. George Wickes. New York: Dutton, 1964.

Fish, Stanley E. "Literature in the Reader: Affective Stylistics." *Reader-Response Criticism: From Formalism to Post-Structuralism.* Ed. Jane P. Tompkins. Baltimore: Johns Hopkins University, 1980.

Frank, Joseph. "Spatial Form in Modern Literature." *Sewannee Review* 53 (1943). Rpt. in *The Widening Gyre: Crisis and Mastery in Modern Literature.* Bloomington: Indiana University, 1968.

Iser, Wolfgang. *The Implied Reader: Patterns in Communication in Prose Fiction from Bunyan to Beckett.* Baltimore: Johns Hopkins University, 1974.

―――― . "Indeterminacy and the Reader's Response in Prose Fiction." *Aspects of Narrative.* Ed. J. Hillis Miller. New York: Columbia, 1971.

Kellman, Steven G. *The Self-Begetting Novel.* New York: Columbia University, 1980.

Young, Kenneth. "A Dialogue with Durrell." *Encounter* 13:6 (December 1959).

13

From Pudding Island: A Personal View

Peter Baldwin

Beryl Bainbridge, Sir John Betjeman, Malcolm Bradbury, Anthony Burgess, Margaret Drabble, Lawrence Durrell, John Fowles, Leon Garfield, William Golding, Graham Greene, Ted Hughes, John Le Carré, Laurie Lee, Rosamond Lehmann, Iris Murdoch, V. S. Naipaul, V. S. Pritchett, Rosemary Sutcliff, Laurens van der Post, Rebecca West

The Best of British Authors

I have in mind writers in whom Mr. Eliot has expressed an interest in strongly favorable terms: . . . Henry Miller, Lawrence Durrell of The Black Book. *In these writers . . . the spirit of what we are offered affects me as being essentially a desire, in the Lawrentian phrase, to "do dirt on life."*

F. R. Leavis, The Great Tradition

And this an "agon" for the dead, a chronicle for the living.

Lawrence Durrell, The Black Book

I first "discovered" Lawrence Durrell with *Tunc* in 1974 and have since then read his writings avidly. I find, therefore, great pleasure in joining this celebration of a masterly writer. My subject is primarily Durrell's reputation in England

("Pudding Island" is his nickname for the United Kingdom in the poem "Cities, Plains and People"). However, I shall progress to one of many but, I think, the most fascinating and radical of Durrell's themes, which I loosely term the fiction of personality: how Durrell takes us through the contrast in Eastern and Western thinking about the concept of individuality leading to a meditative state culminating in inferential consciousness.

I have prefaced this essay with two contrasting views of Durrell's work against which to set his current reputation in the UK, as well as a quotation from his first major novel which—so to speak—sets the scene. It is ironic that the quotation from Leavis comes from *The Great Tradition,* given that Durrell in *The Black Book* was reacting against the stifling literary and cultural traditions he felt to prevail in the 1930s in the UK, which he left for Corfu: "How can a man withstand the atmosphere / This hell compounded of such strange alloys?" (*Collected Poems* 32). In a most remarkable poem written, it would seem, before Durrell departed for Corfu in 1935, he looked forward with almost visionary promise:

> Old year, kind year:
> Image of sunshine and nightingale-passion
> Urge us so gently and smoothly away,
> My lovely accomplice and I,
> To the dead selves of lovers,
> The voiceless, forgotten, the faded companions
> Old year, lost year, lead us away.
>
> (*Collected Poems* 43)

Since the time of that poetry, Durrell has enjoyed an increasing reputation for his writing, principally his verse, especially the collections *A Private Country, Cities, Plains and People,* and *On Seeming to Presume.* On these volumes from the thirties and forties, his reputation as one of the leading "minor" poets lies. There, but for the meteoric rise to fame of *The Alexandria Quartet,* his reputation might have stayed: a literary exile with a respected reputation for poetry, along with a couple of travel books for good measure.

Yet even Durrell's achieving international reknown has not completely caused a change in the way he is regarded in the UK. In considering Durrell's current reputation here, Dr. Keith Brown, Professor of English at the University of Oslo, recently described Durrell as subject to "a persistent scepticism of the London literary world" (597). I should add that such scepticism has never been absent from the critical view of Durrell's work. Yet so distinctive is Durrell's style and method, the difficulty of pigeonholing him with other contemporary novelists will probably continue.

The scepticism in critical circles arises partly from a distaste in certain corners for his bold and overtly vivid prose style. Also, his novels are set against manifestly bourgeois social groups, and such settings are viewed with suspicion and even distaste by the predominately left-wing influenced literary academics of the postwar university campus. However, my argument is that the central vision of Durrell's recent writing, as evinced by *The Avignon Quintet,* operates against a profoundly different psychological and philosophical contemporary background from the traditional modern literature of the UK. Until that cultural thinking finds itself redirected (possibly in literary terms under the influence of Durrell), his work will continue to be subject to that scepticism and critical distance.

The distinction between Durrell's philosophic viewpoint and the tradition from which the British reader observes it was characterized by Durrell himself in an interview on BBC Radio 2 on 29 May 1985 with John Dunn:

> The two philosophies [Eastern and Western] are coming together in a head-on collision. The basic thing which differentiates them is determinism and materialism in the West and precisely this pentagram formation about human personality in the East. They say that psychology instead of being divided into male and female, conscious and unconscious, is divided into five groups—baskets, skandhas. So it is a sort of pentagram I envisioned instead of a Freudian square.

Again, in his essay "From the Elephant's Back," Durrell reminds us of two more germane and fundamental points: "The Indians had always said that the notion of matter was an illusion. . . . Long ago [they] had told us that the notion of the discreet and separate ego was also an illusion" (6).

Possibly from the earliest time of Western thinking, from its Greek origins, our philosophy has borne the twin characteristics of determinism and materialism. Little wonder, then, that a novel infused with such a different metaphysic is viewed with caution by the reading public. Contemporary fiction is still very much imbued with the fragmentation of spiritual and emotional values with the only course for the individual leading into the realm of the material in the by now constant struggle to maintain individuality as technology increasingly affects our lives.

Durrell anticipated the current techoculture with *Tunc* and *Nunquam,* the double-decker novel of 1968 and 1970. It portrays an era of computerized society in which the individual seems and feels hopelessly lost against a culture of micro-electronic-thinking machines. What the hermetics tried to do by calling down spirits into human models and what the Firm in *Nunquam* failed to do by the synthetic reconstruction of a woman, Iolanthe, the computer culture is now starting to achieve in computer graphics with the animation of human features on the computer screen. This is a culture which has taken over the individual and collective spirit of mankind.

In many respects, *Tunc* and *Nunquam* may be the most difficult of Durrell's novels; but they provide a metaphor very germane to these cultural considerations. The wider audience could appreciate them for the very revaluation of traditional values which they pose. The whole concept of memory, so essential to deterministic thinking, is attacked by the idea of Abel, Charlock's machine, which given "a sign or the birth cry of a baby . . . can tell you everything" (*Tunc* 11). A perceptive reader, alert to Durrell's intent and method, can experience in reading one of Durrell's novels a greater awareness, understanding, and maturity toward contemporary culture, the one to which all must function and respond. Through his novels Durrell can cause the reader to revalue traditional ways of thinking and so achieve a heightened awareness, leading to "liberation through self knowledge" and "acceptance through understanding," phrases Durrell used in his essay, "Studies in Genius VI: Groddeck."

That Durrell intended a revaluation of traditional Western ideas of love, life, and death is evident in the characters and themes of all his novels: love in *The Quartet* and death in *The Quintet,* for instance. Durrell has never shied away from being candid about the sexual liaisons enjoyed by his characters, the most infamous of which appear in both *The Alexandria Quartet* and *The Avignon Quintet.* I fear, however, that the reader will find great difficulty in approaching the gulf created by situations such as these:

> The woman . . . should be perpetually manipulating the scrotum, manufacturing the sort of product which will biologically enrich the race.

> Making love with a sincere belief in this kind of reversed affect relationship leading to a simultaneous orgasm. (*Constance* 285)

I am not here considering the biological relevance of passages such as these on which much of *Constance* turns. However, it takes a broad mind not to react with initial caution against such ideas even to the point of rejection, as did many critics at the time *Constance* was published. However, Durrell's intent has not been to be deliberately offensive, but rather, by this radically different approach to his art, to cause the reader to revaluate both self and culture, as he made quite clear in the epigraph from Wordsworth that introduces *Quinx,* the last novel of *The Avignon Quintet:* "[Each original work of art] must create the taste by which it is to be judged" (8).

In *The Avignon Quintet,* Durrell has thrown away the discreet, individualistic ego, such a concept being, in Eastern terms, "a fiction": "Identity is the fragile suggestion of coherence with which we have clad ourselves" (*Monsieur* 87). To struggle with the understanding and implications of the five *skandhas* is to struggle with concepts most central to Eastern thinking. Individual consciousness in Eastern terms is perceived by these five *skandhas*— "symptoms," which can be briefly listed as follows: *rukpa* (matter), *vedana* (sensation of feeling), *sanna* (perceptions), *sankhara* (mental formations), and *vinnana* (consciousness).

The proof of the merging of Durrell's ideas with those of the East appears readily in a comparison of two texts. In the words of Shingyo Sutra:

> When the Bodhisattva Avalokitesvara was engaged in the practice of the deep Pranjnaparamita, he perceived that there are the five Skandhas; and these he saw in their self nature to be empty.
>
> O Sariputra, form is here emptiness, emptiness is form; form is no other than emptiness, emptiness is no other than form; that which is form is emptiness, that which is emptiness is form. The same can be said of sensation, though, confliction, and consciousness. (Suzuki 26)

In *Quinx,* Durrell sums up his synthesis of Eastern and Western thought in the words of Blanford, one of the writers whom he has always had a penchant to create:

> Your consciousness bears witness to the historic *now* which you are living while your memory recalls other nows, fading slowly into indistinctiveness as they move into the pre-history you call the past. This temporal series, indistinct and overlapping, you attach to one individual whom you call "I." But . . . in the course of a few years, about seven I think, every cell in the body of this "I," this individual, has been modified and even replaced. His thoughts, judgements, emotions, desires have all undergone a similar metamorphosis! What then is the permanence which you designate as "I"? Surely not simply a name which marks his ("its"?) difference from ("its?") fellow man . . . a discreet sequence of rather distorted recollections which began some time in infancy and terminate with a jolt *now* and in the *present*—such is his time as a datum of consciousness! . . . When all this raw material has undergone a strange refining process which we know as physical intuition it is transformed into something close to a meditative state—a version of "calm abiding" as the Tibetans would say . . . [a] backcloth of everything we do or every kiss we exchange. When if ever one has the luck to arrive at an inferential consciousness the steps of the reasoning process that preceded it are no longer necessary, one can let go! Kick away the ladder. . . . It illustrates the nothingness we have decorated with our trashy narcissim. (176–77)

The similarity of the ideas is obvious, as is the reason. From at least the time he wrote *The Black Book,* Durrell has been discontent with the answers offered him by Western culture. Increasingly, Durrell has turned away from the simple alternatives of acceptance or rejection, contentment or despair. Granted his affirmations may be qualified, but he has found in the merging of Eastern and Western metaphysics answers that provide some stability, some peace, even enlightenment.

The challenge of Durrell's writings is clearly not limited to the readers in the United Kingdom, though they are my main concern in this essay. Yet those readers, in particular, are forced to revalue "the great tradition" against which the literary experience Durrell presents is set. If the reader is not prepared to undertake such revaluation, even assuming he is perceptive enough to see what Durrell is asking of him, only scepticism and a failure of understanding will result.

Works Cited

Brown, Keith. "Up to the Pisgah-sight." Rev. of *Quinx*. *Times Literary Supplement*. No. 4287 (31 May 1985), 597.

Dunn, John. Interview with Lawrence Durrell. BBC Radio 2 (29 May 1985).

Durrell, Lawrence. *The Black Book*. London: Faber, 1973.

––––––. *The Collected Poems*. London: Faber, 1980.

––––––. *Constance, or Solitary Practices*. London: Faber, 1980.

––––––. "From the Elephant's Back." *Poetry London* 1:2 (1982).

––––––. *Monsieur, or the Prince of Darkness*. London: Faber, 1973.

––––––. *Nunquam. London: Faber, 1970.*

––––––. *Quinx, or the Ripper's Tale*. London: Faber, 1985.

––––––. *Tunc*. London: Faber, 1968.

––––––. "Studies in Genius VI: Groddeck." *Horizon* (London). 17 (June 1948).

Durrell, Lawrence, ed. *Poems* by William Wordsworth. Edited and selected with an introduction by Lawrence Durrell. Harmondsworth: Penguin, 1972.

Leavis, F. R. *The Great Tradition*. London: Chatto and Windus, 1960.

Suzuki, D. T., ed. *Manual of Zen Buddhism*. New York: Grove, 1960.

\

14

Durrelland

Jean Blot

It was the fifties. Were they gay? Plenty of the worst went on, of course, but the century's monsters, Hitler and Stalin, were dead *at last*. A new world war was beginning. The reader was tired to tears of war heroes, even more by the ex-Communist and his ordeal. We were bored to the same lachrymose limit by the so-called New Novel which, collaboration inspired, did its very best to evacuate all kinds of meaning from the world—with the hope that working with the Jerry would also go down the drain to be forgotten. Grey ashes everywhere: no story, no character, only objects of the most abstract nature. It was in that void that the Durrell thunder rolled in *joyously* and that the quartet from Alexandria exploded with a bang.

It was new; it was great. It was as intelligent as the New Novel tried to be. It was more alive, more full of color than anything English we had read on the Continent since Joyce had gone mad at an over-Irish wake. Here were again the two Englands we treasured: Falstaff, full of sack, gross sexuality, enough guilt to keep Freud busy till the end of time, incredibly but indissolubly wed to the English gentleman with an elegance and glamour that he would bring to saloons, whores, and all related vices. Here was Durrell! A grand talent was born. We were overcome. We could not believe that such an event would visit our generation. The years have passed, alack so many! But that amazement still remains.

I shall not try to explain it away. If only because I want to keep its magic. But the sweet poison of the Durrell-exploded novel has sunk in deep. From it, I gather these few impressions that I would love to share with whomsoever. Some authors are like lands. You can't say they are good or bad. They are. They generally find some pyramid or molehill with which they identify. Proust, to take our greatest, is Combrais and Balbec and it would not be at all silly to start from there to explain his quest: from the over-bourgeois sea, its sophisticated chatter, its blending with the golden silent plain leading to the cathedral.

Durrelland, of course, is Alexandria.

The sea again. And ever present because always moving, changing on the verge of the desert. But this is background. In the center, the city, capital of the metamorphosis, there is no past, as it sinks in the quicksand and the marshes, and therefore no present to stand up against it. No future to dream about or to invent. It is this historic reality—two-thousand two-hundred years, but no land-marks—that brought to light and maturity something which lived buried in the sand of the past of Durrell who—after all—was born at the foot of the Hima-layas. It is not that things, women, men are deprived of reality but that this reality weighs little in comparison to the flux that carries them toward other forms and realities. There is one big, silent, dark current that flows right through *The Alexandria Quartet;* and Justine, Clea, Darley, Nessim are moments of the incarnation of that one over-fertile current. From one novel to the next, they are the same and yet different. One form has appeared here. Another in the next volume. So that we find concretely expressed, lived through to its dangerous limits, the basic yet relative truth of One Life occupying the whole of space and time with all beings, episodes, loves, tragedies, and even huge Durrellian laughs—as provisional, fragile, and at most times absurd forms of that One Life.

Durrelland is a pagan land. Not one God in the middle of the sky but a huge quantity of little gods present everywhere, in the duck that is hunted—only a provisional form of reality—as well as the pit of the olive that Justine will spit out with that amazing blend of refinement and vulgarity that belongs to the land where only demons dare to tread. Gods here multiply as in the Alexandrian art at its sunset. When identity is refused to man and the poet of the past—full of the reality borrowed from the life stream—he becomes the poet of the present with no clear limitation between the one—yet he is Greek, homosexual, etc. and the other—yet he is English, loves women, etc. When one feels between the prostitute and the high-society lady an overbearing continuity—life in its wom-anhood stronger than all differences between women—the identity of the super-natural becomes weak indeed. No sky above our heads, for individual destiny. No ground beneath our feet, for personal death. Only the endless and joint mirage of the desert and of the sea.

Transcendence becomes magic. Nothing beyond, nor yonder. All is here and now, the dead in the living, the woman in man, the harlot in the saint. Here and now—but not all is said. Because of endless and perpetual metamorphosis Durrelland is in perpetual turmoil. What is here today will be something else tomorrow. Untold dangers threaten every form. And all existence is but form. There might be a meaning or even a message in Melissa, a prostitute, Narouz, a murderer, or the color of the sky; but it is not anthropomorphic, or not enough to be gathered and strangled in the chains of meaning. Magic: if you look at the world, it will change; man, woman, child—nothing can be trusted. And politics, through which the bodies of nations are constantly transformed, least of all.

Magic—that is to say another meaning beyond meaning, present here and now, beyond the intellect and the sense. Perhaps it is hidden close to the sexual organs through which life goes on transforming itself.

A despair inhabits Durrelland in spite of its wealth in all the goods of the world, because the identity of none can be guaranteed, and therefore none can be justified, explained, enjoyed. Through politics, fishing, hunting, through sex and love, wealth and hunger, a strange Nostalgia, soft and dark like velvet, walks secretly through Durrelland. It is she whom I love: a strange, English goddess with a Greek education, an Indian background. It is she I long to meet, I and all those who with me or after me will visit one of the most wonderful countries that this century has opened to dreams and longings: Durrelland.

Lawrence Durrell, *The Greek Priest,* 1974
Acrylic, signed by Lawrence Durrell/Oscar Epfs.

15

The Paintings of Lawrence Durrell: An Interview with Marthe Nochy

Alice Hughes

The two principal exhibits of the paintings of Lawrence Durrell have been held at Galerie Marthe Nochy, 93 rue de Seine, Paris, in 1970 and 1974. Nochy has, in fact, been the sole agent for his paintings, most of which are signed Oscar Epfs, a name concocted by Durrell and Nadia Blokh, a painter who has contributed a drawing to this collection.

AH: When did you first meet Larry?

MN: I met him at U.N.E.S.C.O. We had friends in common, Jean Blot, Alex Blokh, and his wife. When I left U.N.E.S.C.O., it was in sixty-four. Then later, he came with Alex Blokh and asked me if I would like to make an exhibition of Oscar Epfs paintings. I said yes. I didn't think about it. I was very happy. It was to me very important at the beginning of my bookshop. We did the exhibition two years later, in 1970. That was when DeGaulle died, so we had problems with the press. They had something more important. But then Larry came to Paris in his escargot, his car, with his paintings and said: "If you don't like them, burn them immediately."

AH: Had you seen any of his paintings before?

MN: No. I only knew his writings. I discovered him when *Justine* was published. It was very much a shock to me. Of course, I like books, have the bookshop and the gallery. So it's perfect for me, having a writer, Durrell, and to tell people he's also a painter is wonderful.

AH: Did you know him well at the time of the first exhibit?

MN: When I have an exhibition, it's what I call a cohabitation. He never left the shop without saying thank you for all you have done. Not many artists do that.

AH: So you and Larry got on well from the first?

MN: Yes. Very well. Many people thought we were lovers, but we were much more than that.

AH: Did you ever see Henry Miller's paintings?

MN: Only in a book. Larry told me he began to paint because of Miller, that painting worked well for them in expressing themselves.

AH: What was the second exhibition like?

MN: It was really a great event. I had to fight against the journalists because he was a celebrity. Everyone wanted to see him. And I think it was important to him because as he's living in Languedoc sometimes he must think everybody is forgetting him.

AH: But when he comes to Paris, the newspapers, the radio, the television, he's on everything.

MN: Yes, but it was different when he was staying here all day long and saw a lot of people who liked his work, the writings, and all the rest. He says he is not a painter. As a matter of fact, he's not a painter. He paints. He said once, he doesn't draw, it's easier to make paintings without learning how to draw. This is the real creator. It's not technical. I don't like painters who are more technical than artistic. Of course, it is necessary to know some practical things, but when technique takes over the artist, I think that is very bad. You can see in Larry's poems sometimes that he wanted to say so much that he would not allow the crafting to get in the way of the expression. He puts in everything. He doesn't make a choice.

AH: Have you seen changes in Larry's paintings over the years?

MN: Yes. A great deal of change. In the beginning, he had in his mind Miró, Léger, some Picasso, you see, and Matisse. Some of his first paintings were like that. Then later he was freer. He always used high colors, like the places he has been, India, Ireland, Languedoc, now.

AH: Would you say that in his first exhibit in 1970 he was beginning to paint like himself?

MN: No. It was with the second exhibition. In 1970 he was still impressed by the other painters, especially Matisse I should say. In the first, he had made brush drawings for his walls that were a little like Matisse. It was not exactly Epfs. Afterwards, he took confidence and became himself.

AH: Where did the name Oscar Epfs come from?

MN: That's Larry because it's funny. It's difficult to pronounce. Everybody made mistakes. In the newspapers, the *f* was forgotten, making it Eps, you see.

AH: In this folder you have a record of the press receptions of Larry's exhibits?

MN: Yes. All of them.

AH: Has he only shown here?

MN: Yes. He did, though, have his first little exhibition in '65. But nobody knew it was Larry. It was Oscar Epfs.

AH: His exhibitions were always well received in Paris?

MN: Yes. And we became friends during that time. He was here for a fortnight. When you know somebody who remains with you all day long, you know him. I can't say I know him in another manner. But he is so so nice, so kind, so clever, so funny. He's a man it's so easy to love, nice, easy, and witty—very witty.

AH: Was he married when you met him?

MN: No, it was before his last marriage. We were going someplace, to an interview. And I said, "Why did you marry her? Everything she does seems to make you unhappy." And he said, "You must know what it's like. Women are so happy when you marry them." That's Larry. I told you that I went for him to an exhibit at Lyon he couldn't go to, an exhibition of works by painters who had been influenced by his writing. I gave Larry's paintings to the salon, and the painters of the salon worked for one year to prepare the exhibition on the work of Larry.

AH: In fact, weren't you president of the salon? Which is quite an honor.

MN: Yes. It was doubly an honor for me because I was able to bring Larry's paintings to the salon.

AH: Do you see any relationship between his writing and his painting?

MN: No, as a matter of fact I don't.

AH: Not even the poetry?

MN: The poetry, yes, in the colors. But it's quite different from his prose. For me, it's another way he has of expressing himself.

AH: The painting I bought from you, of the Greek priest, was signed both Oscar Epfs and Lawrence Durrell. Did he do that very often?

MN: No, never. A lot of people wanted that one because a lot of people bought the paintings because they were Larry's. They wanted the signature of Lawrence Durrell and Epfs.

AH: There's a smile on the face of that priest that looks very much like the smile on the face of Lawrence Durrell.

MN: Exactly. I saw that too.

AH: Then you think Larry paints himself into his paintings as well?

MN: Yes, I do.

AH: There was one you had of a face looking out through vegetation, perhaps in the jungle. It was Larry's face, but it was a very savage face.

MN: Yes. But I think sometimes he must feel like that, to write what he does. He's not always happy with himself, you know. That's why I like him. He is not always sure of himself. He's always surprised. When he came last time, he was with Jean d'Ormesson, a famous French writer whom I also know very well. It was wonderful to see how pleased everybody was to see Larry. He lives far from Paris, working, and doesn't have time to write to people, but really people like him very much.

AH: In the reception of his paintings by the Paris art critics what do you think is important in what they see?

MN: They saw another aspect of Larry. It was like a bomb. Durrell is an author and a painter. When we did the exhibit, I prepared for four months, six months before. I had an *attaché de press*. And everyone knew Lawrence Durrell was going to have an exhibition.

AH: I know I would have liked his paintings if he hadn't done them. But how important do you think it is that the author of *The Alexandria Quartet* has done these paintings?

MN: It's very important. Nowadays, you know, when you are famous, people look at you with other eyes. As we say in French: "You invite people to have supper with you who don't need to, but never really invite the people who need to."

AH: Alex Blokh is International Secretary of the P.E.N. Society?

MN: Yes. When he left U.N.E.S.C.O., he was chief interpreter.

AH: His wife paints, also?

MN: Nadia, yes. I had her paintings here, also, an exhibition for her. Alex wrote a book on Greece, and she did the illustrations.

AH: How do the French editions of Larry's writings sell?

MN: They sell well in my shop. I can't tell you about the last book, but *The Alexandria Quartet* is always a best-seller.

AH: Are the young people reading him now?

MN: Yes, I think so. But I want always people who don't know his work to know it. When people want a good book, I always speak of him. I give my advice, but he is famous, very famous. His first editor for *The Alexandria Quartet* was Buchet-Chastel; and he was very sad to lose him. Now Larry is with Gallimard. That is very nice. It is *etiquette*.

AH: Ezra Pound said that sometimes, maybe once in a generation, a writer becomes part of a culture other than his own. Has Larry done that in France?

MN: Absolutely. He had very good translators, but his work is very much appreciated here. He's a very, very good writer.

AH: He thinks in French?

MN: Yes, but then he has chosen France as his place to live. He could have lived in England, Ireland, anywhere. He has lived in Greece. He likes Greece. But now he goes there for a few months or for his holidays or for some time away from everyone to prepare another book. But he likes France. He likes French cooking. He likes French wines. He likes all parts of life. That's why it's very sad when he is depressed, as he was some time ago.

AH: I understand he was depressed before his daughter Sappho died. And he must have been intensely so afterwards.

MN: Exactly. He had been told by a doctor, maybe a year before that he must not drink anymore. Then after what happened, he couldn't do anything. He was scared to drink, not even a glass of wine to make him feel stronger, to forget. I must say that all the artists I know, writers, painters, all drink some. They are all scared somewhere inside. And they need it. To drink to forget they are scared. And I think it's exactly the same with Larry.

AH: I mentioned to him that I thought his house seemed like the one he wrote about in *The Avignon Quintet.*

MN: Yes, so do I.

AH: The swimming pool, the overgrown garden.

MN: When a writer writes a novel, he forgets what he is. But he has not forgotten where he lives or his memories. And you can find them in his books.

AH: I thought the house was an experience from which he invented. He lived there, but he made the house in *The Avignon Quintet* something other than what he experienced. I don't think he would have written what he did without that particular experience of that house.

MN: I think so, too, but you know he's a real writer. The books you read now, it's only the life of people; they have real names. That's how books are written now. When someone has a name, a politician or an artist, an editor will ask him to tell about his life. And then he is speaking on the recorder, but he is not writing. Somebody else tells the story after, but it's not what I call being a writer. There is no more literature. People are telling their own stories, their family life, their personal life, so you see everybody like everybody.

AH: But Larry's people in his novels are very special. We can feel what they feel, but they are so much themselves.

AN: Yes! He has got a universe which is not his life, but it is very rich inside. He has traveled a lot. He has had a lot of experiences. He has seen a lot of different people. He has been in love with several women. That's the real experience of life, and when you have talent as he does something comes from it. It's a need for a real writer. That's what I told you before. When people tell their lives, it's not interesting. With Larry, it's different. It was a big family with Miller, Anaïs Nin, and Durrell. It was very important that through Larry I thought I knew Miller, and I knew Anaïs Nin. When you know people, not just read their writings, it is quite different. You see through them. If you didn't know Larry's house, you wouldn't have said what you did about *The Avignon Quintet.*

AH: How long has it been since Larry painted?

MN: I haven't seen anything since the last exhibition. Maybe now that his novels are done, he will start painting again. I will send him a note and say: "What do you think about that, a new exhibition."

Paris, 4 November 1986

16

Love, Culture, and Poetry

Jeremy Robinson

I am no longer of this world, I am far from myself, I am no longer a part of my own person. I am within the the essence of things themselves.

Constantin Brancusi

Lawrence Durrell's major concern, like that of all serious artists, is with the "essence of things," which begins and ends, like culture, in people. And Durrell rightly recognizes that it is not what people do that is interesting, but what they actually are. Lawrence Durrell is one of the few people (Freud, Marx, Darwin, Stalin, and Hitler are not among them) to have targeted exactly the nub of human life: love (to use that well-worn word for the most profound, complex experience known to humankind). All Durrell's major fictional works have as their prime theme the hyper-trenchant, comic, ironic, tragic-heroic experience of love. Through the character of Pursewarden, at the end of *Balthazar*, Durrell explains that his object is "to interrogate human values through an honest representation of the human passions" (211). Yet the hardest task for the artist is always the transmission of content—that old "raid on the inarticulate" as Eliot fondly called it (182). The post-modern novel, however, is well-suited for an in-depth voyage into what Henry Miller called the "trackless oceans" of love (*Sexus* 211).

In *The Alexandria Quartet*, Durrell follows the dictum given by Pursewarden, who so often speaks for his creator: "good art points" and cannot, really, do any more (*Clea* 122). His absent colleague in *The Alexandria Quartet*, the French quasi-psychoanalytic writer Arnauti, outlined this new type of novel which "might dispense with the narrative articulation"—a book which has "on the first page a synopsis of the plot in a few lines" (*Justine* 66). The writer is then free to get down to the real heart of the work. The essence of a novel is not the plot, the story, or even the background description (though "spirit of place" has a massive effect on all the protagonists in Durrell's novels). The plot, then, the storyline, and all those other literary devices delineated by E. M. Forster in *Aspects of the Novel*, are not important. The real essence of the novel lies in its poetic, spiritual, and human content and, also, in its prose style and syntactical structuring: "Language is not an accident of poetry but the essence. The lingo is the nub" (*Clea* 249).

It is somewhat of a surprise, then, to find in Durrell's fiction immediately after *The Alexandria Quartet*—*Tunc* and *Nunquam* (also known as *The Revolt of Aphrodite*) a viciously swift plot with a multitude of scene and character changes. But then Durrell is really a child of the literary tradition of the 1930s and 40s, when the literature of Europe was dominated by Joyce, Lawrence, Eliot, Proust, Rilke, and Yeats. Yet most of Durrell's work has a free-wheeling form which allows for the real spice of social life—differences in opinion and character—to flourish. *Tunc* and *Nunquam*, however, are packed full of plot and story and read somewhat like slick thrillers. Durrell admits that the characters are deliberately "puppet-like" and that they are thrust through a strongly driven narrative which has the look and feel (intentionally) of a commercial film (Fraser 149). One might mention in passing Ian Fleming's Bond pastiches, but this is not to cheapen Durrell's wildly kaleidoscopic "double-decker." In fact, all of Durrell's books are a delight to read—delicious montages and creations which offer a phenomenal range of poetic insights, incisive and ironic comments, and a subtle and generous philosophy which melts into quasi-Taoist quietism at the drop of a stitch in the Interlinear. Durrell is the unsurpassed wizard of word-magic, who can conjure up the essence of a landscape or a person more success-fully than anyone else. Listen:

> In such light, and at such a time of day, the darkness hides the squalor and ugliness of the capital, leaving exposed only the pencilled shapes of its domes and walls against the approach-ing night; and moreover if one embarks on water at such an hour one instantly experiences a lift of the senses. The sea-damp vanishes. God, how beautiful it is. Light winds pucker at the gold-green waters of Bosphorus; the gorgeous melancholy of the Seraglio glows like a rotting fish among its arbours and severe groves. (*Tunc* 109)

Tunc and *Nunquam* (the titles derive from Petronius's *Satyricon*, "the first European novel": "Aut Tunc, aut Nunquam"—"it was then or never") are my-thographic expositions of a "mystical leap"[1] into the clack-bang-whistle-and-whir of our post-Holocaust post-everything age, in which the excellent (and apposite) metaphor of *le cinéma* is used to depict the trashy, vapid, banal, psychic condition of the "well-fed" life-styles in all the world's cities.[2] The narrative is racy, the characters are affluent jet-setting cognoscenti, and the theme (as ever) is that culture has long ago passed into mere "civilization" as described in Oswald Spengler's *The Decline of the West:*

> Every Culture stands in a deeply-symbolical, almost a mystical, relation to the Extended, the space, in which and through which it strives to actualize itself. The aim once attained—the idea, the entire content of inner possibilities, fulfilled and made externally actual—the Culture suddenly hardens, it mortifies, its blood congeals, its force breaks down and it becomes Civilization. (90)

This parallel with Spengler comes about honestly. At the end of *Nunquam,* Durrell states that the "double-decker" is "a sort of novel-libretto based on the preface to *The Decline of the West"* (285).

Curiously, *The Revolt of Aphrodite* (as the one-volume edition of the two novels was titled) is one of the few of Durrell's fictions to take place in a time "now," placed distinctly within the context of the late sixties. The parallel themes of *Tunc* and *Nunquam* are the typical fodder of middle/late twentieth-century literature: existential crises of self-identity in a world which continually smothers all traces of any individuality; the decay of culture and *moeurs;* the Faustian/Frankensteinian dream of creating a human being from the detritus of an alchemy now bastardized into the new "science" of technology and politics; diplomatic/administrative powergaming; and the general decline in the quality of life.

Durrell explores these themes through a central trio of superintellectual protagonists—Felix, Julian, and Benedicta—ego, shadow, and anima respectively (God, Satan, and Virgin Mary). The basic thrust of the story is one of discovery. Felix is drawn slowly into the complex web of the mysterious "Firm," an arcane superpowerful capitalist machine with a finger in everybody's pie: the Firm acts as a metaphor for any secret society intent on control (for example, world governments, secret services, corporations, or of course civilization itself). But over and above the smooth panic of the plot there are the power-love struggles of the puppet-heroes. As in *Justine,* there is a central quartet of sexual relationships: Felix and Iolanthe, Iolanthe and Julian, Julian and Benedicta, Benedicta and Felix. In this particular "comedy of wheels within wheels," to use Durrell's phrase for similar structures in *The Black Book* (49), the same configurations of relationships occur that form the central battleground of *The Alexandria Quartet* and *The Avignon Quintet.* The hero moves from romantic/erotic entanglements with a "fallen" Goddess character to a more stable kind with a woman who seems softer, kinder, and more psychically sympathetic to the hero (the ego finds his anima at last!). The spiritual movement of love relationships in Durrell's oeuvre is a (nonlinear, multidimensional) journey toward transcendence ("The struggle is always for great consciousness," as

Pursewarden says in *Clea* (123)). But like the arrogant Christian mystics (John of the Cross, Eckhart, Augustine, Aquinas) the ego/hero/self must pass through a "dark night of the soul" (sleeping with Justine/Melissa/Iolanthe/Livia) before achieving the long-desired transcendence. But it is not as simple as that—for none of Durrell's characters is one-sided. All possess many (sometimes conflicting) personalities: "We each have as many destinies stacked up inside us as a melon has seeds. They live on 'in potentia,' so to speak. One does not know which will mature" (*Quinx* 169).

The characters in Durrell's three major works—*Tunc* and *Nunquam, The Alexandria Quartet,* and *The Avignon Quintet*—do in fact begin to merge. Durrell acknowledged this as his intention in *Clea:* "Arnauti, Pursewarden, Darley—like Past, Present and Future tense!" (154) and "the three women who also arranged themselves as if to represent the moods of the great verb, Love: Melissa, Justine and Clea" (154). Other relationships and events which are common to all the major works of Durrell include incestuous love affairs, shocking suicides out of the blue, strange, violent, and often disfiguring occurrences, and the ubiquitous brothel sequences which are always described in the most grotesque, cynical, ribald fashion. All of these events take place in *The Revolt of Aphrodite,* although they are not given the full resonance of meaning and emotion that so marks Durrell's best work with genius—insights moving backward and forward in time. By the time of *The Avignon Quintet,* Durrell has moved on to the remarkable idea that "all people are slowly becoming the same person" (*Quinx* 26). This astonishing concept closes up all the resonances, insights, and meanings of his previous fiction into one whole unit, a singular universe of life concentrated into one cell.

Central to much of Durrell's poetic architecture is the psychic dichotomy between the individual and the mass, between the artist and society, which finds its most potent expression through the aphorisms of his fictitious novelists (Arnauti, Pursewarden, Sutcliffe, Blanford). The hyperintellectual prosopopeias of these dry counterheroes offer the most honest and razor-sharp critiques on life, art, people, and love in the Durrell canon:

> Pursewarden: "My unkindest critics maintain that I am making lampshades out of human skin." (*Balthazar* 211)

> Sutcliffe: "A thermonuclear Jehovah is watching over us." (*Sebastian* 133)

The battle between the individual and the group (between the poet and the culture) finds another parallel in the strange mixture of cultural influences that makes Durrell such a fascinating writer. On one side is the rationalist-realist masculine train of thought; and on the other is Durrell's magnificent poetic sensibility, which impregnates his writing with mystical brilliants.

The two influences—the rational and the poetic—create a beguiling *mélange* of insight and meaning throughout Durrell's writings, not the least being his increasing use of Gnostic philosophy—which in his hands becomes intermeshed with his basic metaphysical stance: the quietist Taoist, where "genius is silence" (*Quinx* 165). The Gnostic religious theories form a sizeable part of *The Alexandria Quartet;* but as an undercurrent to a glossy psychological thriller such as *The Revolt of Aphrodite,* the result is very strange indeed. Characters in Durrell's novels have always had an acidic hypertrophic intellectual apothegm ready for every occasion, but to have characters spouting verbose convolutions concerning archaic mysteries, such as Gnosticism (which has been dead as a mass religion for centuries) is very, very odd. For instance, when Felix finally meets up with the elusive head of the Firm on a mountainside in Switzerland, Julian comes out with the following wonderfully unreal (yet historically and philosophically accurate) peroration:

> Felix, it's my belief that you can touch the quiddity, the nub of the idea only if you realize that it comes out of an art of associations of which the primal genetic blueprint in the strictest sense is the uniting of the couple, man and woman. (*Nunquam* 87)

The spiritual marriage of man and woman, the unification of opposites found in Gnosticism and later in alchemy was explored in depth by Jung in *Mysterium Coniunctionis.* But Durrell develops these ideas in the face of pure Freudian psychoanalytical theory to mean that immortality cannot be found through a mere coupling but only in the sacred voluptuousness of the shared orgasm. These quasi-Gnostic, quasi-Taoist ideas occur throughout *The Revolt of Aphrodite,* but mature in *The Avignon Quintet,* in this passage from *Quinx* for instance:

> Reality has several dialects, and the most powerful are sexual ones. The sexual code, if ignited between two people who recognize how momentous an act it is, will automatically be conducted with reserve and timidity. "Of course," said Sutcliffe approvingly, "because the seed of all meditation is in the orgasm itself!" (97)

These powerful theories (based partially on Tantric and Taoist sex-mysticism) are discussed further by Durrell with Jolan Chang. An account of their curious meeting in Provence can be found in *A Smile in the Mind's Eye.*

Among Durrell's many other laudable capacities are his healthy dislike of the English, as in his calling for a banding together of "Poets and Idealists against Protestant shopkeepers" (*Quinx* 199). Then there is his accurate apprehension that Christianity perpetuates the two worst crimes known to mankind: the psychotic exaltation of the ego and the prolongation of the over-simplified religion of dualism (that dangerous theosophy which reduces multifarious reality into two elements, such as good and evil). Indeed, Durrell's intelligent and sensitive assimilation of Eastern spiritualities is most welcome in a culture clogged with the dross of philistine occultism, astrology, UFOlogy, fake cults, sinister religions, gurus, and other hokums and ologies dressed up as genuine magic. Durrell's over-reliance on orthodox Freudian "theology" is perhaps the only complaint one can level against his general philosophic outlook: love, not sex, is god.

"Tread softly, for here you stand / On miracle ground, boy" (*Collected Poems* 111). Durrell shares a distaste for counterfeit culture with one of his greatest influences. D. H. Lawrence's nature-mystical religion of the "sacred body" features strongly in Durrell's work, as it does in Henry Miller's, where the "sacred body" appears as a chapter title in *The World of Lawrence*. And it was Lawrence who also inspired the other two of that "happy trinity of lovers," Anaïs Nin and Henry Miller, to write. The massive influence of the literary giant who "fucked a flame into being," to quote from one of the many famous lines in *Lady Chatterly's Lover* (316), can be felt through *The Quartet,* and *The Revolt of Aphrodite,* right up to the last pages of *Quinx.*

Sutcliffe said grimly, "Sex—the human animal's larder" (200). But Durrell was always a much softer writer than those bright luminaries of obscenity, Lawrence and Miller. His affectionately irreverent appraisals of Lawrence, suitably infrequent, are often spoken through a character (the writer's defense against critics). Pursewarden: *"My dear DHL. This side of idolatry—I am simply trying not to copy your habit of building a Taj Mahal around anything as simple as a good f—k"* (*Balthazar* 94). The unconscious Jungian multiplicity of Anaïs Nin was more his style—though he wouldn't have admitted it at the time.

Durrell's real literary parent is Cavafy, that brilliant supersensuous poet of El Iskandariya with his blend of eroticism and gnostalgia, best illustrated in the gorgeous poem "In the Evening," surely one of the most superb pieces of poetry created in this century, along with other mythical and beautiful poetry such as Rilke's *Sonnets for Orpheus* and Graves's "The Snapped Thread." Cavafy's gnomic genius is the inverted homosexual spiritual inheritor of the haptic preternatural supplications of the woman-poet Sappho: "TO EROS / You burn me." Durrell is the heir of Cavafy's erotic mnemonics (those poems filled with the hot dust of the blue-white Mediterranean landscape), a Classical sensibility that somehow mixes memory with desire. The mnemonic sense provides a rich range of resonances throughout Durrell's poetry and prose—every place, every gesture, and every emotion has many equivalents creating harmonies backward into the tapestry of time and experience. The trick is to integrate memories, then forget them:

> Yes, the past now had attained a curious nervous density, a weight which was not composed (as one might suppose) of multiple nostalgias. It was rich and full, plump as an autumn fruit. It had been so fully lived that there was nothing about it one could dare to regret. (*Monsieur* 19)

Some poets are brilliant (pitifully few, however). Durrell is one of those true poets.

The "spirit of place" has always played a large part in the psychospiritual content of Durrell's edifications. Yet his work has a cosmopolitan feel to it, being partially the result of roseate pantheistic travels through a "heraldic" universe. Durrell's descriptions of landscapes are among his most memorable sequences, for which he is rightly famous. From the seventh paragraph of *Justine:*

> Notes for landscape-tones. . . . Long sequences of tempera. Light filtered through the essence of lemons. An air full of brick-dust—sweet smelling brick-dust and the odor of hot pavements slaked with water. Light damp clouds, earth-bound, yet seldom bringing rain. Upon this squirt dust-red, dust-green, chalk-mauve and watered crimson-lake. (12)

And from the beginning of one of his famed "island books," *Bitter Lemons:*

> These thoughts belong to Venice at dawn, seen from the deck of the ship which is to carry me down through the islands to Cyprus; a Venice wobbling in a thousand fresh-water reflections, cool as a jelly. It was as if some great master, stricken by dementia, had burst his whole color-box against the sky to deafen the inner eye of the world. (15)

Places are deeply emotionally important to a poet like Durrell, and the feelings surrounding them become crystallized and illuminated when the reluctant departure separates the lover from his landscape:

> To really appreciate a place or time—to extract the poignant essence of it—one should see it in the light of a departure, a leavetaking. It was the sense of farewell in things which impregnated them with this phantom of nostalgia so important for the young artist. (*Livia* 164)

Durrell's perception is sometimes so delicate and beautiful that it shoots way past Housman's test for true poetry—"Does it make the hairs of one's chin bristle if one repeats it silently while shaving?"—as paraphrased in Graves's *The White Goddess* (21). Listen:

> The most haunting thing about human reality is that there is always something unexpected happening in the room next door about which one will only find out later on! Moreover it will prove surprising, totally unpredictable, and more often than not unpalatable! (*Sebastian* 178)

Sometimes, of course, Durrell is ruthless, incisive: "In a new age of plastic caryatids we shall be permitted to change women in mid-scream" (*Quinx* 52). There are echoes here of Henry Miller's blistering polemics that stink of wombs, ecstasy, death, and decay in *Tropic of Cancer*. Again: "She was beautiful with her swarthy rose-black skin and apricot-fashioned mouth sticky as a fresh hymen—the silkworm's tacky passage across a mulberry leaf" (*Constance* 360). Here are poetic economies at their best. Consistently, Lawrence Durrell has written the best poetic prose in English this side of the last Ice Age; and because he is a great writer, his less-than-brilliant work is superior to many authors' most concerted efforts. But of course, writing is just writing, after a while, merely "A paper recreation of lost loves" (*Collected Poems* 234). And Durrell, as Conon, knows that "the past harms no one who lies close to the Gods" (108).

To transcend art is the poet's true psychic objective—to throw the whole package into the trashcan and get on with living—to let slip the baggage weight of the masquerade, the labyrinth, the charade that passes for "culture" or "life" and to start living life for real with all its sweetest passions and mnemonic ecstasies. We doubt, though, that either Durrell or one of his creations would agree with Nabokov that "literature and butterflies are the two sweetest passions known to man." Though as the young Huxleyesque novelist Aubrey Blanford so gorgeously and innocently says: "a plea for bliss as being the object of art. Am I talking rubbish? It's euphoria, then!" (*Quinx* 16).

Transcendence is the prime objective of the poet-artist-mystic-lover who has discerned and recognized the "essence of things" through a cathartic process that strips away meaningless culture to reveal the naked soul. The being is left with only the most valuable of knowledge, of experience: among these the most important is love. After this catharsis, the romance with life can begin; and reality becomes inverted into the sublime negative philosophy of Taoism, Confucianism, and Buddhism—where multiplicity in unity is a practical reality and not just another dream away.

"True poetic practice," writes Robert Graves, "implies a mind so miraculously attuned and illuminated that it can form words, by a chain of more-than-coincidences, into a living entity—a poem that goes about on its own (for centuries after the author's death, perhaps) affecting readers with its stored magic" (*White Goddess* 490). Durrell's magic words will live on for a long, long time. In a letter to Henry Miller, Durrell said he had "developed a newish kind of prose—not surrealistic but gnomic. It is lucid and yet enigmatic—I think nearer to me as a person than I have got yet." He was writing of *The Alexandria Quartet,* in which he was "looking for a diamond-bright lucidity which will be QUOTABLE and MEMORABLE, not because of marvelous metaphors and bright lights, but because the thread of the EXPERIENCE shines through, as when you turn a tapestry round" (Wickes 106). And of course, he has succeeded magnificently: *The Alexandria Quartet* is one of the most densely packed fictional works in literature, with a plethora of luminous insights on every page. "D has begat" a most eminently memorable poesie out of the urban desuetude of the twentieth century. "Try to keep them, poet, / those erotic visions of yours," (48) wrote Cavafy; but the painful longings eventually slip away (like the Gnostic

Orphite snake's skin) from the poet-mystic who is interested in spiritual-emotional content rather than form, which is always transitory.

In an epigraph to the poem "Conon in Exile," Durrell writes: "I want my total poetic work to add up as a kind of tapestry of people, some real, some imaginary" (*Collected Poems* 107). Durrell's characters bleed into one (many of them even have similar-sounding names—Affad, Akkad). The trick is not to be fooled into thinking that a merging into unity implies a loss of infinity or immortality or even multiplicity. *Tunc* and *Nunquam*, though mythic, are limited by their violently delineated context, but by the end of *The Quintet*, Durrell's last major work of fiction, all the characters are back together again with their masks, personas, disguises, costumes, facts, lies, truths, all dancing their way into the labyrinthine caves where lies the Gnostic megatreasure, a symbolic journey into the womb of the Earth / the primal chaos / the Underworld / the psychoanalytic couch to touch the Grail, to talk to God. In "The Anecdotes," Durrell writes:

> Sometime we shall all come together
> And it will be a time to put a stop
> To this little rubbing together of minimal words.

> (*Collected Poems* 206)

In this postatomic postreal world (in which nothing is sacred—two world wars have seen to that), it is marvelous that one can still find a writer who is creating poetry that is simply magnificent, "glittering," dazzling, profound, and spiritually enriching.[3] Durrell's real genius is that he has created a whole new form of novel writing, wonderfully adapted to a serious investigation into the nature of human experience. No one else has gone further into the human heart or written better or more glorious, hugely enjoyable prose and poetry than Lawrence Durrell. "Comedy or tragedy? Which side up, old boy?" (*Monsieur* 250).

Notes

1. The expression is from part 16 of "The Anecdotes" (*Collected Poems* 213):

> Yet the thing can be done, as you say, simply
> By sitting and waiting, the mystical leap
> Is only a figure for it, it involves not daring
> But the patience, being gored, not to cry out.
> But perhaps even the desire itself is dying.
> I should like that: to make an end of it.

2. Rebecca West wrote in *The Young Rebecca*: "Sex, which ought to be an incident of life, is the obsession of the well-fed world" (119).

3. One of the many sublimely exaggerated notices (this from *The Times Literary Supplement)* on *The Alexandria Quartet* proclaimed: "If ever a work bore an instantly recognizable signature on every sentence, this is it. In fact it is a formidable, glittering achievement."

Works Cited

Brancusi, Constantin. *Constantin Brancusi.* Trans. David Lewis. New York: Wittenborn, 1957.

Cavafy, C. P. *Collected Poems.* Trans. Keeley and Sherrard. Ed. George Savidis. London: Routledge & Kegan Paul, 1974.

Durrell, Lawrence. *Balthazar.* London: Faber, 1963.

———. *The Black Book.* Paris: Olympia, 1959.

———. *Clea.* London: Faber, 1961.

———. *Collected Poems 1931–1974.* London: Faber, 1980.

———. *Constance, or Solitary Practices.* London: Faber, 1982.

———. *Justine.* London: Faber, 1979.

———. *Livia, or Buried Alive.* London: Faber, 1978.

———. *Monsieur, or The Prince of Darkness.* London: Faber, 1974.

———. *Nunquam.* London: Faber, 1970.

———. *Quinx, or the Ripper's Tale.* London: Faber, 1985.

———. *Sebastian, or Ruling Passions.* London: Faber, 1983.

———. *A Smile in the Mind's Eye.* London: Wildwood, 1980.

———. *Tunc.* London: Faber, 1968

Durrell, Lawrence, and Henry Miller *Lawrence Durrell–Henry Miller: A Private Correspondence.* Ed. George Wickes. New York: Dutton, 1963.

Eliot, Thomas Stearns. *The Complete Poems and Plays of T. S. Eliot.* London: Faber, 1969.

Fraser, G. S. *Lawrence Durrell: A Study.* London: Faber, 1968.

Forster, E. M. *Aspects of the Novel.* Ed. Oliver Stallybrass. Harmondsworth: Penguin, 1974.

Graves, Robert. *The White Goddess.* London: Faber, 1948.

Greek Lyric Poetry. Trans. Willis Barnstone. New York: Schocken, 1972.

Jung, Carl Gustav. *Mysterium Coniunctionis. Collected Works* Vol. 14. London: Routledge and Kegan Paul.

Lawrence, D. H. *Lady Chatterly's Lover.* Harmondsworth: Penquin, 1960.

Miller, Henry. *The World of Lawrence: A Passionate Appreciation.* London: Calder, 1985.

———. *Sexus.* London: Calder & Boyars, 1969.

Spengler, Oswald. *The Decline of the West.* Trans. C. F. Atkinson. Abr. ed. Eds. H. Werner and A. Helps. London: Allen and Unwin, 1961.

West, Rebecca. *The Young Rebecca.* Ed. Jane Marcus. London: Macmillan, 1982.

17

Durrell's Major Works:
Classic Forms for Our Time

Lee J. Lemon

Where the devil do we put Lawrence Durrell's major novels? Modernist? Post-modernist? Experimental? Metafictional? In typical fashion, his own answer, from the introductory "Note" to *Balthazar,* opens rather than closes the question.

In order to explain the strange thing his readers held in their hands, he described *The Alexandria Quartet* as an attempt to "discover a morphological form one might appropriately call 'classical'—for our time." But why should we need help to recognize a form that is "classical" for our own time?

The problem of classifying Durrell's major novels is not as sterile an exercise as it might seem. The point is neither what intellectual news and fictional techniques Durrell learned from which twentieth-century inventors nor whether he reported accurately—as if he were a student we were testing.

The question is important because, as T. S. Eliot reminds us in "Tradition and the Individual Talent," the works of writers—especially great writers—are not judged in isolation. They are judged and survive in a curious double relation with tradition: they must fit into a tradition even as they alter it. A great work, and Durrell's major novels are indeed great, must both share its character with a community of works and impose that character upon them.

In the following pages, I shall try to describe both that community of novels which for post–World War II Anglo-American readers makes up the classic contemporary form (it may be more Durrellian and it will certainly be more correct to say *a* classic contemporary form) and to sketch the role *The Alexandria Quartet* and *The Avignon Quintet* play in it. But we are back to that paradox—"classic contemporary form." Offhand, I can think of four distinct ways of describing "classic contemporary form." The description most useful here sees a classic literary form as dependent on those literary means most appropriate to embody deeply held values, assumptions, and concerns common to many of those likely to read the literature. This is not to imply that all members of a community of readers share all of the same values, nor that the community of readers is defined by nationality, historical period, or even class. Such a community is an *ad hoc* group of individuals who tend to respond positively—or at least to be willing to entertain—a loosely associated group of values, and who find values related to that group at least provisionally interesting. The values may be moral, social, psychological, philosophical, literary, or whatever. We recognize, for example, that the ideas, beliefs, values, or attitudes that seem perfectly appropriate in the works of one period, one nation, one intellectual community, are inappropriate (but definitely not impossible) in those of another.

A classic form, then, is a form appropriate for the expression of the values recognized (at least provisionally) as significant by a community of readers. To give a simple example, the longish codas of much earlier fiction, in which justice is precisely meted out, are likely to be part of the classic form of the narratives of an age which sees a just God as a kind of moral scorekeeper; even individuals in the community who did not share that belief were likely to be more tolerant of poetic justice than we moderns—who tend to find it embarrassingly naive.

Before sketching the values on which the classic contemporary novel form is based, I must put one more piece into place. It is the assumption that one of the purposes of literature (I would say the highest purpose) is not to iterate values but rather to display their human significance. Thomas Aquinas taught Renaissance Catholics how to think about the world; Dante showed us the human implications of what it means to live in a world in which people thought and felt that way. The most endearing literature neither merely repeats beliefs nor necessarily creates them; rather, it shows—to use Durrell's word—their "poignance." If we read Dickens for an intellectual understanding of the Victorian family structure, we read him badly; if we read him in part to share the human experience of being a member of such a family, we read him for what he does incomparably. Joyce's *A Portrait of the Artist as a Young Man* will give much information about Irish Catholic retreats led by Jesuits at the turn of the century—but there are better and more accurate sources for that information. There is no better source for the feeling of what it must have been like for a sensitive young man to have experienced a retreat.

Let us agree, then, that the classic literature of a period invites the reader to share the human experience of living according to the values which dominate that period. How does it feel to be a warrior returning to Greece after ten years of fighting at Troy? How does it feel to be a proud young man like Prince Hal, raised in a society whose values include both jealous insistence upon one's own aristocratic rights and subservience to king and father?

And, more to our purposes, how does it feel to be a human being in the last half of the twentieth century? How does it feel to be a human being subject to the frustrations and opportunities that characterize our society? How does it feel to live in the shadow of Einstein and Freud and multinational corporations and easy access to more variety of taste and standards and values and experience than our ancestors dared dream?

The second paragraph of the "Note" to *Balthazar* poses still another very nice problem. Durrell writes that "modern literature offers us no Unities, so I have turned to science and am trying to complete a four-decker novel whose form is based on the relativity proposition." The irony, of course, is that the relativity proposition is partly responsible for our inability to find the "unities." There is, the relativity proposition tells us, no one way to truth, no center upon which we may stand with absolute confidence.

The loss of a center in modern belief has been discussed so often—cause, effects on themes of fiction, effects on forms of fiction, and so on—that it is useless to belabor the issue. I want, rather, to make a more specific argument. It is that until roughly the midpoint of this century, the classic form of the then modern novel facilitated the expression of anguish at the loss of the "unities." More specifically, the Jamesian experiments in point of view and the tortuous sentences—which surround the meaning but never quite get to its center—are appropriate means to express how it felt to live in a world in which social and moral values were becoming increasingly ambiguous. Conrad's experiments with Marlow suggest that the only center we have is the point of view from which we perceive reality—and that that is not *the* center but *a* center. One way of describing Marlow's understanding of the horror in *Heart of Darkness,* for example, is to note that there is no center other than himself, his own re-sources—and that is merely *a* center in a vast and uncaring universe. Joyce creates forms that enable us to share the anguish of the young Dedalus as he breaks from the false centers of race, religion, language, nationality, and fam-ily, and as he suffers the pain of searching for a new center, a new father figure. And Hemingway's protagonists nostalgically ache for the old unities even as the style in which he describes them demonstrates lack of faith in the absolutes in which they were based. His search for a substitute in a kind of stoicism and a faith in the particular are not greatly different from the supports that Conrad gave Marlow.

But in 1946, Viking published Malcolm Cowley's "Introduction" to *The Portable Faulkner,* and the expectations of the community of readers began to change. Hemingway's stock began to drop, Faulkner's to rise. The isolation of the Hemingway hero (despite the allusive title of *For Whom the Bell Tolls*) is replaced in Faulkner's world by a sense of community, and the forms differ accordingly. Hemingway's descriptions of exteriors are replaced by Faulkner's passionate portrayal of the interior lives of his characters. And again, the forms differ accordingly.

Moreover, a kind of faith runs throughout Faulkner's novels, a faith that life may sometimes be worth the struggle no matter how desperate and painful the struggle might be. Put another way, in a world in which the center is lost, Hemingway seemed awed by death. Asked why so many of his works ended with death, he remarked that any human story, if pursued far enough, ends that way. Faulkner's works, on the other hand, show a nice balance of life and death—some emphasize one, some the other, and some, like *Light in August,* are shaped to remind us that each is part of human experience and that we must be equally in awe of each.

The faith in Faulkner's novels is nothing like the faith of the earlier fictions. Throughout the classic novels of the eighteenth and nineteenth centuries, the forms always make space for a safety net. God will mark Joseph Andrews with a strawberry birthmark and take care that Mr. Wilson arrives in time to discover it; Providence or some principle of order will assure that each of the Bennet daughters gets the man she deserves; if David Copperfield just works hard enough and remains decent enough, society will eventually reward him with the comforts of a good wife and a respectable income. (The famous revision of the ending of *Great Expectations* illustrates what happens when an author attempts to violate the values of his community of readers.)

Faulkner recognizes that the safety nets available to characters in earlier fiction (the same nets that Hardy's Jude fell through and that Dedalus had to flee) are badly worn. The ambiguities Faulkner presents to his characters and readers make those presented by James read like a primer.

Some time shortly after World War II, a definite shift in the attitudes of Anglo-American readers began. The classic novels of the first half of this century were, to a great extent, designed to show the pain of living in a world without a center. Faulkner's works, which I am treating as transitional, seem shaped to show the possibility of nobility in such a world (and, of course, the conditions of that nobility in such a world or lack of it). But transition to what? What is the classic form emerging after World War II?

A look at some of the novels that felt newest then and have survived best provides part of the answer. Within a decade after the publication of *The Portable Faulkner,* Ellison published *The Invisible Man;* Bellow, *The Adventures of Augie March;* and Barth, *The Floating Opera.* Perhaps as much as any novel except *Jude the Obscure, The Invisible Man* is about the disappearance of what I have called safety nets. It is, in fact, a peculiar kind of *Bildungsroman*— peculiar because it is less the story of the development of its major character than the story of the failure of the individuals and systems that traditionally would aid that development. Like Jude, the Invisible Man tries education and hard work; instead of the church, he has the Brotherhood. Near the end, he must reject the various paths represented by Ras and Rinehart. Finally, he must shed his past—so he hibernates, knowing that when he awakens he will be something special, but has no idea what that something special will be. He still has no name because he has no identity, no center. The kaleidoscopic mélange of style in the novel reflects the swirling confusion of the world in which the Invisible Man must shed his identities. In fact, one of the subthemes of the novel is the major theme of *The Avignon Quintet*—the protean nature of the human ego. As the novel's last sentence reminds us, although *The Invisible Man* is a Black novel, "on the lower frequencies" it speaks for all of us.

Augie March is certainly no Invisible Man, but both share many of the same problems. Augie must find his values in a world in which—since ultimately they amount to the same—there are either no values or too many sets of values. Like the ending of *The Invisible Man,* the ending of *The Adventures of Augie March* is more an affirmation of a possibility of wholeness than an example of it. In that respect, the affirmation that ends both novels is much like the affirmation that ends *The Alexandria Quartet*. There is no center; there are no solutions. But there is absolute faith in the potential inherent in just living. To present a solution—in the manner of classic novels of the eighteenth and nineteenth centuries, in which an acceptance of the mainstream social values of marriage and a modest but adequate income is the ideal solution to all life's problems—would be to impose a new center, to imply an absolute certainty about the proper values in life. And to do that would be to deny the question that modern fiction has to answer: Can we thrive in a world without a center, a world in which the unities are lost?

Barth's *Floating Opera* takes quite a different tack, but comes to an ending compatible with those of the other two novels. Todd Andrews, protagonist and narrator, is as much an existential man as Camus's Stranger. An intellectual, the circumstances of his life (a heart that may stop at any moment, a battlefield encounter, his father's suicide), or even matters of lesser importance have convinced him that all things are equally valueless. He plans a dramatic suicide; but in reviewing the notes he keeps, he makes a startling discovery—one that is at once painfully obvious and that simultaneously reverses completely the morbidity of orthodox existentialism. If there is no reason for anything, including living, there is equally no reason for dying. With just a bit of extrapolation (justified, I believe, by the joyousness of much of Barth's later work), unhappiness and happiness are each equally unreasonable. The only sensible thing to do, then, is to exercise our existentialist prerogative and choose. In this context, the choice is obvious. As Todd Andrews realizes in Barth's *Letters,* although it is true that in the long run (the very long run—Barth takes the cosmic view here) nothing has value, in the short run, the scale on which we live, everything has value.

Note the lack of specificity. It is not life in the country, marriage to Squire B or Fanny, flight from Ireland, the Lawrentian discovery of good sex, or the discovery of an absolute set of rules for life. It is everything. If there is no center, there is an infinity of centers. If there are no absolute rules limiting our potential, our potential is absolutely unlimited. In less grandiose but more human terms, life is valuable simply because it is the experience of life.

By the mid 1950s, then, we had a community of novels whose reception by critics and readers alike suggested acceptance of values unacceptable in previous decades. It is as if a group of our finest novelists had individually concluded that fiction had sufficiently bewailed our loss of a center. Time had come to recognize that those centers, those values, those unities, were dead. And it was time to get on with life. A community of readers, without whom a classic tradition within literature is meaningless, seemed ready to agree.

In England, perhaps largely because of World War II and the devastating political, economic, and social effects of its aftermath, the development was generally just a bit slower. Many of the best postwar talents were angry young men, a generation of writers whose experience in England seemed to belie belief in a world of unlimited possibilities. Others—like C. P. Snow and Angus Wilson—seemed motivated less by anger than by a need to chronicle social conditions. The result was little formal experimentation within the works of either group. A few novelists, most notably Iris Murdoch, seemed alive to the sort of epistemological and personal issues raised by our new sciences—depth psychology and relativistic physics—and accordingly strove to develop the appropriate forms. But with no significant exception I can think of, even the most "modern" of the English novels of the early 1950s failed to appreciate the richness of life in a world without unities. We may speculate that those English writers most inclined to experiment were subject not only to the bleakness of England's future, but also heavily impressed by the pessimism associated with French existentialism.

It was not until the late 1950s and 1960s that British novelists were ready for a more optimistic reading of the implications of relativistic physics and depth psychology. Durrell's *Justine,* Doris Lessing's *Golden Notebook* (and in 1969, *The Four-Gated City*), and John Fowles's *The French Lieutenant's Woman* explored both the loss of the old unities and the fact that the loss enabled at least the possibility of freedom.

We have here two curious formal problems, both stemming from the fact that thematically the classic contemporary form I am describing requires that the protagonist be both content (if not actually happy) and free. As a form, the novel has difficulty with both contentment and freedom. One of the truer clichés is that contented protagonists do not make for good fiction. Perhaps the only essential ingredient of a story is conflict, and conflict tends to make protagonists unhappy. Conflict must be resolved. Traditionally, a story begins when a source of conflict intrudes and ends when the source of conflict is overcome. Unless the protagonist is seriously threatened, we are likely to feel little suspense or even interest. Hence, in fictions with a positive theme the happy ending is also a stable ending—the way has been found, the unity discovered, the center established. And the protagonist will live, without substantial change, happily ever after.

And this leads to the second problem. Within the body of the novel, only minor characters are allowed to live long in contentment—often in those sections of the novel we skim most rapidly. They function, like Mr. Wilson in *Joseph Andrews,* as a kind of example of the life the hero, if he is successful, will snuggle into. But the problem is that an example is a pattern, an embodiment of a set of rules, a mold that restricts freedom. As a result, none of the protagonists of the novels in the classic contemporary form have guides who represent the ideal. Martha Quest and Anna Wulf must find their own ways because they have no adequate models on which to pattern their lives; Herzog has a series of "reality instructors" who introduce him to the unpleasant aspects of life and shield him from its richer possibilities; Giles Goat-Boy, whose mentors (including the frequently wise Max Spielman) are imperfect, will become a prophet who is in many ways unlike all past prophets. Fowles's Sarah Woodruff and Daniel Martin must find their own ways to their freedom; poor Charles is left at the end of *The French Lieutenant's Woman* drifting toward it, presumably still bemused by Sarah. Conchis, the Magus, gives Nicholas Urfe not a pattern for life but the possibility of a set of attitudes toward it. We do not know, at the end of these novels, what the protagonists will do, what choices they will eventually make. But we know that they are free, and we know that their choices will be made freely.

If this analysis holds, even in outline, we can describe the characteristic features of this particular classic form. Not all characteristics will necessarily be present in any one novel because a form is not a recipe but a loose association of techniques. And, of course, individual novels will exhibit their own peculiar variations and techniques. What follows, then, is not an existentialist definition—even that unity has been lost—but rather a Wittgensteinian cluster of characteristics.

1) Our classic contemporary form will be a variety of the *Bildungsroman* because it will be concerned primarily with showing the development of the protagonist as he or she learns how to cope with the loss of unities in the modern world.

2) The protagonist will often be somewhat older than the usual Bildungsroman protagonist, I suspect because he or she must learn how to become independent of society rather than dependent upon it; and that lesson requires a certain ripeness.

3) One of the major themes will be epistemological because the loss of

unities is a loss of orientation. The source of our particular loss of orientation results from the post-Kantian disappearance of absolutes (of which modern physics and mathematics perhaps offer the most conclusive demonstrations) that placed human experience at the center of all knowledge, and the subsequent extrapolations of depth psychology which either immensely complicated or put into doubt the notion of a stable human ego.

4) Structurally, emphasis will be upon the demonstration of the extent of the loss, its nature, and the problems the protagonist faces in responding to it. Thematically, however, the emphasis will be not upon the lost unities but upon the achievement of freedom. That is, the Invisible Man, Anna Wulf, Daniel Martin, Sarah Woodruff, Herzog, Henderson, the positive characters in Barth's fiction, and our other protagonists will, because stories require conflict, spend most of their time in the novel struggling for whatever freedom they attain—whether it is as muted as the "cure" of Anna Wulf or as exultant as Darley's new beginning at the end of *Clea*. This point needs emphasis because we can become so easily overwhelmed by the intensity of the struggle that we minimize the victory, because the rewards of the victory are intangible, and because freedom is an invitation to danger rather than a promise of safety.

5) Because the victory brings not the security of absolutes but the perils of freedom, this particular form of the Bildungsroman must avoid even the suggestion that there is an ideal pattern of life for either the protagonist or the reader. As a result, all guides will be flawed. Anna Wulf learns from Mother Sugar, Nicholas Urfe from Conchis, Darley from Pursewarden—to cite just three examples—but none of the mentors is a model. Mother Sugar is merely an analyst, interpreting the omens. Conchis has created so many identities for himself that he has none that Nicholas might imitate (Conchis, although more sober, is in many respects like Burlingame in Barth's *Sot-Weed Factor*). Pursewarden's judgment waxes hot and cold; Balthazar is a friend but not an example, and until the end Clea is—like Darley—still earning her freedom.

6) For the same reason (the eventual freedom of the protagonist) conclusions are inconclusive, endings are open. The Invisible Man is still hibernating in his coal cellar, awaiting his metamorphosis. We do not not know if Urfe and Alison will get together. We know that Anna Wulf has written "Free Women," but that is past business and tells us little about her future. Herzog has stopped writing his letters, for a while, and Henderson has begun a new career. We are given our choice of endings in *The French Lieutenant's Woman,* and so can never be certain whether or not Sarah and Charles marry, or (even if we take the third ending as most likely) whether or not Charles attains his freedom. We know that Darley will write and Clea paint, but not what kind of lives they will choose.

7) Because of the relativity theme, the novels will include various means for forcing the protagonists and/or the reader to reassess not only the interpreta-

tion of events but, in many cases, even their factuality. The means will range from such very large-scale structural devices as repetition of events from alternate points of view—including multiple narrators, and such interlinear texts as Balthazar's Interlinear, "The Shadow of the Third" in *The Golden Notebook,* even Dr. Grogan's proto-Freudian remarks about female hysteria in *The French Lieutenant's Woman*—to inclusions of discussions of relativity, to such small-scale motifs as mirrors, glasses, eyes, (missing, blind, etc.).

8) Use of such devices and other considerations will often necessitate chronological displacements. The most significant effect of the displacement will be to juxtapose events in order to require the reader to compare or contrast them—thereby reinforcing the relativistic necessity of viewing the world from multiple perspectives.

9) Point of view will often be limited—first person, limited third, or shifting among a number of limited narrators. An omniscient narrator (except, ironically, as in *Mountolive*—ironic because after two volumes the reader has available certain information apparently not available to the "omniscient" narrator) is not suitable in a fictional world that denies omniscience.

10) The classic contemporary novel will sometimes be self-referential. In a relativistic universe, all knowledge of reality is, in a sense, fictional—a product of a particular stance rather than a universal view. Reminders that the events of the novel itself are fictions, in place of the usual illusion of reality more orthodox novels attempt, help substantiate the relativistic theme. Moreover, the form is better served by what might be called a radical honesty rather than by an attempt to create an illusion because the epistemological theme calls into question the nature of all reality. To summarize both points: if, in Derrida's very apt formulation, all the world is text, the novelist reflects and clarifies the nature of the world outside the fiction by drawing attention to the textuality of the work.

11) The general effect of such means will be to force the reader to do what stage directors call a "double take"—a superficial reaction closely followed by another, quite different, reaction. The style of *The Invisible Man* frequently undercuts the naivete of the narrator. Lessing's varying descriptions of characters and events in the four notebooks and in "Free Women" repeatedly force us to revise our initial impressions. The narrator of *The French Lieutenant's Woman* repeatedly lets us make one evaluation of an event—say, Sarah's bedding with another woman—then tells us that our initial reaction is improper. The second half of *Giles Goat-Boy* turns into one of the longest double takes on record, and Burlingame in *The Sot-Weed Factor* (like his descendants in *Letters*) constantly keeps other characters and readers off base. Durrell in both *The Alexandria Quartet* and *The Avignon Quintet* is the master of the double take: there is no major character in *The Alexandria Quartet* whom the reader does not have to reevaluate; even after four volumes, the "Workpoints" at the

end of *Clea* suggests still further reevaluations. And the self-referentiality of the initial fiction within the fiction and the interweaving of characters from various levels of the fictions in *The Quintet* give rise to a similar need for reassessment.

12) Although not required, humor often appears and serves two general thematic functions. Humor, by its nature, requires a double perspective, and awareness of all sides of an incongruity. In the relativistic universe of these novels, the title of Pursewarden's trilogy—*God Is a Humorist*—is perfectly appropriate. The universe of the humorist is the world of the unexpected, of the uncertain, of multiple possibilities. To be moral in such a universe is to accept the multiplicity of possibilities with delight and gratitude and responsibility. Moreover, the humor makes the multiplicity of possibilities inviting both to the reader as reader and the reader as possible convert. That is, not only is the humor fun in itself, it suggests to the reader that the breakthrough into freedom will be enjoyable. Despite the justice that prevails in Doris Lessing's more visionary works, to provide a negative example, her lack of humor in presenting her vision contributes to an atmosphere of drabness that makes her utopias peculiarly uninviting. Barth, Fowles sometimes, and Durrell use their humor to persuade us that freedom is not only our heritage, it might even be our delight.

Up to this point, I have concentrated primarily on the ramifications of relativity, with only an occasional glance at the implications of depth psychology. If Freud taught us that the human personality is a many-layered mentality, Lacan radicalized Freud by arguing that we never get to the bottom layer because there is no bottom layer, that the human psyche is less an entity, however structured, than refractions of a series of events. It has been argued, persuasively, I believe, that relativity theory and Lacanian psychology (to give particular names to what in actuality is a general Weltanschauung) are special developments of a profound ontological scepticism. Not surprisingly, then, the effects of both on the form of the novel are in some ways similar.

The disappearance of the stable ego, however, does lead to some special problems, some special techniques, and some change of emphasis on the techniques already discussed. Art, by its very nature, requires organization. Even if the theme is chaos, the necessary particularity of art requires that it be this chaos rather than that chaos. And, of course, the very presence of the theme of chaos necessitates organization around that theme. In the relativistic form which I have described, the fiction is held together by the developing stability of the ego of the protagonist—hence the picaresque structure of such novels as *The Invisible Man* and *The Adventures of Augie March*.

In older fictions—*Wuthering Heights* and *The Turn of the Screw* come immediately to mind—the uncertainty about the ego of the characters is interesting in large part precisely because it is a mystery that we feel can and should be solved. The uncertainty exists against a background of certainty. Mrs. Dean's narration in *Wuthering Heights* exists against a background of the tradition of omniscient narrators, of narrators who cannot but tell the whole truth. The uncertainties about the stability of the egos who play major roles in James's short novel are so unsettling because in large part we expect the uncertainties to be resolved. The effect of uncertainty about the stability of the ego in past fictions has been to make readers feel, "Isn't *that* mysterious?" In our classic contemporary form, the effect has been to make us feel, "Isn't everything, including humanity, mysterious?"

As yet, unless a number of very relevant novels that I do not know of are lurking somewhere, we have neither a community of novels which explore the uncentered ego nor (if reception of *The Avignon Quintet* is indicative) a sizeable community of critics and lay readers prepared for it. Most of the post–World War II novels we have considered thus far have, in effect, been built around a search for an ego strong enough and flexible enough to survive in a universe in which the traditional unities no longer provide support. The theme could, for example, legitimately be read into *The Invisible Man, Herzog* and *Henderson the Rain King, The Golden Notebook,* and *The French Lieutenant's Woman* and *Daniel Martin,* most of the work of Barth, and even (with some qualification) *The Alexandria Quartet.*

There are hints that a new classic form is birthing: Barth's *Letters,* which makes explicit the Proteus theme implicit in his earlier work; much of Günter Grass's work since *Flounder,* some of the experimental French fiction; and— most significantly—Durrell's *The Avignon Quintet.* Although the features are not yet fully formed, we may assume that it will look somewhat like its predecessor. But some features will be different. There will probably be less of the Bildungsroman, for example, because the new form, after all, will not be about the development of an ego. In its fully grown form, it will simply assume that the stable ego cannot exist. There will, concomitantly, be a search for some means of attaining coherence without the presence of a protagonist with a well-defined set of traits. We might expect, for example, an increase in the number of Proteus figures, one model which the emerging classic form might take, such as the Polyeidus figure in *Letters,* the figure which becomes the marsh mosquito which infects the Burlingames and Bray, which passes along its history to Barth as narrator, and which becomes the figure of both the eternal trickster and the eternal artist. The muse in Fowles's *Mantissa,* Erato, is a similarly Protean figure.

As both *Letters* and *Mantissa* suggest, the emerging form is likely to be highly self-reflexive. Both use the readers' awareness that they are reading a fiction to blur the lines between reality and fiction. If the fiction within the fiction is as real as the fiction in which it nests, where does the nesting end? The breaking of the lines between the outer fiction and the inner fiction also breaks the lines between the characters in each. The nurse in Miles Green's story within *Mantissa* blends into Green's muse in the outer novel, just as Green merges with his creator, Fowles. Barth the author merges with Barth the narrator in "Dunyazadiad," as he does in *Letters*.

Perhaps the contrast between the self-referentiality of the new classic form as manifest in *The Alexandria Quartet* and the emerging form as manifest in *The Avignon Quintet* might be illustrated by the different uses of two nested narratives—the excerpts we have from *Moeurs* in the former and the introductory short story, "Monsieur," in the latter. The primary (certainly not the sole) function of *Moeurs* is to provide alternative points of view about both Justine and Darley. We see Darley forced to respond to another's interpretation of his lover. We also see that Darley writing *Justine* and Arnauti writing *Moeurs* are engaged in precisely the same activity—recreating their experience of Justine from a totally egoistic perspective, the perspective that flatters them most. One of the implications is the relativistic theme that no single perspective permits an adequate view of reality. (An analogous reading of "The Shadow of the Third" in *The Golden Notebook* could be made; Anna Wulf's creation, Ellen, forces us to see a hidden Anna—not the real Anna, but an aspect of herself which she can imagine.)

"Monsieur," on the other hand, exists less to present an alternative view of Blanford than to establish a fictional level as fiction and, equally important, to establish certain motifs, themes, characters, and events that will later merge with the outer layers of the novel. If certain characters and events appear in what we are told explicitly is a fiction, how are we to react to them when they appear in that part of the novel in which we usually expect the illusion of reality? Just as "Monsieur" is a product of the imagination whose elements take on a reality within *The Avignon Quintet,* so Sutcliffe is a product of the imagination of Blanford, who is in part a product of his own imagination—and outside the novel, he is a product of Durrell's imagination (and ours).

We cannot yet be certain how the emerging classic form will look; there is not enough evidence yet to describe its features with any assurance of accuracy. It may, because of the self-conscious gamesmanship involved in making the theme of the disappearance of the self incarnate, preclude the development of an adequately large community of readers. It takes a certain critical mass—in both senses of "critical"—of both novels and readership if the form is to become classic. But with talents the likes of Grass, Barth, Fowles, and Durrell at work—and a new generation of writers and a new audience whose background includes not only these novelists but also such critics as Derrida and Lacan—the promise is there. If that promise is fulfilled, I am willing to predict that *The Avignon Quintet* will occupy the same central position in that tradition as *The Alexandria Quartet* occupies in its own.

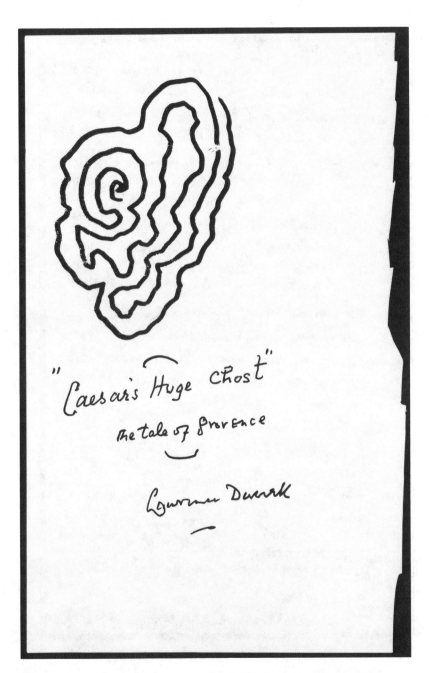

Lawrence Durrell's Cover Mock-Up for Work in Progress on Provence, 1989

MSS of a Book
on "PROVENCE" nearly finished
She drew her laughter from
a fountain of undefiled risability which
wells eternally from the heart of the cryptic
volcano engendered by human time and the
whole theory of change — the mutation harboured
by human kisses. She told me "I know that
God Loves me and I know why. It is
because I am completely unprincipled" also
Human love is based on thrift. As a good Jewess
I study cash-flow in my lovers. Only thus can
you count the dimples in the Creator's chin.
Another saying of of Demon are was
"Try and make everything inadvertent,
fortuitous, given, spontaneous yet secretly
willed"! only the impossible is worth
trying for as an objective I know it.
There is no reason for things to be to.
as they are. Yet as a poet I am dying
of blood-poisoning for I know that it is fatal
for my art for me to preach.
If you could have life as a reality would you
want it? Its Its unreality which charms and
seduces? Investing in rubber that was
different... The Nimes arenas with their
rubber capsule
                Lawrence Durrell   1989

Draft Page from Lawrence Durrell's Work in Progress on Provence, 1989
Original in blue, black, red, and green ink.

18

Thirty Years Already

F. J. Temple

Life is a dream, Calderón once said. Sometimes I wake up and find it difficult to believe that so many years have come across this dream. A banal remark. But how can one not be astonished? I met Larry thirty years ago. I have just turned sixty-five. Mathematics is merciless. One has to submit to it.

One day in July of 1956, I went to find Richard Aldington, author of *Death of a Hero,* Imagist poet, and friend of D. H. Lawrence. He was then living in Montpellier, and we were supposed to eat lunch together in the countryside. When I arrived at the Villa des Rosiers where Richard lived, he was speaking to a small stocky man in his prime, with youthful eyes and an explosive laugh; he looked exactly like a rugby player. "Jacques, this is Lawrence Durrell," Richard said. "Would it bother you if he joined us?"

Lawrence Durrell! I had read that name at the beginning of *The Colossus of Maroussi,* when Henry Miller recounts how the song of the sirens impelled him to go to Greece. I had not yet read anything by Larry, who had not been translated in France. But it was love at first sight. I knew right away that we would not leave it at that.

Lunch in the shade of the linden trees featured Richard's sense of humor and Larry's explosive laugh and went beyond all expectations. What could I do but listen?

It didn't take me long to visit Sommières, where Larry had rented a small house, the Villa Louis. It lay above the city, among the pines. It was pleasant up there. The serenity was broken only by the rustling of branches and the squawks of a friendly magpie who would come pick crumbs from under the table. I came to know Claude, whom Larry had met in Cyprus. Their life was then more than modest. Larry had left Cyprus with a few pieces of clothing, his typewriter, and a toothbrush. What little furniture they had came from flea markets. Nevertheless, life was becoming settled at the Villa Louis, in spite of a few legal worries. The landlord, it seems, had suddenly discovered that he wanted the villa back for his own use. One day, at Larry's request, I brought a lawyer friend of mine to resolve the situation. A compromise was reached, and everything fell back into place.

In the year 1957 *Bitter Lemons, Esprit de Corps,* and *Justine* were published. *Bitter Lemons* would receive the Duff Cooper Prize in November, and that "put a little butter in the spinach"—as Larry phrased it. Larry was grinding away at the end of *The Alexandria Quartet.* The publication of *Justine* in France was deemed a literary event, to be confirmed by the Award for the Best Foreign Book. Larry's reputation was rising. This sometimes amused him: "The butcher's wife has discovered that I am a literary giant, and now they cut the steaks thicker for us. Long live France!"

Claude and Larry lived in the Villa Louis until the fall of 1958. In October, they moved into Mazet Michel near Nîmes. They stayed there for eight years before returning to Sommières, their first port.

Thirty years have passed since the most Languedocian of Britishers came to stay with us. Thirty years of work, of happiness, of fame, of friendship, of grief, and of deaths.

I will stop here, for the past always weighs too heavily, and I raise a glass full of the good red wine of friendship.

Translated by Françoise Rosset

Contributors

Peter Baldwin is a lawyer practicing in England. He is also the proprietor of the Delos Press, which publishes Lawrence Durrell, Iris Murdoch, and David Gascoyne.

Michael H. Begnal is Professor of English and Comparative Literature at the Pennsylvania State University. In 1986 he directed the Fourth International Lawrence Durrell Conference. He has published widely on James Joyce and modern literature. His most recent work is *Dreamscheme: Narrative and Voice in* Finnegans Wake.

Alexandre Blokh (pseudonym Jean Blot) has been Professor of English at the Ecole Rabbinique of Paris, interpreter for the United Nations and U.N.E.S.C.O., Councilor General of the Royaumont Foundation, President of the Menorah Association and Director of the the collection "Presence of Judaism," and Secretary of the P.E.N. Society. He has published novels, criticism, and translations and has been awarded the Prix des Critiques and the Prix Valéry Larbaud.

Nadia Blokh is an artist and illustrator. She and Lawrence Durrell created the pseudonym under which he paints: Oscar Epfs.

James A. Brigham is Professor of English at Okanagan College in British Columbia. He edited Lawrence Durrell's *Collected Poems 1931–1974* and with Alan G. Thomas compiled *An Illustrated Guide to the Writings of Lawrence Durrell*. He founded and, with Ian S. MacNiven, edited *Deus Loci: The Lawrence Durrell Quarterly* from 1977 to 1984.

Peter G. Christensen teaches in the Department of English at Marquette University. He has published many articles on such writers as Lawrence Durrell, D. H. Lawrence, John Cowper Powys, and Graham Greene.

Gregory Dickson has published various essays and reviews concerning modern literature, especially on the writings of Lawrence Durrell.

Jean Fanchette was born in Rose Hill, Mauritius, on 6 May 1932. In 1951 he came to Paris, where he studied medicine and specialized in neuropsychiatry. Trained as a psychoanalyst, he is a member of the Paris Psychoanalytical Society and of the IPA and practices in Paris. With Anaïs Nin, he founded the literary magazine *Two Cities* in 1959. He recently revived Editions Two Cities and published his early correspondence with Durrell and the proceedings of a seminar, *L'Humour dans l'oeuvre de Freud*. He has published some twelve books: essays, novels, and poetry. He has won the Prix Paul Valéry and the Prix de la Langue Française of the French Academy.

Vincent Gille lives in Suresnes, France, where he edits the review *La Vie exactement*.

Alice Hughes is Assistant Professor of English at St. Mary's University, San Antonio, Texas. She has published on various modern authors and is currently writing a study of Edna O'Brien.

Steven G. Kellman is Professor of Comparative Literature at the University of Texas at San Antonio, Texas. Author of *The Self-Begetting Novel, Loving Reading: Erotics of the Text,* and *Approaches to Teaching Camus's "The Plague,"* he has served as Fulbright Senior Lecturer in American Literature to the Soviet Union in 1980 and as Partners of the Americas Lecturer in Cinema to Peru in 1988. Member of the PEN American Center and of the National Book Critics Circle, he received the H. L. Mencken Award in 1986 for his cultural commentary.

Frank L. Kersnowski is Professor of English at Trinity University, San Antonio, Texas. He has published widely on modern literature, including such books as *The Outsiders: Poets of Contemporary Ireland, John Montague,* Tomas Rivera's *Always and Other Poems* (ed.), and *Conversations with Robert Graves* (ed.). He is currently president of the International Lawrence Durrell Society.

Lee J. Lemon is Professor of English at the University of Nebraska. His books include *The Partial Critic, Russian Formalist Criticism, Glossary for the Study of English,* and *Portraits of the Artist in Contemporary Fiction,* as well as many reviews and essays. He is editor of *The Prairie Schooner.*

Ian S. MacNiven is Professor of English at the State University of New York Maritime College. He has edited *The Durrell-Miller Letters, 1935–1980* and coedited *Literary Lifelines: The Richard Aldington–Lawrence Durrell Correspondence* and *The Modernists: Studies in a Literary Phenomenon.* He is currently writing the authorized biography of Lawrence Durrell.

Alfred Perlès was born in turn-of-the-century Vienna. The first of his many books and stories of an autobiographical nature were published during World War II, *The Renegade, Alien Corn,* and *Round Trip,* followed later by books such as *Art and Outrage; Henry Miller in Villa Seurat; My Friend, Alfred Perlès; My Friend, Henry Miller; My Friend, Lawrence Durrell;* and *A Snail's Pace Suits Me Fine.*

Carol Peirce is Professor of English and Communications Design at the University of Baltimore, Maryland. She has guest-edited two issues of *Twentieth-Century Literature* devoted to Lawrence Durrell and coedited *On Miracle Ground II: Second Lawrence Durrell Conference Proceedings.* Currently associate editor of *Deus Loci: The Lawrence Durrell Journal,* she is also completing *Lawrence Durrell's City of the Imagination.*

Jeremy Robinson is a young poet living in London. His poetry has appeared in many magazines throughout Great Britain, and volumes of his poetry include *Black Angel, Gloryland,* and *Magnificence.* He is currently working on studies of J. M. W. Turner, Thomas Hardy, and Lawrence Durrell.

F. J. Temple is a poet and novelist born in Montpellier, France, where he now lives. He has been a friend of Blaise Cendrars, Henry Miller, Joseph Delteil, and Richard Aldington. Author of biographies of Henry Miller and D. H. Lawrence, he has also edited, with Alister Kershaw, a collection of essays about Richard Aldington. He was Director of Radio and Television in Languedoc until 1986 and in the sixties made a television film on Lawrence Durrell.

Gordon K. Thomas is Professor of English at Brigham Young University, Provo, Utah. He has published many articles and books on nineteenth- and twentieth-century literature, among them *Wordsworth's Dirge and Promise, Lord Byron's Iberian Pilgrimage,* and *Wordsworth and the Motions of the Mind.* He is a regular participant in The International Wordsworth Conference at Dove Cottage and the International Byron Symposium.

Index